Americans on
Italo Montemezzi

Italo Montemezzi photographed in New York, 1920

Americans on
Italo Montemezzi

Henry E. Krehbiel
Philip Hale
William J. Henderson
Lawrence Gilman
Deems Taylor
Olin Downes
Herbert F. Peyser
Harold C. Schonberg

Edited, annotated, and introduced by
David Chandler

Foreword by Duane D. Printz

First published in this form by Durrant Publishing, 2014

Copyright © 2014 David Chandler
All rights reserved

Hardback   ISBN 978-1-905946-34-1
Paperback ISBN 978-1-905946-35-8
ePub   ISBN 978-1-905946-36-5

First Edition, corrected

∞ The paper used in this publication meets the minimum requirements of the American National Standard for Information Sciences – Permanence of Paper for Printed Library Materials, ANSI Z39.48-1992. The paper is acid-free and lignin-free.

Printed and bound by Lightning Source
Published by Durrant Publishing
82 Earlham Road, Norwich, NR2 3HA

For Pam and Tony Dignum

Great pro-America friends whose visit to the United States in 1991 changed my life, and whose own lives epitomize the wisdom of Norman MacEwan's

*'We make a living by what we get,
but we make a life by what we give.'*

David Chandler is a Professor in the English Department at Doshisha University, Kyoto, having obtained his D.Phil at the University of Oxford. His published work is mostly in the field of English literature, but in addition to the present book he has also edited *Alfredo Catalani: Composer of Lucca*, *The First Lives of Alfredo Catalani* and *Essays On The Montemezzi-D'Annunzio 'Nave,'* as well as publishing a number of articles and reviews on musical theatre in various journals.

His website is at: http://www.davidjchandler.co.uk/

Duane D. Printz is the Artistic Director of Teatro Grattacielo, a company she founded in 1994 with a view to reviving the neglected operas of the verismo era. She studied at the Manhattan School of Music and the Accademia di Santa Cecilia in Rome, and has sung in many opera and concert productions in the U.S. and Italy. She has been on the voice faculties of the 92nd Street Y and the H.E.S. Music School in Brooklyn, and has also worked in the world of international finance.

The Teatro Grattacielo website is at: http://www.grattacielo.org/

Contents

Foreword by Duane D. Printz xi
Acknowledgements xiii
List of Illustrations xiv

Introduction 1
    Note on the Texts. 42

Part One: *L'Amore dei Tre Re*

New York, 1914

1. Herbert F. Peyser, *Musical America*, 10 January 1914 47
2. Henry E. Krehbiel, *New-York Tribune*, 3 January 1914 63
3. Richard Aldrich, *New York Times*, 3 January 1914 75
4. Unsigned review attributed to
    Leonard Liebling, *Musical Courier*, 7 January 1914 85
5. Henry E. Krehbiel, *New-York Tribune*, 22 January 1914. 91
6. William J. Henderson, *Opera Magazine*, February 1914. 95
7. John van Broekhoven, *Musical Observer*, February 1914. 101
8. Lawrence Gilman, *North American Review*, February 1914 109

Boston, 1914

1. Philip Hale, *Boston Herald*, 10 February 1914 121
2. Olin Downes, *Boston Post*, 10 February 1914 127
3. Philip Hale, *Boston Herald*, 15 February 1914 131
4. Roger Sessions, *Harvard Musical Review*, February 1914 135
5. H. T. Parker, *Boston Evening Transcript*, 19 February 1914 137

Later Criticism, 1915–1962
1. Richard Aldrich, *New York Times*, 14 February 1915 147
2. Unsigned review attributed to
    Gilbert Seldes, *Evening Ledger* (Philadelphia), 24 March 1915 . . . 151
3. Karleton Hackett, *Chicago Evening Post*, 7 October 1915 157
4. Otheman Stevens, *Los Angeles Examiner*, 7 March 1916 161
5. Unsigned review attributed to
    Henry E. Krehbiel, *New York Tribune*, 15 March 1918 165
6. James Gibbons Huneker, *New York Times*, 23 March 1919 167
7. Reginald de Koven, *New York Herald*, 23 March 1919 173
8. Carl Van Vechten, extract from
    Interpreters and Interpretation, 2nd edition (1920) 175
9. Henry T. Finck, *New York Evening Post*, 10 January 1924 179
10. Deems Taylor, *World*, 10 January 1924 183
11. Olin Downes, *New York Times*, 28 October 1928 187
12. Lawrence Gilman, *New York Herald Tribune*, 30 October 1928 191
13. Oscar Thompson, *New York Evening Post*, 3 November 1928 195
14. Herbert F. Peyser, *Opera News*, 10 January 1949 203
15. Ethel Peyser and Marion Bauer, extract from *How Opera Grew: From Ancient Greece to the Present Day* (1956) 211
16. Harold C. Schonberg, *New York Times*, 26 February 1962 213
17. Winthrop Sargeant, *New Yorker*, 3 March 1962 217

Part Two: The Other Operas

La Nave, Chicago, 1919
1. Karleton Hackett, *Chicago Evening Post*, 19 November 1919 225
2. William L. Hubbard, *Chicago Daily Tribune*, 19 November 1919 . . . 231
3. Herman Devries, *Chicago American*, 19 November 1919 235
4. Unsigned review attributed to
    Jeannette Cox, *Musical Courier*, 20 November 1919 239

Giovanni Gallurese, New York and Philadelphia, 1925
1. William J. Henderson, *Sun*, 20 February 1925 249
2. Deems Taylor, *World*, 20 February 1925 257
3. Olin Downes, *New York Times*, 20 February 1925 261
4. Lawrence Gilman, *New York Herald Tribune*, 20 February 1925 267
5. Ernest Newman, *New York Evening Post*, 20 February 1925 275
6. Oscar Thompson, *Musical America*, 28 February 1925 279

La Notte di Zoraima, New York and Philadelphia, 1931–32
1. William J. Henderson, *Sun*, 3 December 1931 287
2. Olin Downes, *New York Times*, 3 December 1931 295
3. Lawrence Gilman, *New York Herald Tribune*, 3 December 1931 299
4. Oscar Thompson, *New York Evening Post*, 3 December 1931 305
5. Deems Taylor, *New York American*, 3 December 1931 311
6. A. Walter Kramer, *Musical America*, 10 December 1931 315

L'Incantesimo, NBC Broadcast from New York, 1943
1. Olin Downes, *New York Times*, 10 October 1943 321
2. Viva Liebling, *Musical Courier*, 20 October 1943 327
3. Oscar Thompson, *Musical America*, October 1943 329
4. Marion Bauer, *Musical Leader*, November 1943 333

Appendix 1: The Plots of Montemezzi's Operas 335
Appendix 2: Biographies of the American Critics 342

Foreword by Duane D. Printz

D R. DAVID CHANDLER continues his scholarly exploration of Italo Montemezzi's extraordinary operatic career with this fascinating book focused particularly on the composer's reception in America. *Americans on Italo Montemezzi* answers many questions and raises others – what caused a work like *L'Amore dei Tre Re* to so capture the imagination of the operatic world and why doesn't it seem to do so anymore? This, of course, is the eternal question in all art as particular fashions come and go, and yet the appeal and allure of this opera is still there for those with ears open to its remarkable power and beauty.

Montemezzi certainly swept America off its feet with *L'Amore dei Tre Re*. That is hardly surprising, for the opera is superbly well-constructed, without any superfluous passages, and the action moves swiftly along and, by operatic standards, is relatively short, lasting only about 85 minutes. Yet it immediately captures the imagination given Montemezzi's talent for descriptive musical details that highlight the action and text so perfectly.

Several examples come to mind – the theme of the rampaging horses galloping through Italy with their riders' swords glinting in the sunlight in Archibaldo's first act aria; Fiora's theme in the flutes whenever she appears, so floatingly lovely that is seems like a perfumed mist has suddenly filled the air; and the wonderful orchestral accompaniment when Fiora goes to the parapets to wave her scarf to her departing husband. It is a theme so filled with her torment and the danger surrounding her as to be palpable to everyone in the audience.

Montemezzi never lost this descriptive musical talent; it is abundantly displayed in the opening sequence of his last opera, *L'Incantesimo*, with the simplest of repeated eighth notes, unremarkable in themselves, but which somehow in his hands denote not only the falling snow but also the boredom and emptiness of Giselda's existence; and who can ever forget the incandescence of this opera's final miracle scene: the music just seems to somehow glow. In *La Nave,* the Venetian lagoon is right there in the music complete with circling seagulls overhead and Montemezzi's gift for religious music is also apparent in the beautiful chorales sung by the populace in front of the basilica.

This was Montemezzi's great talent, and the novelty of it, combined with the intense dramatic situations of *L'Amore dei Tre Re*, excited the American critics and public for many years, as the many reviews collected in this book demonstrate. Perhaps, too, it was the American dream, in a way, that Montemezzi captured: the inspirational and aspirational character of his music so perfectly matching American ideals at that time. In any event, capture the American public he certainly did, and thanks to this new book we can, in a sense, recapture the excitement ourselves. For this, all of us who love this period in operatic history owe David Chandler a great debt of gratitude for his work in retracing the steps of Montemezzi's operatic triumphs here in America, and we look forward with great anticipation to his continuing exploration of Montemezzi's life and career.

Teatro Grattacielo
New York City, November 29, 2013

Acknowledgements

GIVEN THE theme of this book, it is appropriate and pleasant to acknowledge that it could not have been put together without the generous help of many Americans. First among these are Kris Lipkowski, my always obliging research assistant, and Duane D. Printz, a great Montemezzian who has contributed the Foreword. Several American librarians have also gone to considerable trouble on my behalf, especially Allan Holtzman of the Enoch Pratt Free Library, Baltimore. I was interested in Montemezzi's Baltimore reception because I hoped that H. L. Mencken might have written something on *L'Amore dei Tre Re*. Alas, Mr. Holtzman's digging suggests this was not the case, but he has turned up much other material of interest. Other librarians who provided invaluable assistance are: Henry F. Scannell and Cecile W. Gardner of the Boston Public Library; Richard Foster and Yesenia Castro of the New York Public Library; Alain Wolfe of the Chicago Public Library; Ann Mosher of the Samuel L. Paley library, Temple University; and the staff of the Newspaper Department, The Free Library of Philadelphia. For obtaining copies of materials, I am additionally grateful to Stephanie Challener of the *Musical America* archive, the Music Teachers National Association, Mark Russell Gallagher of UCLA, and Roy C. Dicks.

For the many illustrations that add considerably to the value of the book, I am grateful above all to John Pennino of the Metropolitan Opera House Archive who generously provided me with a treasure trove of scans of photographs related to the productions of Montemezzi's operas at the Met. I am also very grateful to M. J. Duffy of James Cummins Bookseller, New York, for the photograph of Herbert F. Peyser, probably Montemezzi's greatest American admirer; Charles Mintzer for the photographs of Rosa Raisa and the rehearsal for *La Nave*; and Stephanie Challener (again) for some images from *Musical America*. Thanks, too, to Allan Lacki.

Two resources which have been of enormous service also deserve mention here. Tom Tryniski's marvellous website, Old Fulton NY Post Cards, contains millions of scanned pages of New York newspapers. It can be extraordinarily frustrating to use, but it is also extraordinarily useful, and the unpredictable results it produces have led me to many things I would not otherwise have discovered. Mark N. Grant's enthralling book, *Maestros of the Pen: A History of Classical Musical Criticism in America* (1998), has also been an inestimable resource, for it offers a wonderful overview of the personalities and the issues involved in the decades when Montemezzi's operas were introduced into America.

So far, all these acknowledgements have been to Americans, but several people outside America have also given invaluable help. In particular, I must thank Paul Durrant, who has put everything together with his customary care and patiently watched me change my mind about the shape of the book several times; and Valerie Langfield, who read, corrected and advised on an earlier draft of the introduction. Giuseppe Martini of the Istituto Nazionale di Studi Verdiani generously devoted a great deal of time to two Verdi queries. The Mitchell Library, State Library of New South Wales, kindly supplied the photograph of Louis P. Verande. Michael Sharp helped me search for the mysterious quotation concerning the 'ancient tree of death.'

The copyright status of much of the material here is ambiguous. Everything published prior to 1924, which makes up around half this collection, is out of copyright. The five selections from the *New York Times* subsequent to that date have been licensed and paid for, and I am grateful to Victoria Vazquez of PARS International for sorting out the paperwork. Similarly, Winthrop Sargeant's review from the *New Yorker* has been licensed. The copyright in Herbert F. Peyser's 1949 article for *Opera News* does not belong to the magazine, but to Peyser's heirs. He had no children, however, and I was unable to trace anyone who might be able to make a claim of ownership on the piece. I have therefore, in consultation with F. Paul Driscoll, the present Editor in Chief of *Opera News*, decided to reprint the essay, confident that Peyser, of all the critics represented here, would most support a project like the present publication. The material from *Musical America* is reprinted with the permission of Stephanie Challener, who manages the archive of that paper. The brief extract from *How Opera Grew* is judged to fall within the terms of academic 'fair use.' Most of the other post-1923 material comes from now defunct publications and it is not clear who could claim or grant copyright on it. The *Evening Post* is a special case, for though it lives on in a debased form as a Murdoch tabloid, it has changed ownership (and character) so many times that I am not sure the present owners can, or would, claim copyright on material published before 1933, when the paper entered a very uncertain period in its history. That is the view of Tom Tryniski, who has put tens of thousands of pages from this paper on his website. Most of the *Evening Post* material in this collection is, at the time of writing, freely available on the internet. Anyone who claims copyright in this or any other of the unlicensed material should contact the editor, who will be pleased to discuss the matter with them.

David Chandler

List of Illustrations

Italo Montemezzi, 1920 . . . . **Frontispiece**
Programme for the first Los Angeles performances of *L'Amore dei Tre Re* . **15, 16**
The Metropolitan Opera House, 1913 . . . . **44**
Programme for the Met *L'Amore dei Tre Re** **46**
Set designs for the Met *L'Amore dei Tre Re** **50–52**
Pasquale Amato and Lucrezia Bori in *L'Amore dei Tre Re*. **65**
Edoardo Ferrari-Fontana and Lucrezia Bori in *L'Amore dei Tre Re** **71**
Adamo Didur as Archibaldo carrying Fiora (Bori)* **80, 81**
Adamo Didur as Archibaldo after killing Fiora* **92**
William J. Henderson, early 1910s. **94**
The Final Scene of *L'Amore dei Tre Re* **111**
Jules Speck, 1916* **117**
Programme for the final Boston *L'Amore dei Tre Re* **120**
The Boston Opera House, c. 1910 . . . . **125**
Set designs for the Boston *L'Amore dei Tre Re*. **129**
Louis P. Verande, c. 1912[1] **133**
Jean Vanni-Marcoux as Archibaldo. **141**
Cartoon of Montemezzi, 1916 . . . . **146**
Pasquale Amato as Manfredo* **153**
Lucrezia Bori as Fiora* **156**
Luisa Villani and Edoardo Ferrari-Fontana as Fiora and Avito **158**
Claudia Muzio as Fiora, 1918* **164**
James Gibbons Huneker, 1918 . . . . **169**
Mary Garden as Fiora. **177**
Replacement set for Act 2 of the Met *L'Amore dei Tre Re** **186**
Rosa Ponselle as Fiora, 1926* **190**
Montemezzi instructs Grace Moore in the strangulation scene, 1941* **202**

---

* All these photographs are © the Metropolitan Opera Archives and are reproduced by kind permission.

1 © The State Library of New South Wales – P1/1872. Reproduced by permission.

Herbert F. Peyser with Christopher Hayes[1]	205
Virgilio Lazzari and Dorothy Kirsten as Archibaldo and Fiora, 1948*	210
Phyllis Curtin and Giorgio Tozzi in the NBC Love of Three Kings	215
Giorgio Tozzi as Archibaldo	219
Montemezzi at the rehearsals for Giovanni Gallurese	222
The Auditorium Theatre, Chicago, 1929	224
Montemezzi rehearsing La Nave, 1919	228
William L. Hubbard	230
Rosa Raisa as Basiliola	237
Set designs for La Nave	241
Cleofonte Campanini, 1913	245
Programme for the Met Giovanni Gallurese	248
Giacomo Lauri-Volpi, Maria Müller & Giovanni Martino	251
Giuseppe Bonfiglio and Rosina Galli in Sardinian costume,	255
Olin Downes, 1925	260
Rehearsing the final scene in Giovanni Gallurese	263
Giuseppe Danise as Rivegas	266
'Ne l'occhio tuo nerissimo ...'	271
Autograph quotation from Giovanni Gallurese	274
Hardman piano advert, 1925	278
Programme for the Met La Notte di Zoraima*	286
The central scene in La Notte di Zoraima*	290
Detail of Rosa Ponselle and Mario Basiola*	291
Rosa Ponselle and Frederick Jagel in La Notte di Zoraima*	294
Santa Bionda and Rosa Ponselle in La Notte di Zoraima*	301
Rehearsing the central scene in La Notte di Zoraima*	304
Tullio Serafin, 1931*	310
Alexandre Sanine, 1931	314
Studio 8-H, Radio City, 1940	320
Montemezzi rehearsing L'Incantesimo	323
Front page of the New York Sun, 9 October 1943	326
Poster for the first staged performance of L'Incantesimo	331

---

[1] Reproduced by kind permission of James Cummins Bookseller.

Introduction

'SIGNOR MONTEMEZZI has come to New York, and New York is his.'[1] So declared Henry E. Krehbiel, undisputed dean of New York's music critics, after the triumphant premiere of *L'Amore dei Tre Re* ('The Love of Three Kings') at the Metropolitan Opera House on 2 January 1914. The American critics hailed Italo Montemezzi's opera as a masterpiece, as the greatest Italian opera since Verdi stopped composing, and also as a seminal and timely work, one that resolved doubts, pointed the way to the future, and even seemed, in Krehbiel's optimistic conclusion, to herald the 'operatic millennium.'[2]

The extraordinary success of *L'Amore dei Tre Re* in the United States in 1914 and later represents a fascinating chapter in the history of opera in America, but one not yet studied or documented despite the fact that Montemezzi's masterpiece was an article of faith for a majority of two key generations of American music critics. This book rectifies that situation by presenting an edited selection of some of the best, most influential, and most interesting writing on Montemezzi by critics of the United States (the slight exception, Ernest Newman, was writing for an American newspaper). It includes fifty reviews and essays by thirty critics. Cumulatively, the collection has much to say about a particular epoch in the history of opera in America, and the way Montemezzi's music first fulfilled, and later failed to fulfil, cultural needs and expectations. But the book is not intended merely as a historical record; it is also meant to force a re-evaluation of

---

1 See below, p. 74.

2 See below, p. 93. 'American' here is taken to denote, as it often does, the United States, but should not be understood to suggest that Montemezzi's opera was only successful there. *L'Amore dei Tre Re* received its South American premiere in Buenos Aires on 11 July 1914, and its enthusiastic reception in Argentina would merit another study.

Montemezzi today, now that his star has greatly dimmed. Were such wonderfully qualified critics as are represented here wrong to judge *L'Amore dei Tre Re* a masterwork, one of the greatest, if not the greatest, of twentieth-century operas? Although I have, to be fair – fair, that is, to the ratio of positive and negative criticism in the past – included some unfavourable assessments of this opera, I am of the Krehbiel party, and hence this book. It is the positive criticism which rings true. Many readers prepared to read through this anthology alongside listening to (or seeing) a good performance of *L'Amore dei Tre Re* will agree.

The central figures in the older generation of American critics who welcomed Montemezzi's opera were listed and given appropriate epithets by James Gibbons Huneker in his 1913 autobiographical work, *Old Fogy*: 'the brilliant Mr. Finck, the erudite Mr. Krehbiel, the witty Mr. Henderson, the judicial Mr. Aldrich, the phenomenal Philip Hale.'[1] These five, with Huneker himself, were the acknowledged leaders of their profession: where they led dozens of lesser critics followed. Apart from Huneker (who was in Europe), they all heard *L'Amore dei Tre Re* in 1914, in most cases attending every performance they could, and William J. Henderson, Richard Aldrich and Philip Hale all joined Krehbiel in welcoming the opera with intense enthusiasm, as this book demonstrates. Only Henry T. Finck of the New York *Evening Post* demurred, yet his objection to *L'Amore dei Tre Re*, that it was not melodic enough, placed it in such distinguished company as to turn out, with hindsight, an unwitting tribute to Montemezzi's achievement: 'The whole history of music teaches that you cannot make the public accept operas like "Boris Godounoff" or "Pelleas et Melisande," because they lack the charm of melody.'[2] In any case, Montemezzi's opera

---

1 *Old Fogy: His Musical Opinions and Grotesques* (Philadelphia: Theodore Presser, 1913), 43.

2 'A New Italian Opera,' *Evening Post*, 3 January 1914, 4.

gradually grew on Finck (as it has on many listeners), to the point where he finally judged that 'apart from Puccini no other Italian composer since Verdi has created an opera superior to Montemezzi's.'[1] For opera lovers today that might be sufficient endorsement, but many of Finck's colleagues ranked *L'Amore dei Tre Re* well above any Puccini opera.

By the mid-1920s most of Huneker's generation of critics were dead or retired, but the younger men who stepped into their shoes were, for the most part, equally great admirers of *L'Amore dei Tre Re*. Major figures in this generation were Lawrence Gilman, Olin Downes, Herbert F. Peyser, Oscar Thompson and Deems Taylor. Gilman is a particularly interesting part of this history, for he was, like Finck, one of the few critics unenthused by Montemezzi's work in 1914, judging it inferior to Puccini's operas. But his conversion was even more complete than Finck's; he later became one of the most eloquent champions of *L'Amore dei Tre Re*, in his revised judgement 'the noblest music drama that has come out of Italy since Verdi's "Otello,"' an opera in a different league from those of the 'facile and shallow Puccini.'[2] By contrast, critics like Downes and Peyser had been enthusiastic about Montemezzi's opera from the beginning, and for decades passionately promoted it in newspapers and magazines.

As much of the American writing on Montemezzi appeared in newspaper columns and periodical publications, it has always been difficult of access (and some has been entirely lost), but the majority view of the United States' critics found its way into books, too. In his classic *Short History of Opera* (1947), for example, Donald J. Grout affirmed categorically that '*L'amore dei tre re* is without doubt the greatest Italian tragic opera since Verdi's *Otello*.' It was all the more beautiful, in Grout's reading, for coming as the final consummation of the Italian tradition,

---

1 See below, p. 180.
2 See below, pp. 192, 191.

'the ripe and languid fruit of a dying age, the sunset of a long and glorious day.'[1] But there was something of sunset about Grout's evocation of the opera in more ways than one. By the late 1940s the number of American newspaper and magazine critics prepared to make such claims for the opera was much smaller than it had been in the decade after 1914, at the height of Montemezzi's popularity in the United States. As the typewriters of critics such as Gilman, Peyser and Downes fell silent one by one, no critics of comparable authority emerged to take over their consistent advocacy of *L'Amore dei Tre Re*. Nevertheless, occasional revivals of the opera in the United States since 1950 have always been accompanied by very appreciative commentary.

Although well over half this anthology is devoted to *L'Amore dei Tre Re*, by far the most written about Montemezzi opus, the reception of his other operas in the United States is also documented. Because of the enormous success of *L'Amore dei Tre Re*, three other Montemezzi operas were staged in America: *La Nave* (1919), *Giovanni Gallurese* (1925) and *La Notte di Zoraima* (1931). None of them achieved anything like the following of *L'Amore dei Tre Re*, and critical responses often took the form of a damning comparison with the established work. It is remarkable how even critics devoted to the earlier-produced opera generally expressed little enthusiasm for these other Montemezzi efforts. Montemezzi, who had married Katherine Leith (née Levy) of New York in 1921, moved to America in 1939, and his final opera, *L'Incantesimo*, was first performed as an NBC broadcast in 1943. This did receive more positive reviews, but it was too slight a piece to shake the established consensus that Montemezzi was

---

1 *A Short History of Opera*, 2 vols (New York: Columbia UP, 1947), 2: 444–45. It is worth noting that Grout chose a key scene from *L'Amore dei Tre Re* to form the frontispiece of this volume.

the ultimate one work composer, a man who had risen into the realms of genius on one, but only one, glorious occasion.

In selecting material for this anthology I have, in general, preferred to include writings by the unquestionably major critics already mentioned who played a central role in mediating Montemezzi's operas to the American public. On the other hand, I have also mixed in a number of reviews by other critics, ranging from the very famous (Ernest Newman) to the very obscure (Viva Liebling), for their intrinsic interest, as well as some reviews by important people not in general known as opera critics (Roger Sessions, Gilbert Seldes, Marion Bauer), for their opinions are fascinating given their prominence in other areas of American musical life. This introduction provides an overview and background for the reception of each Montemezzi opera in the United States. I have divided it by opera, but as *L'Amore dei Tre Re* has a much more complex and extensive reception history than the others, I have considered it in two parts, the first covering the period to 1930, the second the period to 1962.

L'Amore dei Tre Re to 1930

L'Amore dei Tre Re, Montemezzi's third opera to be staged, received its premiere at La Scala, Milan, on 10 April 1913. It was a *Literaturoper*, setting to music a shortened version of Sem Benelli's 1910 play of the same title.[1] It was favourably received by the public and the critics, and further productions were soon planned. A second production opened at the Emilia Romagna Teatro, Cesena, on 23 August 1913; this was seen by Toscanini, then acting as the artistic director of the Metropolitan Opera; he was impressed, and an American premiere was scheduled. The

---

1 For some discussion of Montemezzi and the *Literaturoper* tradition see my introduction to *Essays on the Montemezzi-D'Annunzio 'Nave,'* 2nd edition (Norwich: Durrant Publishing, 2014).

first performance took place on 2 January 1914 with Toscanini conducting: this was the first time the opera had been seen outside Italy. Fortuitously, it was quickly followed by a second American production. The recently founded Boston Opera Company had planned to stage the world premiere of Riccardo Zandonai's *Francesca da Rimini* early in 1914; when this prestigious event had to be cancelled, *L'Amore dei Tre Re* was substituted.[1] The first Boston performance took place on 9 February, with three of the four principals who had sung in the Met production. Thereafter the two productions ran simultaneously, with the final Boston performance taking place on 18 February, a day before the final New York one. An overwhelming majority of the New York and Boston critics praised Montemezzi's opera in very enthusiastic terms, many of them reviewing it more than once.

To a great extent the American critics who praised *L'Amore dei Tre Re* agreed on its merits. Though they made little of its being a shortened, but otherwise largely unadapted play, there was a near unanimity of opinion that the libretto was superb, and this included the few negative critics, too. Thus the young Roger Sessions, unimpressed by Montemezzi's music, found it a 'beautiful libretto … a decided contrast to the average contemporary Italian libretto,' while Huneker later judged '[t]he book by Sem Benelli … admirable, a better one seldom has been written.'[2] The vast majority of the critics agreed, further, that Montemezzi's response to his libretto had been exceptionally profound: he had placed his music at the service of the drama, expanding Benelli's words into agitated melody which seemed to catch their every nuance, making music and text meet as equals rather than subordinating one to the other. As Krehbiel later put it, 'Theirs [Benelli's and Montemezzi's] is as perfect a wedlock as has been accomplished in the field of

---

1 See below, p. 135, n. 2.
2 See below, pp. 135, 167.

art.'¹ Montemezzi had done this with an exceptional seriousness of purpose, thinking only of his opera as a whole, and not attempting any shortcuts to please his audience. In this, and in the opera's general air of nobility, its concern with highborn personages whose destinies affect whole peoples, *L'Amore dei Tre Re* was understood, surely correctly, as a reaction to – rather than as a continuation of – *verismo*.

Montemezzi's command of the orchestra was also highly praised. The comparative restraint of his style, his subtle instrumental effects, his contrapuntal mastery, rhythmic force and variety, and use of dramatic motifs were all highly praised. The question of whether the score was, strictly speaking, melodious divided the critics, but only a few joined Finck in holding a perceived lack of melody against Montemezzi. Perhaps the most remarkable aspect of the reviews is the variety of explanations of Montemezzi's style, especially as, in more recent times, it has become a critical commonplace to call it Italianized Wagner. A recent American critic, Alan Mallach, for example, judges that 'Montemezzi's harmonic language is echt Wagner, the language of *Der Ring des Nibelungen*.'² By contrast, in 1914 Richard Aldrich assured readers of the *New York Times* that 'There is as little as may be of Wagner in this [Montemezzi's] score – little of direct suggestion, little but what is in the general musical atmosphere of the modern world and from which none may hope to escape entirely'³ – and none of the 1914 reviewers regarded *L'Amore dei Tre Re* as excessively Wagnerian.⁴ Some of them heard Montemezzi's style as original and personal, some heard it as an intelligent and convincing synthesis of other composer's styles,

---

1 See below, p. 166.

2 *The Autumn of Italian Opera: From Verismo to Modernism, 1890–1915* (Boston, MA: Northeastern UP, 2007), 323.

3 See below, p. 78.

4 Leonard Liebling is a partial exception. See below, pp. 86-87.

only a small minority dismissed it as synthetic in a negative way, characterless. Taken together, the reviews reinforce the old truth that even the best-trained ears hear things differently.

As well as the many qualities the critics consciously discovered in *L'Amore dei Tre Re*, and that can be verified today, there were larger cultural factors behind the American enthusiasm for Montemezzi's opera. The leading critics of Krehbiel's generation were mostly ardent Wagnerians, given to extolling the German tradition of music above all others (several of them had German backgrounds). But they found little to celebrate in modern German opera. Only two German opera composers subsequent to Wagner had gained any fame in America: Engelbert Humperdinck and Richard Strauss (an attempt to launch Eugen d'Albert's *Tiefland* at the Met in 1908 was unsuccessful, and led Henderson to make the exasperated and revealing comment that '[t]he complete failure of this opera illustrated the impossibility of measuring New York taste by that of Germany'[1]). Finck's 1913 judgement that Humperdinck's *Königskinder* was 'the best opera written since Wagner's death'[2] really just shows how desperate things appeared to a leading Wagnerian critic looking for a meaningful Wagnerian tradition. Finck's colleagues did not support him on this,[3] and the American public, too, showed only a lukewarm enthusiasm for *Königskinder*, even though the Met, which had secured the world premiere in 1910, tried hard to establish it as a repertoire work in the years before the First World War. Thus Humperdinck was left as a 'one work' composer, his perennial favourite *Hänsel und Gretel* now two decades old.

---

1 'The Metropolitan Season,' *Sun*, 11 April 1909, 10.

2 'Music News and Gossip,' *Evening Post*, 1 March 1913, 3.

3 Krehbiel regarded *Königskinder* as damaged by a weak libretto: 'stilted in language, its symbolism too much in evidence and not sufficiently sympathetic, and its construction faulty.' See *Makers of Modern Opera, The Mentor* 1:47 (5 January 1914), 10.

Strauss, by contrast, had shown that he could be undeniably prolific, but his music, as music, was still controversial in America, many critics finding it too modernist and too clever for its own good; the subjects of his operas, moreover, shocked and offended the more puritanical strain in the American character. A single performance of *Salome* at the Met in 1907 was enough: it was not repeated there until 1934. Krehbiel warned in January 1914 that:

> Richard Strauss reflects the tendency of the times away from all ideal things. Physical, moral, and mental degeneracy are the subjects which he has attempted to glorify in 'Salomé' and 'Elektra,' and shameless immorality in 'Rosenkavalier.' To the celebration of such things and to the promotion of his material interests he is prostituting the finest musical gifts possessed by any composer known to the present day.[1]

The American public, and some of the other critics, would come to disagree on the matter of *Der Rosenkavalier*, but that work was still very new and not yet established in 1914. The German 'tradition' of opera had thus become mainly a matter of repeating Wagner's canonical music dramas as often as possible.

In remarkable contrast, the Italian tradition seemed to be thriving, at least in terms of producing operas that audiences wanted to see. If even opera devotees find it difficult to name a single German opera composed between *Parsifal* (1882) and *Hänsel und Gretel* (1893), they have no difficulty naming several Italian operas from the decade after Verdi's youthful swansong, *Falstaff* (1893). Well before the death of Verdi – whom the American critics tended to pay lip service to as the 'other' giant of nineteenth-century opera – it was already clear that a younger generation of composers had emerged to carry on the Italian tradition of

---

1 Ibid.

popular opera with broad international appeal. Puccini, in particular, established himself in the eyes of the opera-going public as the older composer's heir. The American critics generally had far more tolerant feelings toward Puccini than toward the Strauss of *Salome* and *Elektra*, but though they recognized his expertise in what he did, and even his absorption of certain Wagnerian tendencies, they could, and did, deplore the fact that he seemed to be aiming much lower than the Verdi of *Aida* and *Otello*, let alone Wagner. In other words, whether they looked to Germany or Italy opera seemed to be in a state of decline.

With the post-Wagnerian Germanic tradition so disappointing and the Italian tradition producing so many popular operas, it is not surprising that the early years of the twentieth century witnessed significant shifts in the American repertoire, the proportion of Italian works steadily increasing as Wagner's gigantic grip on that repertoire eased. A Wagner cult of extraordinary intensity had developed in the United States in the 1880s.[1] Wagner was not only critically elevated far above Verdi, but his operas came to be programmed far more regularly. It was in the 1880s, Herbert F. Peyser later remarked, that 'certain persons who should have known better labored under the delusion that Italian opera was dead in New York for all time.'[2] For a while things did have that appearance. As George W. Martin notes, 'It seems incredible but in the season of 1888–1889 in New York there was only a single performance of an Italian opera, *Lucia di Lammermoor*.'[3] It was

---

[1] For a detailed and wonderfully readable account of this see Joseph Horowitz, *Wagner Nights: An American History* (Berkeley: U of California P, 1994).

[2] 'New York' in *Musical U.S.A.*, ed. Quaintance Eaton (New York: Allen, Towne and Heath, 1949), 19–56, pp. 26–27.

[3] 'The Reception of Verdi's Operas in the United States' in *Verdi Reception*, ed. Lorenzo Frassà and Michela Niccolai (Turnhout: Brepols, 2013), 173–91, p. 189.

no temporary phenomenon. Martin also points out that as late as the 1903–04 season, the Met put on all ten canonical Wagner operas alongside just five Verdi operas.[1] But those figures, though confirming Wagner's continuing ascendancy, also demonstrate that Italian opera was on the rise, and thereafter the proportion of Wagnerian to non-Wagnerian opera gradually fell. This is not surprising, for the Wagner cult was a top-down cultural phenomenon depending a great deal on the evangelising exertions of music critics and the missionary efforts of conductors and opera managements seeking to 'improve' audiences devoted to *Il Trovatore*.[2] A significant section of the audience for opera had never been won over to the Wagnerian cause. The 'boxholders,' Peyser recalled, sympathy tempering his scorn (he himself preferred Italian opera), 'disliked Wagnerian opera from the depths of their beings'[3] – and they were a powerful group. The rise of Puccini, an effortlessly popular composer who appealed to the boxholders, epitomized the anti-Wagnerian reaction. After the Met produced four Puccini operas in 1907, Krehbiel lamented that 'Mr. Conreid [the director had] sold the Metropolitan's birthright for the Puccini pottage.'[4] When Giulio Gatti-Casazza, the former director of La Scala, took over at the Met the following year the critics feared, with reason, that he would further Italianize the repertoire, more 'Puccini pottage' being offered in place of Wagner gold.

In this context *L'Amore dei Tre Re* made its explosive impact in the United States. As it has become a critical cliché to describe Montemezzi's opera as singularly 'Wagnerian,' it is tempting to

---

1 Ibid.

2 George W. Martin remarks on the great popularity of *Il Trovatore* in America from 1855 onwards: it 'had everything the American audience at the time wanted.' Ibid. 185.

3 'New York,' 26.

4 'Accusing Excuses,' *New-York Tribune*, 22 February 1908, 7.

jump prematurely to the conclusion that America's Wagnerian critics liked it for that reason: that they welcomed Montemezzi as a worthy heir of Wagner in a way Strauss was not. There may be a little truth in this – Herman Devries in Chicago hailed him as 'a young Wagner'[1] – but, as noted already, they did not, consciously at least, hear Montemezzi's music as particularly Wagnerian. Rather, they understood Montemezzi as restoring and extending a 'noble,' grand tradition of Italian opera which had peaked in *Aida* and *Otello* before degenerating in the hands of the *verists* (the American critics appear to have known little of such earlier attempts to restore the grand tradition as Leoncavallo's *I Medici* and Mascagni's *Parisina*). This tradition had already, in their understanding, absorbed a good deal of Wagner, and hence the greatness of *Aida* and *Otello*. *Aida* had emerged as Verdi's most popular opera around the turn of the century, but Krehbiel judged in 1914 that 'The greater charm which "Aïda" exerts now is due as much to the advanced ideals of the public, which Wagner was largely instrumental in creating [and American institutions had been instrumental in propagating], as to the refined and deepened sense of dramatic propriety and beauty which Verdi discloses in its melody, harmony, and instrumentation.'[2] Montemezzi, in this reading, had not needed to make any special effort to 'Wagnerize' Italian opera. He had taken his artistic bearings from late Verdi and developed his own, original, elevated style, a style influenced, but not excessively, by his own response to Wagner's operas, as well as by Debussy, Mussorgsky, and possibly other composers too.

Many of the leading American critics who praised *L'Amore dei Tre Re* in 1914 would doubtless have preferred to listen to Wagner. But the previous two decades had taught them that the larger world of opera on which they commentated demanded Italian

---

1 See below, p. 235.
2 *Makers of Modern Opera*, 3.

opera alongside, or even in preference to, the great German works they worshipped. And if the repertoire was going to contain Italian works, Montemezzi's opera was one they could wholeheartedly endorse, for it seemed to represent a restoration of the very best of the Italian tradition, synthesized, to some extent, with the best of the German tradition. The public enthusiasm for the work was very satisfying to the critics, for it seemed to support the thesis that, in Krehbiel's words, opera audiences now had more 'advanced ideals' after their exposure to Wagner. And the popular success of the work, in turn, was understood as saying something very positive about the opera. Edward Ziegler (1870–1947) of the *New York Herald* believed he was summarising the views of other critics when he later stated 'the reason why the masses love Mr. Montemezzi's opera is that it is a sincere writing. Instinctively the public feels this and willingly it responds.'[1]

Whether 'the masses' would have agreed with this assessment, or indeed have accepted this designation, is inevitably a question difficult to answer, and one complicated by the fact that many critics soon began to maintain the opposite: that *L'Amore dei Tre Re* was not an opera of 'mass' appeal. As early as February 1915 Aldrich was concluding: 'It [*L'Amore dei Tre Re*] is not an opera likely to become widely popular. In this respect its composer has undoubtedly something to learn of Puccini.'[2] Montemezzi's opera lacked the obviously popular elements audiences may have expected in an Italian work. Their positive response, despite this, perhaps owed something to a perception of Montemezzi's uncompromising 'sincerity,' but sincerity in art can take many forms, and it was perhaps the sheer intensity of the opera, with its near continuous dramatic tension, and the assumption that

---

1 'New Opera Clever, but Not Inspired,' *New York Herald*, 29 March 1914, 3rd section, p. 10 (the title does not refer to Montemezzi's opera).

2 See below, p. 150.

Montemezzi wrote it that way (though Toscanini did speed it up) because he could write it no other, which won them over. Ziegler put this nicely when, comparing Montemezzi's opera with Ermanno Wolf-Ferrari's *L'Amore Medico*, he suggested that: '"L'Amore dei Tre Re" sounds as if the composer must have written it even if he had been sent to jail for his deed; "L'Amore Medico" sounds as if its composer had written it as a pastime.'[1] The opera conveyed a business-like urgency, the sense of a goal ardently pursued and achieved, that resonated with American values and may explain why it achieved its greatest popularity in the United States. *L'Amore dei Tre Re* is considerably less than half the length of most of Wagner's operas, so the pacing is quite different, and closer to that of the embryonic art of the cinema. Analysing the failure of d'Albert's *Tiefland* in America, Henderson had reluctantly concluded that there was something in the American character averse to German prolixity: 'The American craves brief speech and swift action. Even in opera he wishes to come to the point.'[2] *L'Amore dei Tre Re* unerringly came to the point.

After the great success of *L'Amore dei Tre Re* in New York and Boston in 1914, the two companies repeated it the following year and set about making the opera more widely known. In 1915 the Met production was taken to Philadelphia and Atlanta, while the newly constituted Boston Grand Opera Company took their production on tour to Chicago, St. Louis, Louisville, Detroit, New York, Philadelphia, Washington, DC, and Baltimore. The Chicago performances, in October 1915, are particularly important, for the Chicago Opera Association, headed by Cleofonte Campanini, soon afterwards mounted their own production of the opera, first performed on 4 December with Edoardo Ferrari-Fontana of the New York and Boston productions again taking

---

[1] 'New Opera Clever.'

[2] 'The Metropolitan Season.'

MASON OPERA HOUSE

CHARLES FROHMAN | Lessees
KLAW & ERLANGER |
W. T. WYATT, Resident Manager

Matinees 2:15   Evenings 8:15

PUBLISHED BY THE PROGRAM PUBLISHING COMPANY
226-227 BLACK BUILDING, FOURTH AND HILL
Phone: F 1178

L. E. BEHYMER PRESENTS
By arrangement with Max Rabinoff
A Limited Engagement of the

Boston Grand Opera Company
IN CONJUNCTION WITH THE
Pavlowa Imperial Ballet Russe

WEEK MARCH 6, 1916
SIX NIGHTS—MATINEES, WEDNESDAY AND SATURDAY
MASON OPERA HOUSE
MAX RABINOFF, Managing Director

Among the Distinguished Artists are:

Felice Lyne	Coloratura Soprano
Tamaki Miura	Japanese Prima Donna
Maggie Teyte	Lyric Soprano
Maria Gay	Mezzo-Soprano
Elvira Leveroni	Contralto
Riccardo Martin	Dramatic Tenor
Giovanni Zenatello	Lyric Tenor
Thomas Chalmers	Baritone
Giorgi Puliti	Baritone
Paolo Ananian	Basso
Jose Mardones	Basso
Roberto Moranzoni	Conductor
Adolf Schmid	Conductor
Alexander Smallens	Assistant Conductor

Orchestra of 60 selected musicians of the Boston Opera House.
Chorus—entire Boston Opera corps of 70 choristers.
And

PAVLOWA	PAVLOWA BALLET RUSSE
Ivan Clustine	Director Choreographique
Alexandre Volinine	Premier Danseur Classique
Stephanie Plaskovietzka	Premiere Danseuse Classique
Stasia Kuhn	Premiere Danseuse Caractere

With Complete Corps de Ballet which Pavlowa has maintained in Former Seasons.

Montemezzi reaches the West Coast
The programme for the first Los Angeles performances

"L'Amore Dei Tre Re"
(The Love of Three Kings)
A Tragic Opera in Three Acts by
ITALO MONTEMEZZI

CAST.

Fiora	Maggie Teyte
Manfredo	Graham Marr
Archibaldo	Jose Mardones
Avito	Riccardo Martin
Flaminio	Romeo Boscacci
Ancella	Luisa Pavani
Una Vecchia	Elvira Leveroni
Un Giovanetto	M. Alliotto
Una Giovanetta	Fely Clement

Conductor—Roberto Moranzoni.
Chorus Master—Amedeo Barbieri.   Stage Manager—Armando F. Agnini.

SYNOPSIS OF SCENES.

ACT I. A hall in the castle of Manfredo, Altura, Italy.
ACT II. The terrace on the summit of the castle walls.
ACT III. The crypt in the castle chapel.

The action of the opera takes place in a remote castle of Italy forty years after a barbarian invasion.

FOLLOWED BY "SNOWFLAKES"
From Tschaikowsky's "Nut Cracker" Ballet.
Arranged by IVAN CLUSTINE.

Valse of Snowflakes.................................Mlles. Plaskovietzka, Kuhn, Butsova, Collinette, Verina, Griffova, Crombova, Leggierova, Fredova, Lindowska, Brunova, Naumova, Shelton, Stuart, Daganova, Cortnova, Saxova, Florence; MM. Vajinski, Kobeleff, Zelewski, Loboiko, Domislovski, Marini, Bain, Hubart, Veseloff, Marum

---

PROGRAM—*Continued*

Pas de Deux	ANNA PAVLOWA and M. VOLININE
Pas de Cinque	Mlles. Plaskovietzka, Crombova, Leggierova, Stuart, Daganova
Variation	ANNA PAVLOWA and M. VOLININE
Pas de Trois	Mlles. Butsova, Collinette, Griffova
Coda	ANNA PAVLOWA, M. VOLININE, and entire company and entire chorus

Conductor—Adolf Schmid.   Choreographic Director—Ivan Clustine.
STEINWAY PIANO USED.

the role of Avito, Clarence Whitehill as Archibaldo, Graham Marr as Manfredo and Louise Edvina as Fiora. Thus by the end of 1915 the three major resident American opera companies had all produced *L'Amore dei Tre Re*. In 1916 the Boston Company continued its tour, presenting Montemezzi's opera in Buffalo, Cincinnati, Cleveland, Pittsburgh, Denver, Portland, Los Angeles, San Francisco, Seattle, Kansas City and Omaha. In terms of the number of cities visited, this 1915–16 Boston tour must count as a world record for a production of *L'Amore dei Tre Re*. Many of these cities had no professional music critics; nevertheless, Montemezzi's opera attracted a great deal of press attention, nearly all of it enthusiastic. The enthusiasm was sometimes rather gauche, but the reviewers were generally sensitive to what was genuinely special about the opera, and they clearly experienced the same kind of excitement as the more sophisticated East Coast critics. Otheman Stevens' review for the *Los Angeles Examiner*, included in this anthology, gives a good idea. By the end of the Boston tour it was clear that *L'Amore dei Tre Re* had a bright future in America, and in October 1916 *Musical America* placed Montemezzi in its 'Gallery of Celebrities,' a striking cartoon image by Giovanni Viafora accompanied by one version of what seems to have been an established joke: 'Effery time he [Montemezzi] hav' three King he draw a fulla house – you know – just lika poker!'[1]

No history of *L'Amore dei Tre Re* in the United States would be complete without a mention of the Ravinia Opera, founded in 1912 to offer summer seasons of opera at an easy distance from Chicago. *L'Amore dei Tre Re* was first given there on 3 August

---

1 For the cartoon, see below, p. 146. The earliest version of the joke I have come across appears in Louis Elson's column 'Cadenzas' in the *Musical Observer* for February 1914: '*L'Amore dei tre Re* is making its way in the American repertoire. It is not astonishing that three kings should win. The complete hand in this case is three kings, a queen and a knave' (168). The knave (in the sense of a male servant) is Flaminio.

1918 with Claudia Muzio as Fiora. Ravinia specialized in short works (longer operas were inevitably cut), and Montemezzi's opera became a staple of their repertoire, being given two or three performances every single season through to 1932 (thirty-four performances in all), when the company collapsed due to economic problems caused by the recession. To the best of my knowledge, this is a world record in terms of regular, annual repetition of Montemezzi's masterpiece, and it is most unlikely that it will ever be broken.[1]

Ravinia's embrace of *L'Amore dei Tre Re* from 1918 and the Chicago Opera Association's production of *La Nave* (discussed in the next section of this introduction) in 1919 suggests that Chicago was coming to displace New York and Boston as Montemezzi's American heartland. This was to some extent confirmed when the Opera Association mounted a second production of *L'Amore dei Tre Re* in 1920. First played in Chicago on 9 January and then brought to the Lexington Theatre, New York, on 26 January 1920, this production is important for two reasons. First, it was not only the most frequently performed, but the most widely performed production of the opera in the 1920s, for the Opera Association took up the defunct Boston Company's project of touring Montemezzi's opera: as well as annual New York performances between 1920 and 1922, it was presented in Cleveland in 1920, Denver in 1921, Los Angeles and San Francisco in 1921 and 1922, Baltimore, Milwaukee and Pittsburgh in 1922, and Boston in 1923, 1925 and 1929. Second, it featured Mary Garden as Fiora. Garden always managed to attract immense publicity wherever she went, and her passionate interpretation of Montemezzi's heroine proved a sensation. Her performance was so intense that Montemezzi himself, on seeing her sing the role in New York, felt 'overcome' at the end of the

---

1 For a history of the Ravinia Opera, see Robert C. Marsh, *150 Years of Opera in Chicago* (DeKalb: Northern Illinois UP, 2006), 94–103.

second act and had to be 'led to the foyer by kindly friends, trembling with the thrill of fired emotions.'[1]

Initially, in Chicago, critical interest focussed mainly on the fact that Garden, for the first and only time in her career, was singing a role in Italian. This seems to have had much to do with her own high regard for Montemezzi's work, which she considered second only to *Pelléas et Mélisande* among twentieth century operas: 'How I loved that opera [*L'Amore dei Tre Re*]! I sang it in the original Italian, the only opera I ever sang in that language, and I adored every word of it.'[2] The Chicago critics were divided on how successfully she had managed the transformation, but the majority declared in her favour, and Karleton Hackett, Montemezzi's leading champion in Chicago, was unequivocal:

> Mary Garden achieved one of the greatest triumphs of her career as Fiora. She was the incarnation of the poetic spirit of the story, and there was about her portrayal a warmth that was instinctively Italian. The French quality which we have always considered as somehow her essential mode of thought seemed to have dropped from her as one would lay aside a garment, and she stepped forth Italianized.[3]

After the Chicago *L'Amore dei Tre Re* came to New York, the discussion shifted to Garden's particular interpretation of the role, on which there was an energising difference of opinion. Of the many vivid accounts of her performance, I have chosen Carl

---

1 Felix Deyo, 'Montemezzi's "L'Amore dei Tre Re" Opens Metropolitan Opera Season,' *Standard Union* (Brooklyn), 30 October 1928, 19.
2 Mary Garden, *Mary Garden's Story* (London: Michael Joseph, 1952), 152.
3 'Opera Audience Cheers Artists in "Three Kings,"' *Chicago Evening Post*, 10 January 1920, 7.

Van Vechten's for this anthology – an account the more extraordinary for the fact that Van Vechten had no time for the opera itself. Indeed it may be the case that Garden's performances often most impressed those who had not yet learned to love the opera. Finck, for example, was overwhelmed, and it appears that it was Garden's Fiora, more than anything else, which led him to significantly re-evaluate *L'Amore dei Tre Re*:

> Few things so great have been seen on the operatic stage as her [Garden's] impersonation of Fiora; of the unwilling performance of a hypocritical duty; of the gradual yielding to the primitive passion of her youth after a hard struggle; of the bliss of the long kiss that rivals Kundry's in 'Parsifal' or Siegfried's awakening of Brynhild; and finally, the terrible death struggle. Stage art can go no further.[1]

Some of the critics already convinced by the opera were less positive. Many of them had invested deeply in Lucrezia Bori's interpretation of Fiora as a helpless innocent, a victim of fate, and this interpretation had become central to their understanding of the opera's plot. Garden's Fiora, by contrast, was no innocent victim but a much more worldly-wise creature confident in her adulterous passion, 'a magnificent liar and the most complicated woman in the operatic repertoire.'[2] For critics who preferred Bori, this spoilt the opera. Henderson, for example, judged that:

> ... there was always reason to wonder why her [Garden's] *Fiora* should seem so experienced in the tragedy of love.

---

1 'Mary Garden's Fiora,' *New York Evening Post*, 11 February 1921, 6.

2 This was Garden's own description of Fiora, according to Grace Moore. See Grace Moore, *You're Only Human Once* (London: Latimer House, 1947), 152.

At no time did she clearly denote the grief of the young woman over her inability to give to *Manfredo* what he deserved. There should be an unmistakable strain of repentance in the whole impersonation of *Fiora*, for the woman recognized the worth of her husband. She was simply the victim of an overmastering passion.

Mary Garden's *Fiora* knew too much and appeared in so far as *Manfredo* was concerned, to be plainly bored.[1]

But Mary Garden's Fiora also kept critics and audiences talking. The second stage in the reception history of almost any successful opera tends to involve a comparison of the performances of different singers. In the case of *L'Amore dei Tre Re* in America this process seems to have started with H. T. Parker's remarkable account of Jean Vanni-Marcoux as Archibaldo included in the present collection.[2] As more singers were cast in the opera, so the comparisons began to multiply. But the issues between Bori and Garden were of a different magnitude from those between other rival performers of the main roles, for they profoundly affected the drama as a whole. Every serious lover of the opera had to have an opinion on the matter. Montemezzi later told Verna Arvey that people in America had often pestered him with the question: 'Who do you prefer in the leading role of your opera, Mary Garden or Lucrezia Bori?' He apparently always played safe, responding tactfully that 'no one could express a preference between two such superb artists!'[3]

The 1920s was generally a very good decade for *L'Amore dei Tre Re* in America. Garden and the Chicago company were

---

1 'Miss Garden and Miss Farrar, Artistic Rivals, Discussed,' *Sun and New York Herald*, 1 February 1920, 18.

2 See below, pp. 140–143.

3 Verna Arvey, 'Visits to the Homes of Famous Composers No. XIV: Italo Montemezzi,' *Opera and Concert*, November 1948, 14–15, 28–29, p. 28.

touring the opera widely and getting much attention and acclaim. Ravinia was scheduling it every year. Meanwhile the Met went on playing it, and celebrated their fortieth performance (though they may have miscounted) on 9 January 1924, when a special presentation was made to Montemezzi. In 1925 the San Francisco Opera, founded in 1923, mounted a production of their own, which they repeated in 1928.[1] In 1926 the Cincinnati Opera, founded in 1920, put on their first production, repeating it in 1929. On 29 December 1926 Rosa Ponselle first appeared in the opera at the Met, and became the most talked about Fiora since Garden; she sang the part many times, describing it as 'one of [her] favorite roles.'[2] Montemezzi's prominence naturally made him a target for critics opposed to the type of music he represented, but even this was a backhanded tribute to his importance. Thus Paul Rosenfeld (1890–1946), the rather precious modernist critic, in an essay celebrating the revival of Italian instrumental music, asserted that 'Italian music is no longer chiefly old man Verdi and older man [a misprint for 'son'?] Puccini and the anæmic nephew Montemezzi.'[3] The 'anæmic' was obviously meant to belittle, but the 'chiefly' is oddly flattering, given that Montemezzi was known in Rosenfeld's New York for just one opera, and that he is mentioned here in preference to far more prolific composers such as Mascagni, Giordano and Zandonai.

By the mid-decade, though, it may be the case, at least in retrospect, that a shadowy hand was just starting to write on the wall. Reading attentively through the reviews it does become clear that Montemezzi's opera was no longer always 'draw[ing] a fulla house,' and critics sometimes deplored this, taking it as

---

[1] Arthur Bloomfield, *The San Francisco Opera: 1922–1978* (Sausalito: Comstock Editions, 1978), 8, 372.

[2] Rosa Ponselle and James A. Drake, *Ponselle: A Singer's Life* (New York: Doubleday, 1982), 82.

[3] *Musical Chronicle (1917–1923)* (New York: Harcourt, 1923), 105.

evidence of a wider decline in good taste encouraged by the opera companies themselves. For example, in a 1924 article tellingly entitled 'A Moratorium for Opera,' Henderson declared that:

> The opera of today is in a sorry state, indeed, and the opera going public of New York is in a condition to excite pity. ... If even so recent a reincarnation of the splendid soul of the Italian Renaissance as Montemezzi's 'L'Amore dei Tre Re,' which was new here only ten years ago, had now to gain its place on the New York stage, it would be thrust into outer darkness to make way for Giordano's 'Fédora' and Massenet's 'Thaïs.' For of such operas, with their lollipop music and their jugglery of gestures and posings, the ideal répertoire of the patrons of 'the greatest opera house in the world' is constituted.[1]

There was, then, cause for concern. Nevertheless, with leading singers happy to sing it and major critics happy to praise it, *L'Amore dei Tre Re* seemed securely established in the American repertoire for the time being.

La Nave

La Nave ('The Ship'), Montemezzi's next opera after *L'Amore dei Tre Re*, received its premiere at La Scala on 3 November 1918. It was again a *Literaturoper*, this time setting a shortened version of a complex patriotic play by Gabriele D'Annunzio, Italy's most famous living writer. It enjoyed a reasonably successful run of ten performances at La Scala, for it seemed very topical, celebrating Italy's expansion into the Adriatic just as Italy found herself on the winning side in the First World War. But the

---

1 *American Mercury*, April 1924, 466–68, p. 466.

Italian critics judged Montemezzi's choice of text a bad one, and the very unconventional opera was expensive to produce. It was not staged again in Italy until 1923. Montemezzi himself always claimed that *La Nave* was his masterpiece.

As noted in the previous section, the Chicago Opera Association had put on a production of *L'Amore dei Tre Re* in 1915. This was well received, and though it was not repeated in the following seasons, the company clearly maintained an interest in Montemezzi, for in 1918 they entered into an agreement to give the international premiere of *La Nave* the following year. Not only this, but they planned to perform it in the Lexington Theatre, New York, as well as in Chicago, and to invite Montemezzi to travel to America (for the first time) to conduct. Montemezzi duly came, and *La Nave* opened the Chicago season on 18 November 1919. The production, with the composer present, was understood as a hugely prestigious event for the Chicago company, less than a decade old, and it attracted the intense interest of local newspapers both before and after the premiere. The Chicago critics were mostly positive about the opera, judging it a magnificent musical work, albeit not a very tuneful one. Rosa Raisa won very high praise for her performance of Basiliola, the central character, and to some extent her achievement distracted attention from the opera itself. The same can be said of Norman Bel Geddes' stage and costume designs, which proved controversial and divided the critics.

Ultimately, however, the most significant fact about the Chicago critics' response to *La Nave* is that all those who compared the new with the older opera declared that *L'Amore dei Tre Re* was clearly superior. This was the refrain which, from now on, would vex every attempt to introduce other Montemezzi operas in America.

Just two performances of *La Nave* were given in Chicago: no more had ever been planned in a season which included, astonishingly, over thirty operas. And unfortunately the plan to bring

La Nave to New York was abandoned, despite the fact that it had been announced there for nearly a year. As early as February 1919 it was reported that

> The Lexington lobbies have displayed an interesting forecast of Italy's latest operatic sensation, promised here next year. A great poster set up at the entrance reads 'Lexington Theatre, season 1919–20, Chicago Opera Association … . Opening night, Monday, Jan. 26, 1920, 'La Nave,' (in Italian,) first time in New York, music by Italo Montemezzi, tragedy by Gabriele d'Annunzio.[1]

A late decision was made to cancel the promised 'sensation,' perhaps mainly for economic reasons: it is surely significant that even without taking such a costly production as *La Nave* to New York, the Chicago company managed to make a reported loss of some $200,000 in the course of their five weeks' tenure of the Lexington.[2] But another factor in the decision may well have been Mary Garden's readiness to sing Fiora, for this offered the promise of a Montemezzi sensation of something like equivalent value. Certainly this substitution was made, and the Chicago Opera Association opened their season in New York with *L'Amore dei Tre Re*. Anyone interested in the reception of Montemezzi's operas must feel regret that the major New York critics thus missed the chance to pronounce judgement on *La Nave*.

La Nave was given a third performance in America when Teatro Grattacielo of New York revived it, in concert form, in 2012.

---

1 'Lexington Opera,' *New York Times*, 16 February 1919, 6.
2 'Chicago Opera Company's Losses Here Total $200,000,' *New York Clipper*, 3 March 1920, 6.

Giovanni Gallurese

Giovanni Gallurese was the first of Montemezzi's operas to be performed, and it launched his career in Italy, leading to his being taken up by the powerful publishing firm of Casa Ricordi, who wished to groom him as Puccini's successor. It was originally written in a one-act form for the international competition announced by Casa Sonzogno in 1901. When the twenty semi-finalists were announced in 1903, Montemezzi learned he had not been successful. Convinced this was an injustice, he expanded the opera into a three-act form in collaboration with his librettist, the very obscure Francesco D'Angelantonio. The revised opera was premiered at the Teatro Vittorio Emanuele, Turin, on 28 January 1905, under the baton of Tullio Serafin (1878–1968), Montemezzi's close friend since student days. It proved very popular, running for sixteen or seventeen performances (reports differ). *Giovanni Gallurese* was written in a much more obviously popular, tuneful and *veristic* style than Montemezzi's later operas, with Sardinian local colour and dancing; Italian critics saw it as akin to *Cavalleria Rusticana*. There were many other productions in Italy before the First World War: Montemezzi later claimed it had been performed in 'about fifty' theatres, though one suspects he was rounding up.[1]

The revival of *Giovanni Gallurese* by the Metropolitan Opera Company in 1925 was an event of major importance, not just in terms of Montemezzi's American reception, but of his career more generally. Indeed it was the most significant event of the 1920s for Montemezzi the composer, for, at a time when he seemed incapable of producing new work, it represented the most ambitious attempt to establish him as something more than the composer of *L'Amore dei Tre Re*. Despite the high

---

1 Maurice Halperson, 'How "Gallurese" Saved an Impresario from Bankruptcy,' *Musical America*, 21 February 1925, 3, 27, p. 3.

esteem in which New York critics and audiences had held the later opera for over a decade, the city had not heard another note of Montemezzi's music, apart from a single aria from *Héllera* sung in recital.[1] Serafin had been appointed principal conductor at the Met in 1924, and it was probably partly through his advocacy, and perhaps partly in his honour, that *Giovanni Gallurese* was chosen for his first season. Montemezzi, recognizing the importance of the production, and no doubt hoping for another American success, came to New York to supervise the rehearsals.

It is difficult to categorise the result. In 1948 Montemezzi recollected the production as a 'spectacular success,' and stated that he hoped *Giovanni Gallurese* would be 'done' in America again.[2] There is indeed a good deal of evidence that it was a *popular* success. An unsigned report that appeared in the *New York Evening Post* after three performances gives perhaps the best idea of how the opera was received:

> ... however much the cognoscenti may snicker at such an opera as Montemezzi's 'Giovanni Gallurese,' it continues to be embraced by the Metropolitan audiences with frantic enthusiasm.
>
> ... there were cheers from the large subscription audience for this rather flimsy story of a Sardinian bandit ... Where the critical minded

---

1 The singer was Lenora Sparkes and the recital took place at Aeolian Hall on 7 April 1921. The Montemezzi aria attracted little critical attention, but Krehbiel wrote 'Those familiar with the score of "L'Amore dei Tre Re," found no difficulty in recognizing the authorship of this air ["Héllera's air"], which is akin in character to the music of the opera now so well known.' See 'Miss Lenora Sparkes Is Heard in Recital,' *New York Tribune*, 8 April 1921, 10.

2 Arvey, 'Visits to the Homes,' 29.

may have found musical bromides of a stale school of Italian opera, an aggressive majority found stirring arias, eminently singable and, it may be added, vigorously sung.[1]

Similarly, an unsigned notice in the *Musical Observer* confirms that *Giovanni Gallurese* 'was received by an enthusiasm on the part of the audience not shared by any of the critics.'[2] The critics, however, had the last word. Even those who reviewed *Giovanni Gallurese* with a modicum of favour tended to refer to it, subsequently, as a 'failure,' and it has not been staged since. Whereas the American critics had been happy, in 1914, to align themselves with an audience they praised as enlightened and correct in its judgements, they now, in 1925, mostly disassociated themselves from the popular verdict. The subsequent fate of *Giovanni Gallurese* demonstrates the increasing power of reviewers in the overall economy of opera and reveals something of the emerging paradox whereby opera managements would seek more to please the critics than to win the public.

The critics did not all speak as one on *Giovanni Gallurese*, however. Ernest Newman, who had briefly replaced Finck at the *New York Evening Post*, and Lawrence Gilman were far more hostile than the others: in their view, the opera was simply unworthy of being staged. The other critics stopped well short of this, all of them finding some merits in the opera, and in some cases sounding a note of qualified approval. 'Considered purely as music, it [*Giovanni Gallurese*] is better than much of Puccini, and infinitely above the usual run of contemporary opera music by lesser lights,' declared Deems Taylor.[3] Nevertheless, a general sense of disappointment echoes through the reviews. The critics

---

1 '"Giovanni Gallurese" at the Metropolitan,' *New York Evening Post*, 10 March 1925, 13.

2 'A Composer's First Opera,' *Musical Observer*, April 1925, 26.

3 See below, p. 257.

had hoped for something special, something closer in quality and character to *L'Amore dei Tre Re*. What they heard was a rather ordinary opera crippled by a conventional plot and poor libretto. Their overall message was clear: *Giovanni Gallurese* was worth hearing once, but there was no reason to repeat it when the infinitely finer *L'Amore dei Tre Re* was available.

La Notte di Zoraima

Montemezzi's career never ran smoothly. In the 1910s the international press reported that he was going to write an opera based on Edmond Rostand's play *La princesse lointaine*. This never appeared, and in my understanding was probably never begun. In the 1920s Montemezzi was reported, more confidently, to be working on an opera based on Jacques-Henri Bernardin de Saint-Pierre's classic sentimental novel, *Paul et Virginie*. This was certainly started, but it was abandoned, and in the decade after *La Nave* Montemezzi did not produce a single new composition. Not until 1930 do the first references to *La Notte di Zoraima* ('The Night of Zoraima') appear in Montemezzi's letters in the Ricordi archives. This one-act opera to an original (though very conventional) libretto by the young Mario Ghisalberti (1902–80) was written quite quickly and premiered at La Scala on 31 January 1931. It was modestly successful and La Scala put it on again the following season.

It is a tribute to Montemezzi's high standing in the United States, and perhaps to the rivalry subsisting between New York and Chicago, that Giulio Gatti-Casazza, director of the Met, moved rapidly to secure the American premiere, and *La Notte di Zoraima* was brought out in New York just ten months later, on 2 December 1931. This time the reaction of the more respected American critics was overwhelmingly negative. Whereas they had, for the most part, judged *Giovanni Gallurese* with some indulgence, treating it as a first effort, no excuses could be made for *La Notte di Zoraima*, which was condemned as far inferior to *L'Amore dei Tre Re*. The libretto was dismissed as trashy and clichéd and Montemezzi's music represented as mechanical and uninspired: its similarity to that of his famous opera was allowed, but it was judged as devoid of what Gilman called 'fresh enkindlement, from without or from within.'[1] Of the major critics, only Deems Taylor sounded a positive note, praising the music and the orchestration, though condemning, like his peers, the plot and the libretto. The only aspect of the production to win general praise was Rosa Ponselle's performance as Zoraima.

Like *Giovanni Gallurese*, *La Notte di Zoraima* did have a certain old-fashioned, downmarket appeal. The obscure Joseph A. Miller of the Brooklyn *Standard Union*, who wrote the most positive review of the first night performance, found it 'good lusty opera of the old school, and the music is good, juicy melody': he thought it could become a repertoire work.[2] In a similar vein, Linton Martin of the popular *Philadelphia Inquirer* found *La Notte* 'seductively saccharine, and opulent in orchestration, so that it is always easy to listen to.'[3] Despite such comments, the media reports do not suggest a significant difference of opinion between critics and public as there had been with *Giovanni Gallurese*. This time Montemezzi did not come to America for the production, but his wife, Katherine, did – she attended both the New York and Philadelphia performances – and one must suppose she chose her words carefully when she sent her report to Italy. The only American review she could have enjoyed showing to her husband is that of A. Walter Kramer for *Musical America*. Writing after most of the other critics, Kramer must have been aware of their 'savage slaughter' of the opera,[4] and perhaps, as a

---

1 See below, p. 299.

2 'The Night of Zoraima,' *Standard Union*, 3 December 1931, 6.

3 'Montemezzi Opera in Premiere Here,' *Philadelphia Inquirer*, 13 January 1932, 6.

4 Linton Martin's description. Ibid.

great admirer of Montemezzi, this inclined him to be particularly generous. Certainly his verdict is very much at odds with the others, his praise of the 'exceptional aristocracy' of Montemezzi's style effectively separating him from Miller and Martin.

La Notte di Zoraima is likely to remain the Montemezzi opera for which his admirers find it most difficult to make a case. Rosa Ponselle, who by all accounts did her very best for it, can be given the last word here. She felt that it was a 'weak effort' and when, later in life, she was asked to inscribe her thoughts of various operas on a stack of programmes she simply wrote 'No!' on that of *La Notte di Zoraima*.[1]

L'Incantesimo

Much of the negative criticism of *La Nave*, the revived *Giovanni Gallurese* and *La Notte di Zoraima* focussed on their librettos. Perhaps it was this which led Montemezzi to seek a second collaboration with Sem Benelli, whose contribution to *L'Amore dei Tre Re* had been so very much admired. It is not clear when they decided to work together, but Benelli supplied the composer with the libretto of *L'Incantesimo* ('The Enchantment') – the only purpose-written libretto Benelli ever attempted – in 1933. Montemezzi began work on it straight away, but he found the political situation in Italy unconducive to creative work – so at least he reported after he moved to the United States in 1939 – and made little progress. Most of the composition was done in Beverly Hills, California, after Montemezzi settled there in 1940. He completed the score in summer 1942 and decided to make a 'special request' that NBC broadcast the premiere of *L'Incantesimo* as effectively a radio opera: 'Long an admirer of the NBC Symphony Orchestra, he expressed a wish that his new creation be performed with this orchestra. NBC

---

1 Ponselle and Drake, *Ponselle*, 125, 239.

acceded with enthusiasm.'[1] Montemezzi certainly intended his new work for conventional performance, too, but in the midst of the Second World War there may well have seemed little prospect of a new, one-act opera being staged. In any case, as the critics remarked, *L'Incantesimo* is an opera which seems particularly suited to the radio medium.

L'Incantesimo was broadcast from Radio City, New York, between 1.30 and 2.30 pm on Saturday 9 October 1943, with the composer conducting.[2] Introduced to the world in this way, at the height of the Pacific and European conflicts, it inevitably attracted much less attention than a peacetime premiere at the Met. Nevertheless, the new opera was warmly welcomed by Montemezzi's established champions, Olin Downes (in the *New York Times*) and Oscar Thompson (in the *Sun* and *Musical America*). Both men had been unimpressed by *Giovanni Gallurese* and *La Notte di Zoraima* and they welcomed *L'Incantesimo* as a return to form, as a work worthy of the composer of *L'Amore dei Tre Re*. Downes was particularly enthusiastic:

> we have in the finest pages of 'L'Incantesimo' the same priceless melodic substance, so scarce today in music; the same Italianate song in terms of translated symphonism, which made 'L'Amore'; the same freedom from dross and poetic sentiment. Just some more of it, which is splendid, and likely to be of wide popular appeal.[3]

---

[1] Viva Liebling, 'News and Previews of Radio, Stage and Screen,' *Musical Courier*, 5 October 1943, 8–9, p. 8.

[2] Recordings of the broadcast survive. A restored version, with a translation of the libretto, can be found on the CD *Souvenirs from Verismo Operas – Volume 4* released by the International Record Collectors' Club (IRCC CD 820).

[3] See below, p. 325.

On the other hand, in a demonstration of how different things were from 1914, Virgil Thomson, now the other major critic of the New York music scene, did not review *L'Incantesimo* at all. Rather, he resigned it to one of his underlings at the *New York Herald Tribune*, Jerome D. Bohm (b. 1892), who dismissed it as 'too derivative and undramatic a product to command more than respect for the expertness with which it is tailored.'[1] The other reviews were all very brief, and most took up a position roughly half way between Downes' high praise and Bohm's studied apathy. After Downes and Thompson, perhaps the most significant praise came from the composer Marion Bauer, who found in the new opera 'Montemezzi's finest style of beautiful lyricism, rich harmonization and splendid orchestration.'[2]

Altogether it is clear that the American critics, at least in the context of October 1943, did not regard *L'Incantesimo* as a particularly significant work. It was not staged in the United States until 2010, when it was put on by the Opera Theater of Pittsburgh. It had previously been revived, in concert form, by Teatro Grattacielo of New York in 2007.

L'Amore dei Tre Re, 1930–1962

On 30 April 1929 the Metropolitan Opera Company gave its fifty-third performance of *L'Amore dei Tre Re*. Since 1914 the company had thus averaged a little over three performances of the opera a season. It was the most frequently performed of all post-1910 operas, with *Der Rosenkavalier*, its nearest rival, having been presented forty-eight times (for comparison: *Gianni Schicchi* had been staged twenty times, *Turandot* nineteen times). Yet at this juncture, Montemezzi's opera suddenly started to slide out of

---

[1] '"L'Incantesimo" By Montemezzi Has Premiere,' *New York Herald Tribune*, 10 October 1943, 40.

[2] See below, p. 333.

the Met's repertoire. It was nearly four years before it was staged again, on 17 February 1933. Then, after three performances that season, there was an even longer interval before the fifty-seventh performance was finally reached on 27 December 1939.

The situation in New York was repeated in Chicago. Mary Garden sang the role of Fiora for the thirty-fourth and last time on 22 November 1930, before retiring from the Chicago company the following year. The company collapsed in 1932, as did the Ravinia Opera, which had been faithfully performing *L'Amore dei Tre Re* since 1918. Chicago did not hear the opera again until the Chicago City Opera Company gave single performances in 1937 and 1938. Elsewhere the situation was still worse. Philadelphia, for example, had got used to hearing Montemezzi's masterpiece regularly in the 1910s and '20s. In 1929 Linton Martin (1887–1954) of the *Philadelphia Inquirer* declared that '"The Love of Three Kings" has taken its place as so vital a work that its omission for even a single season would be a serious loss.'[1] Yet Philadelphia witnessed only one more performance of the opera in Martin's lifetime: in 1933. After that Philadelphians did not have the chance to see *L'Amore dei Tre Re* again until 1956, when the Philadelphia Grand Opera Company put on a single performance with Beverly Sills as Fiora.

There is obviously no one explanation for *L'Amore dei Tre Re* suddenly starting to lose ground like this. The economic impact of the recession was clearly significant, especially in Chicago. There were also casting difficulties, with many of the singers who had maintained the opera's place in the repertoire in the 1910s and '20s reaching retirement age. The productions themselves – which in the Met's case was still substantially that of 1914 – were starting to show their age. And, as always, there were many voices calling for a general refreshing and updating of the repertoire.

---

[1] 'Ponselle In "Love Of 3 Kings" Excels,' *Philadelphia Inquirer*, 16 January 1929, 2.

In such a context, there was little for critics loyal to *L'Amore dei Tre Re* to do in the 1930s apart from reaffirming the opera's merits and hoping for better times. Those better times did briefly arrive in the early 1940s, with Montemezzi's move to America in 1939. His presence gave an immediate boost to the fortunes of *L'Amore dei Tre Re* in the United States. The Chicago Opera Company mounted a production in 1940, and the Met and the San Francisco company followed in 1941. Suddenly the opera again had the sort of currency it had enjoyed in the 1920s. The Met's 1941 production was particularly notable. Montemezzi conducted himself (the first time he had conducted this opera in America), and premiered a beautiful orchestral prelude he had written for the third act to replace what had previously been a very brief orchestral introduction. The second performance, moreover, was broadcast: this was the first time that Americans were able to hear the opera on the radio.[1] The critics were virtually unanimous that under Montemezzi's baton, and with Grace Moore as the new Fiora, *L'Amore dei Tre Re* sounded fresher and more powerful than it had for many years. Oscar Thompson enthused:

> 'L'Amore' has never sounded more consistently of a piece than it did last night. One could say again what was said of it at the time of its Metropolitan premiere on January 2, 1914, that in its workmanship here was the finest operatic score that had come out of Italy since the last operas of Verdi, not excepting the successive 'hits' of Puccini.[2]

Later in the year, Montemezzi conducted the opera in San Francisco, the first time a composer had conducted his own

---

1 Recordings of this broadcast survive. A version superbly restored by Richard Caniell, with valuable bonuses and supporting documentation, has been released on CD by Guild Historical (GHCD 2234/35).

2 'Montemezzi Leads "L'Amore,"' *Sun*, 8 February 1941, 28.

opera there, and again won enthusiastic acclaim both for his conducting and his opera. In 1946 the Cincinnati Opera revived *L'Amore dei Tre Re*, again with Montemezzi conducting.

Despite such a promising start to his stay in the United States, though, even Montemezzi's presence was not enough to make *L'Amore dei Tre Re* anything like the annual event it had been in the past. Having done it in 1941, the Met did not revive it until the 1948–49 season, and gave their sixty-sixth, and to date last, production on 15 January 1949 (the second broadcast production). After this, the opera was not staged in New York again until 1982, when it was revived by the New York City Opera. In Chicago, similarly, after the 1940 performance *L'Amore dei Tre Re* was not repeated until 1955, when the Lyric Theater created a new production that played for two performances. This is, at the time of writing, the last occasion on which *L'Amore dei Tre Re* (or indeed any Montemezzi opera) was heard in Chicago; a planned revival in the 2003–04 season was dropped for financial reasons.[1] In San Francisco the opera fared somewhat better, with revivals in 1942 and 1947 (both conducted by the composer), 1952, 1959 and 1966 – but apparently none since then. Other American opera companies have given *L'Amore dei Tre Re* from time to time, and other cities have heard it, but the language surrounding these revivals tends always to describe it as a forgotten, unfamiliar work. The Golden Age for the opera in the United States clearly ended in 1930. The ensuing Silver Age could perhaps be said to have ended in 1949, with the last Met performance, but I shall make the more optimistic case that it ended in 1962, with the NBC's televised production of the opera.

Before considering that production, it is worth paying some attention to one of the finest printed tributes to the continued high standing of *L'Amore dei Tre Re* in the United States in the Silver Age of that opera's fortunes. Indeed it is worth emphasising

---

1 Marsh, *150 Years of Opera*, 215.

that, inevitably, the critical history and the production history do not match: critics did not suddenly stop admiring the opera in 1930, and it was only after the deaths of such influential figures as Henderson (1937), Gilman (1939) and Thompson (1945) that some falling off in critical appreciation of the opera can be felt. Nevertheless, as late as 1949 *Opera News*, the standard opera magazine founded in 1936, devoted a special issue to the opera, in conjunction with (what turned out to be) the Met's final performance and broadcast of the work. The leading article by Herbert F. Peyser – along with Olin Downes the last surviving of the major critics who had welcomed *L'Amore dei Tre Re* in 1914 – is included in the present anthology. Among other features on the opera there is a remarkable essay by Jane Phillips (1926–2013) who, as Mary Jane Phillips-Matz, would later publish major biographies of Verdi (1992) and Puccini (2002). The beginning and the conclusion are worth quoting here:[1]

> Opera in America, we are constantly told, is dying. It is stereotyped, hidebound and strangled by convention. Opera is unnatural and unreal, doomed to failure by the mediocrity of its characters, plots and staging. It lacks popular appeal, say its critics; and, above all, it is lost because opera is art in its lowest form. …
>
> One answer to these critics is to be found in the ever-growing ranks of opera lovers, in the record sales, the increasingly large radio audience and the full houses from San Francisco to New York, from Montreal to Miami. Another answer is the truly artistic performances of our time – but almost the best answer of all is *L'Amore dei tre Re*.

---

1 I had hoped to include the entire essay in this anthology. Unfortunately the copyright does not belong to *Opera News*, but to Phillips-Matz's heirs, who have set a prohibitively high price on the reproduction rights.

It [*L'Amore dei Tre Re*] is intense tragedy, worthy of any stage in the world, and as such it takes its place in tragedy's highest ranks. It is the best, not only of opera, but of drama and poetry, not only for today but for all people in all time. Every scene conveys a lifetime of experience; and further than that it is not possible to go.[1]

And further than *that*, it might be added, it was not possible for critics to go. There is some irony in the fact that the most enthusiastic endorsement of the opera by an American critic should have coincided with its last appearance on a New York stage for over three decades. After 1950 there are still occasional statements to be found of *L'Amore dei Tre Re* being one of the greatest of all operas – for example in Ethel Peyser and Marion Bauer's *How Opera Grew: From Ancient Greece to the Present Day* (1956), the relevant extract from which is included in this anthology. But in general appreciation was cooling, partly, no doubt, because critics were no longer able to see the opera. Every time *L'Amore dei Tre Re* has been revived in America it has prompted enthusiastic criticism, but it has slipped from being one of the great standard operas to being appreciated, if at all, as an unjustly neglected masterpiece. William E. Smith of the Philadelphia *Evening Bulletin*, who was asked to write the programme notes for Philadelphia's 1956 revival of the opera, established the general tone when he emphasized the 'most unjustified neglect of a truly great work.' Critics who have praised the opera have necessarily tended to adopt a more defensive, combative tone, for they can no longer write with the assurance that the operatic establishment shares their views.

Perhaps the last time they could write with some of the old assurance was in 1962. The NBC's well-received television

---

1 'Ay, Every Inch a King,' *Opera News*, 10 January 1949, 12, 14, 31.

version of *L'Amore dei Tre Re*, broadcast in colour on 25 February 1962 and then again on 27 January 1963, represented a powerful statement of belief in the opera some half century after its first appearance in New York and Boston. The NBC Opera Company had been created in 1949 and commenced operations in January 1950 with a broadcast of Kurt Weill's 30-minute opera, *Down in the Valley*. The response was so positive that by the end of the year they were given a 100-minute slot for *Carmen*. The company prospered in the early '50s, and by 1956 were sufficiently established to take their *Marriage of Figaro* and *Madame Butterfly* – sung in English like all their productions – on an ambitious tour of forty-seven cities. In many ways they were, at this juncture, America's leading opera company, and certainly the one with the largest audience. But costs soared; by the end of the decade they were running into financial difficulties, and the company was dissolved in 1964. Despite the growing economic crisis, though, the NBC Company was consistently able to reach an audience numbered in millions; the advance publicity for their Montemezzi production confidently declared that 'millions more people will watch this single performance of "The Love of Three Kings" than have seen it since its premiere in 1913.'

The NBC Opera Company concentrated on producing either new works (in many cases specially written for television) or established repertoire favourites. A glance at their broadcasts in the years 1960–61 gives a good idea. In 1960 they presented *Cavalleria Rusticana*, *Don Giovanni* and their perennial Christmas favourite, Menotti's *Amahl and the Night Visitors*. In 1961 followed *Deseret*, a new television opera by Leonard Kastle, *Fidelio*, *Boris Godunov* and, again, *Amahl*.[1] The decision to produce *L'Amore dei Tre Re*, announced in 1960 – the original intention being to

---

[1] These details are taken from the invaluable catalogue in the second volume of Helga Bertz-Dostal, *Oper im Fernsehen* (Vienna: Herausgegeben mit Förderung der Gesellschaft für Musiktheater, 1970).

broadcast the opera in 1961 – was thus tantamount to declaring it a 'standard' opera, even though most other American opera companies were no longer treating it as such. The key figure behind the decision must have been the aging Samuel Chotzinoff (1889–1964), the company's influential founder and managing director who lived in New York most of his life and presumably had memories of the enormous impact Montemezzi's opera had made in 1914 (Chotzinoff was a great admirer of Toscanini, and published a book about him). As a critic for the New York *World* from 1925 to 1931 and for the *New York Post* from 1935 to 1941, Chotzinoff had, moreover, praised *L'Amore dei Tre Re* on many occasions. And he could boast a personal relationship with its composer, with whom he had corresponded about *L'Incantesimo*. These facts, especially when combined with the ensuing demonstration that Montemezzi's opera *would* work very well as an opera for television, sufficiently explain what may have seemed a slightly eccentric decision to some of Chotzinoff's younger colleagues in 1960. In any case, he was strongly supported by the NBC Company's veteran television director, Kirk Browning (1921–2008), who believed *L'Amore dei Tre Re* was a 'good opera' that would make a 'good television show,' and that it 'contains the most passionate love scenes in all opera.'[1] About six months of preparation were devoted to the NBC production that was to carry Montemezzi's masterpiece to its largest ever audience, and that certainly prolonged its currency in the United States.

The impact of *L'Amore dei Tre Re* in the United States can be represented with the metaphor of a wave. Montemezzi's opera was a tidal wave overwhelming the eastern seaboard in 1914 and starting its spread across the country. Smaller waves coming in

---

[1] Quoted in Harold Stern, 'NBC Opera "Season" Tomorrow,' *Evening Press* (Binghamton), 24 February 1962, 3.

behind it at regular intervals renewed, but with diminishing force, the forward, tidal impetus of that original surge. The first of these was Mary Garden's taking the role of Fiora in 1920, and extensive touring with the opera; the second was Montemezzi moving to America in 1939; the third was Chotzinoff's decision, around 1960, to televise the opera. The NBC broadcasts in 1962 and '63 and the 1966 revival of *L'Amore dei Tre Re* in San Francisco were the last appearances of the opera in the United States still driven, to some extent, by the tidal movement originating in 1914. There have been a considerable number of American productions of *L'Amore dei Tre Re* since then, but they have had to build up their own, modest momentum, perhaps drawing on memories of the past, but no longer borne along by it. The wave of 1914 has retreated into the distance, and into something like legend. But it should not be forgotten.

Note on the Texts

The general aim throughout this anthology has been to present the reviews and essays on Montemezzi's operas in a form that, apart from the reformatting required for their publication in a book like this, is as close to the original as possible. While very obvious typos have been corrected, on the assumption that they reflect errors introduced at the printing stage, other mistakes have been retained. These often reveal something about the critic. The many misspellings of names in Huneker's reviews, for example, may result from his carelessness, but more likely derive from the fact that he refused to use a typewriter. The title of Montemezzi's most famous opera, *L'Amore dei Tre Re*, has been written with every variety of capitalization, and the composer himself was not consistent on the matter. Individual critics have been allowed to make their own choice on this.

Part One:

L'Amore dei Tre Re

(Premiered at La Scala, Milan, 10 April 1913)

**The Metropolitan Opera House,
New York, 1913**

American Premiere

New York, Metropolitan Opera House, 2 January 1914

5 performances

Cast:
Fiora . . . . Lucrezia Bori
Avito . . . . Edoardo Ferrari-Fontana
Manfredo . . . . Pasquale Amato
Archibaldo . . . . Adamo Didur

Director: Jules Speck
Stage Design: Mario Sala
Costume Design: Giuseppe Mancini
Conductor: Arturo Toscanini

FIRE NOTICE: Look around now and choose the nearest exit to your seat. In case of fire walk (do not run) to that exit. Do not try to beat your neighbor to the street. By order of Fire Com.

METROPOLITAN OPERA HOUSE

GRAND OPERA SEASON · 1913~1914
GIULIO GATTI-CASAZZA, General Manager

FRIDAY EVENING, JANUARY 2ND, AT 8.15 O'CLOCK

FIRST TIME IN AMERICA

L'AMORE DEI TRE RE

OPERA IN THREE ACTS BY SEM BENELLI
(IN ITALIAN)

MUSIC BY ITALO MONTEMEZZI

ARCHIBALDO	ADAMO DIDUR
MANFREDO	PASQUALE AMATO
AVITO	EDOARDO FERRARI-FONTANA
FLAMINIO (HIS FIRST APPEARANCE HERE)	ANGELO BADA
UN GIOVANETTO	PIETRO AUDISIO
FIORA	LUCREZIA BORI
ANCELLA	JEANNE MAUBOURG
UNA GIOVANETTA	SOPHIE BRASLAU
UNA VECCHIA	MARIA DUCHENE
CONDUCTOR	ARTURO TOSCANINI
STAGE MANAGER	JULES SPECK
CHORUS MASTER	GIULIO SETTI
TECHNICAL DIRECTOR	EDWARD SIEDLE

CONTINUED ON NEXT PAGE   CORRECT LIBRETTOS FOR SALE IN THE LOBBY

HARDMAN PIANOS USED EXCLUSIVELY

1. Herbert F. Peyser, *Musical America*, 10 January 1914.

Success Unequivocal Crowns 'L'Amore Dei Tre Re' In Its First American Performance

Coming Almost Unheralded, Montemezzi's Opera Produces Electrifying Effect Upon Witnesses of Its Première at Metropolitan – 'One of the Most Deeply Affecting and Full-blooded Scores Since Wagner' – Thrillingly Sung by Bori, Amato, Ferrari-Fontana and Didur

'L'AMORE DEI TRE RE' ('The Love of the Three Kings'), a three-act lyrical tragedy with text by the young but well-known Italian poet and dramatist, Sem Benelli, and music by the young but practically unknown Italian composer, Italo Montemezzi, was given for the first time in this country at the Metropolitan Opera House on Friday evening, January 2, as the second operatic novelty of the season.[1] The production was consummated with a minimum of advance heralding, without increase in the prices of accommodations and without any particular claims of the management in respect to the artistic qualities of the work. And the wisdom of this policy of comparative silence and seeming indifference was demonstrated forcibly and movingly at the première even as had been the case with 'Boris' last season and with 'Königskinder' two years earlier.[2]

---

1 The first 'novelty' was *Der Rosenkavalier*, premiered on 9 December 1913.

2 *Boris Godunov*, sung in Italian, received its American premiere at the Met on 19 March 1913; Engelbert Humperdinck's *Königskinder* had its world premiere there on 28 December 1910.

'L'Amore dei Tre Re' is in relation to the 'Rosenkavalier' a repetition of the case of 'Königskinder' and the 'Girl'[1] – only with a reversal of nationality in the present instance. Gently and unostentatiously it unfolded itself a creation of the purest, most touching, simplest and most resistless beauty, a pregnant new word in the lexicon of modern Italian opera, in many ways the most gratifying example of musical drama from the higher aesthetic standpoints that has come out of Italy since Verdi.

True enough, the drama as such is very far removed from the coarse, sensuous, blood-heating affairs so highly prized by contemporary operatic artisans of that country and so dear, though vitiating, to popular taste. True, as well, Montemezzi has neither essayed nor achieved fire-eyed and revolutionary conclusions in his music for the delectation of progressive pedantry. Nor yet has he pandered, Puccini-like, to obvious musical appetites. In spite of all these impediments, apparently formidable to those of superficial mentality, there need be little apprehension respecting the success of 'L'Amore.' Popular psychology in such matters often seems baffling to those who fail to recognize that the great body of the public is in the last analysis fully responsive to the effects of the genuinely sterling in art. Lofty beauty paired with sincerity is an element to which the popular consciousness eventually reacts despite the controversions of cynicism. And with these qualities Montemezzi's opera is suffused from the first bar to the last. Moreover it has the invaluable asset of brevity; barely two hours and a half are required for the enactment of the tragedy, including the two intermissions, thus bringing it practically within the same time limit as 'Bohème.'

In this brief preamble momentary reference must likewise be made to the magnificently opulent mounting provided by the Metropolitan, and the devoted efforts and superb interpretation accorded the work by Miss Bori, and Messrs. Amato, Edoardo

---

[1] Puccini's *La Fanciulla del West*, which had its world premiere at the Met on 10 December 1910, eighteen days before that of *Königskinder*.

Ferrari-Fontana and Didur, not forgetting the all-comprehensive influence of Mr. Toscanini at the orchestral helm.

Success Unequivocal

Success indeed crowned the new opera absolutely and unequivocally and it may forthwith be considered to have taken its place in the Metropolitan répertoire as a popular favorite destined to rank with 'Boris' and 'Königskinder.' The first act, to be sure, left the issue unsettled, for though the large audience applauded it cordially it was not yet prepared to pledge its faith unreservedly. But doubt and hesitancy vanished with the second act, after the thrilling conclusion of which the house broke into a tornado of applause and hypothetical success became assured triumph. Sixteen times were the four principals summoned before the curtain amidst cheers, and unavailing efforts were made to bring forward Mr. Toscanini. But the conductor, later reported to be indisposed, refrained from appearing. Practically everyone remained to witness the tragic *dénouement* and there was also much enthusiasm when the final curtain fell.

The production was in all its departments worthy of the little master-work. The *mise-en-scène* by Mario Sala is striking in every scene – the sombre hall with its huge blocks of marble supported by thick marble columns; the castellated battlements in the second act with massive fortress in the background and overhead, floating clouds which thicken at the approach of the catastrophe; and the chapel crypt in the third, a reproduction of the church of San Vitale in Ravenna with its architecture and mosaics of Byzantine style.[1]

---

[1] The Basilica of San Vitale, completed in the 540s. This may have served as a general inspiration, but to call the stage design a 'reproduction' is misleading. It is worth noting that this famous church was also taken as a model by Guido Marussig when he came to design the sets for Montemezzi's next opera, *La Nave*. See *Essays on the Montemezzi-D'Annunzio 'Nave,'* 2nd edition, ed. David Chandler (Norwich: Durrant, 2014), 39.

Stage Design for the First Act by Mario Sala

Stage Design for the Second Act by Mario Sala

Stage Design for the Third Act by Mario Sala

Dramatically the four leading artists played into each other's hands in unsurpassable style. Lucrezia Bori, as *Fiora*, put to her credit the best achievement of her American career.[1] A ravishing picture to the eye, a marvel of grace and plasticity, she sang enchantingly and denoted with a world of pathos the soul-struggle of the young woman fully conscious of the worth of her lord, touched by the infinite pathos of his idolatry of her, yet powerless to resist the importunities of one whose ardor overrides all her scruples. Her *Fiora* heightens the young woman's artistic stature very noticeably

Ferrari-Fontana's Début

Mr. Ferrari-Fontana – the husband of Mme. Matzenauer[2] – who had never before been heard in New York, won an instantaneous place in the affections of his audience by his work as *Avito*. He acted it intelligently and revealed a tenor voice of great volume, essentially Italian in timbre but always virile, ringing and resonant and well-handled. Nervousness may have had something to do with the unsteadiness of his tones at the beginning of the opera, for this disappeared as the evening advanced. His further appearances will be expectantly awaited.

In notably good voice, Mr. Amato also covered himself with glory as the noble-hearted, all-forgiving *Manfredo*, the most sympathetic figure in the work. He sang his farewell to *Fiora* with due feeling for its tenderness and was moving in the death scene. Mr. Didur has done nothing better outside of *Boris*[3] than

---

[1] Bori moved to America in 1912, and first sung at the Met on the opening night of the 1912–13 season (11 November), performing the eponymous heroine's role in Puccini's *Manon Lescaut*.

[2] Margaret Matzenauer (1881–1963), the mezzo-soprano who had been singing at the Met since 1911.

[3] Didur sang the role of Boris in the Met's 1913 production of *Boris Godunov*.

the blind *Archibaldo*, prescient in his world of darkness, goaded to madness by the thought of his son's betrayal and eventually, through the supreme irony of fate, bereft of all that made life tolerable for him. The strangling of *Fiora* he made properly gruesome and he looked the embodiment of fate as, with halting steps but firm determination, he carried away the body of his son's wife whom he had loved with jealous affection. Mr. Didur, moreover, sang the music well. Mr. Bada filled the small rôle of the guard, *Flaminio*, adequately while Mr. Audisio, Mme. Maubourg and Mme. Duchène assumed rôles of very subsidiary account. The mourning choruses were beautifully sung.

Despite his reported illness Mr. Toscanini read this score with overwhelming dramatic force and also with a wealth of poetic tenderness. There were moments, though, in which he permitted his enthusiasm for the instrumental parts to militate against discretion with the inevitable consequence of engulfing the singers. The orchestral execution left no flaw open to critical attack.

The Tragedy of Benelli

A detailed summary of the argument of Sem Benelli's drama having been given in last week's issue of MUSICAL AMERICA, the need is obviated of its reiteration at this writing. Suffice it to recall that its scene is a feudal castle in a mountainous region of Italy, its time of action some indeterminate period of the middle ages forty years after an unnamed barbarian invasion. Briefly, the essentials of the plot treat of the illicit passion of *Fiora*, spouse of the warrior *Manfredo*, for *Avito*, an Italian princeling subjugated by the ruling invaders – among whom *Manfredo* and his blind and aged father, *Archibaldo*, are leaders – of the surprisal of the guilty pair by the latter, who straightway avenges his son's honor by strangling the girl and then entraps his son's betrayer by the device of poison spread on the dead *Fiora's* lips. But *Archibaldo* further becomes party to his own unhappiness by unwittingly causing the death of the guiltless *Manfredo* who likewise kisses the lips of his wife as she lies on her bier.

In its operatic form Sem Benelli's tragedy has been subjected to practically no alterations beyond a slight abridgement of several speeches and a few unimportant changes of words made necessary by musical exigencies. The poet has converted the episodes which originally preceded the entrance of *Avito* in the last act to elegiac choruses on the stage and behind the scenes.[1] Beyond that the drama remains intact. With the possible exception of Brian Hooker's 'Mona'[2] no such beautiful libretto has fallen to the lot of an opera composer in many years and certainly none of Italian extraction has been so exceptionally favored. In matter and treatment Benelli's piece betrays something of a kinship to Maeterlinck – the Maeterlinck of 'Monna Vanna' – and d'Annunzio.[3] Admirably proportioned,

---

[1] Act 3 of Benelli's spoken play starts with a mother and daughter visiting the dead Fiora; as they leave, a smith and soldier enter together, and there is an extended conversation concerning the circumstances of the princess's death. As the smith and soldier leave in turn, Avito enters. The removal of these scenes hardly changes the story, but they do include the information that Flaminio has been hung above the castle drawbridge as a 'flag of death': a poignant detail, omitted in the opera, which further emphasizes the terrible isolation of Archibaldo at the end.

[2] *Mona*, an opera composed by Horatio Parker (1863–1919) and with a libretto in old-fashioned 'poetic' English by Brian Hooker (1880–1946), won a $10,000 prize the Met awarded in 1911 for the best opera in English by an American composer. Four performances were given at the Met in 1912.

[3] Maurice Maeterlinck (1862–1949), the Belgian playwright whose *Pelléas and Mélisande* (1893) provided the libretto for Debussy's opera; *Monna Vanna*, a play of 1902, itself inspired several operas, including an abandoned version by Rakhmaninov. Gabriele D'Annunzio (1863–1938), Italy's leading man of letters in the early 1900s, had written several highly poetic plays that were later to be adapted as operas. One of these, *La Nave* (1908), became the basis of Montemezzi's next opera. Italian critics recognized Benelli as strongly influenced by D'Annunzio.

wrought with compelling emotional power, dramatic logic and consistency, simple in motive, it is always atmospheric and poetic. The sense of impending tragedy is established from the outset.

Though a perusal of the libretto conveys an impression of possible slowness and paucity of action the idea completely vanishes in the course of actual representation. As in 'Tristan,' however, the action is pre-eminently psychologic.

It may be urged that the tristful tale offers no feature of novelty, that it is but a variant of 'Francesca da Rimini'[1] and similar in its essentials to countless others of that stamp. The contention is undoubtedly valid but how vain! Whether familiar in its fundamental aspects or not it is in the profoundest measure elemental and human, a story a thousand times repeated in this guise or in that, but never old. Benelli's personages, too, are clearly drawn, and admirably vitalized figures – notably the blameless, large-hearted, all-forgiving *Manfredo*, innocent victim of an inexorable fate, and the blind *Archibaldo*, a sort of Guido Malatesta,[2] stern and terrible arbiter of savage justice, a patriarchal Nemesis, at once awesome and pathetic. Four characters sustain the burden of the drama – the chorus is a picturesque but none the less an episodic element in the last act – yet not for one moment does interest flag. The emotional plan is not of the nerve-rasping order favored by the disciples of the younger Italian school. It is that of tragedy in the lofty Aristotelian sense.

Benelli is a true poet (how unutterably of another world is

---

1 The story of adulterous love in Dante's *Divine Comedy* that inspired a bewildering number of operas and plays including, notably, the play by D'Annunzio (1902) that served as the libretto for Riccardo Zandonai's opera, *Francesca da Rimini* (1914).

2 This appears to be a mistaken reference to Giovanni Malatesta, the cuckolded and vengeful older brother in the *Francesca da Rimini* story. Francesca's father was called Guido (da Polenta).

this text from the concoctions of that clever hack Illica!¹) and 'L'Amore' is in almost every line redolent of the grace of imagination and the beauty of tender poetic fancy. Its verse is pliant and elastic. Unlike Hooker's poem for 'Mona,' it is not of such concentrated richness of expression and imagery as to defy the enhancement of its eloquence by musical investiture. In divining the ideal suitability to operatic purposes of a work of this nature and in adapting it to such in bare-faced defiance of all the tenets of Italian veritism, Italo Montemezzi steps forth without warning into the front rank of contemporary operatic writers, one who if he continues to travel the path which he has trodden in 'L'Amore dei Tre Re' will prove himself an untold artistic boon to his country by restoring its opera to the sphere of poetry, nobility and dignity from which 'realists' have sought in an evil day to divorce it.

In the process of a critical summary it becomes necessary to estimate the new work on the respective basis of poem and score. Nevertheless, the hearer of the opera must be forcibly struck by the extraordinarily felicitous amalgamation of these two factors, their rare unity and ideal coherence.

Montemezzi's Genius Indubitable

Montemezzi is but twenty-eight years of age.² In his present score – his third operatic venture, the previous ones having been 'Giovanni Gallurese' and 'Hellera' – he has well-nigh managed in three or four instances to touch greatness. But if 'L'Amore' is

---

1 Luigi Illica (1857–1919), now best remembered for his collaborations with Giuseppe Giacosa on the librettos for Puccini's *La Bohème*, *Tosca* and *Madama Butterfly*. Among many other librettos, he also wrote *La Wally* for Catalani, *Andrea Chénier* for Giordano, and *Iris* for Mascagni. Montemezzi had collaborated with him on the unsuccessful *Héllera* (1909).

2 Like many of the American reviewers, Peyser was confused about this: Montemezzi was thirty-eight.

big in intrinsic virtues it is bigger still in promise. The young man possesses indubitable genius. In some respects he is already a master. To what heights his bounteous innate gifts will ultimately conduct him can scarcely be surmised as this juncture. Normal advance along the lines indicated by the present score may prove him the legitimate heir to the supremacy of Verdi.

The grasp of the principles of operatic technic and craftsmanship is consummate. Montemezzi's sense of the dramatic is innate and compelling. He comprehends in the fullest the relative functions and capacities of orchestra and voice and writes for the latter with unerring instinct for what is idiomatic and most effective in the best modern sense. No explosive effects nor awkward infractions of the melodic line – so prevalent in contemporary operatic writing – are discernible in this fluent and supple, arioso, veritable type of Wagnerian 'speech-song,' magnificent in the extensive reach and broad span of its melodic phrases.

Viewed in its larger aspects Montemezzi's score discloses itself as one of the most deeply affecting, whole-heartedly sincere, virile, full-blooded and emotionally persuasive that has come to light since the death of Wagner. From the very outset the young composer summarily evinces his absolute independence of Puccini. A Wagnerian influence is, doubtless, inherent in its substance even as it permeates all modern composition to a greater or lesser extent, but Montemezzi is neither a servile copyist nor yet an unmitigated epigone.

A few chord formations savor vaguely of Debussy and a tinge of Russianism is sensed at moments – a touch of the Tschaikowsky of the 'Manfred' Symphony, implied but not directly expressed and filtered, moreover, through the mask of the young composer's own pronounced musical personality. Already his individuality is patent and his speech perceptibly his very own. Invariably modern in spirit his music is guiltless of grotesque harmonic or orchestral aberrations. But its physiognomy is recognizably characteristic.

Prodigality of means is generally a failing consonant with youth in the sphere of musical creativity. But Montemezzi, in this splendidly concise and symmetrical score, never oversteps the bounds of modesty. His orchestral requisitions are not excessive and his scoring is comparatively light. Yet how translucent, how rich in color, how plastic, how amply compact and massive in moments of climax! Indeed, there is probably no living Italian musician who can boast a more comprehensive technic, more solid musicianship or greater facility of creating atmosphere with a few simple strokes.

Melodic Invention

Montemezzi's vein of melodic invention is at once plenteous and opulent. Not a commonplace nor banal phrase defaces 'L'Amore' for the composer's thought is at all times distinguished, poetic, refined. For all its modernity of feeling an intangible element of classicism pervades the score. Intense, impassioned, it is yet music that never transgresses the canons of fundamental artistic continence and lofty beauty.

To a certain extent the score of 'L'Amore' is contrapuntal and in such cases it becomes a golden web of polyphony, each strand and fiber of which glitters and sparkles discernibly. It is emphatically polyphony which 'sounds,' to use a musician's term. Strong and varied rhythmic accents employed solely or else traversing each other's path in counter motion impart zest and frequently deep dramatic significance. Leading motives are traceable to the number of five or six but they undergo no appreciable symphonic germination nor form the warp and woof of the music in Wagnerian fashion. Always they are simple and readily recognizable upon recurrence – as in the case of the stumbling, disjointed, rhythmically broken *pizzicato* figure denoting the blind *Archibaldo*. This theme quickly resolves itself into a sinister, menacing musical symbol of portentous, fateful import. Likewise one finds apposite tonal exemplifications of *Manfredo*'s deep-felt conjugal love, of the tramp of his horses – a dull insistent rhythmic thud that association quickly informs with terrific meaning – and another for the passion of *Fiora* and *Avito*. Vain painting of externals is non-existent. The music is introspective in the main, and when not employed to the ends of pure subjectivity it serves to establish the requisite atmosphere of the scene. With overpowering effect it depicts the awful suspense and tragic horror of the closing part in the second act – the climactic one of the opera.

Montemezzi does not resort to concerted numbers or detachable pieces. From beginning to end the music is closely concatenated. Separate episodes do, however, stand forth by virtue of their sheer beauty and dramatic eloquence – as the blind man's superb narrative in the first act, the tremendous, foreboding orchestral interlude as *Fiora*, in fearful perturbation, mounts the battlements, the impassioned, glowing duo of the lovers, and, in the third act, the impressive choruses of a Gregorian cast sung off-stage *a capella*, as a requiem to the dead princess. Musically and dramatically the second act is the choicest of the three with the third a close second. In the latter Montemezzi has voiced the heart-broken lamentations of *Avito* in music of tear-compelling poignancy.

Comments of other New York critics on the première:

The first hearing of this work prompts the opinion that it is one of the strongest and most original operatic productions that have come out of Italy since Verdi laid down his pen. – Richard Aldrich in *The Times*.[1]

---

1 See below, p. 82.

I can only say that in looking back over Italian opera since Mascagni's 'Cavalleria' I have not noted the distinct promise of genius so unmistakably in anything as in Montemezzi's 'Love of Three Kings.' – Maurice Halperson in the *Staats Zeitung*.

The most significant quality of the work is its freedom from the domination of the style now the most popular in Italian opera. Montemezzi has boldly rejected the idol Puccini. He has chosen his own methods and elected to appeal to the world with an art almost aristocratic in its manner, certainly seeking for nobility of line and purity of color, and yet as capable of delineating passion as the classic verse of Euripides. – W. J. Henderson in *The Sun*.[1]

It is a beautiful score, free from ear-splitting dissonances yet vitally dramatic. It is not reminiscent of any composer; least of all does it resemble any of the musical products of modern Italy. Mr. Montemezzi is not afraid to write melody, for in the various love scenes long phrases of melodic beauty fairly purl from his pen. – Edward Ziegler in *The Herald*.

The composer has provided nothing strikingly original in his music, yet it has individuality. There are evidences of Verdi in his later composing period, of Wagner and even of Debussy. The principal elements to commend are the admirable technical construction, appropriate orchestral color, and the directness with which Montemezzi invariably proceeds. – Pierre V. R. Key in *The World*.

Musically, Montemezzi's opera made even a better impression than it seems to have done at its first success in Italy last year. – W. B. Chase in *The Evening Sun*.

---

1 Henderson's review for the *Sun* is not included in the present anthology, but his later, fuller review for *Opera Magazine* is: see below, pp. 95–100.

Italo Montemezzi was a name that meant nothing to most of us yesterday. To-day it will be on the lips of every music lover, for his opera, 'L'Amore Dei Tre Re,' is a work of genius. – Sylvester Rawling in *The Evening World*.

A work of power and vitality, a work that breathes the spirit of sincerity and throbs from beginning to end with human passion, reaching in the second act a climax of dramatic power, of scorching emotional intensity, that seems almost without precedent on the lyric stage. – Max Smith in *The Press*.

In short, it was abundantly evident that the Metropolitan had secured an opera by a new composer which is a complete success, both with the cognoscenti and with the general public. – H. E. Krehbiel in *The Tribune*.[1]

---

1 See below, p. 74.

2. Henry E. Krehbiel, *New-York Tribune*, 3 January 1914.

'L'Amore Dei Tre Re' Has Premiere

New Italian Opera Proves a Popular and Artistic Success

Montemezzi's Music Original, Striking

Sig. Ferrari-Fontana Wins Ovation – Miss Bori and Messrs. Amato and Didur Excellent

WITHOUT MUCH trumpeting, as if it were a matter of course, indeed, the management of the Metropolitan Opera House brought forward a new opera last night: a new opera, in an especial sense, for 'L'Amore dei tre Re' is scarcely a year old, if it is that,[1] and up to last night had been heard only in two opera houses, and those in Italy.[2] This circumstance, associated as it must be with some of the new productions of the last five years, indicates a closer relationship than ever existed before between the proud operatic establishment in Broadway and the composers and publishers of Europe. That New York should be in advance of the majority of the capitals of the Old World in giving a hearing to orchestral works has been a familiar fact for a quarter of a century at least: but this has not been the case in respect of

---

1 The premiere at La Scala took place on 10 April 1913.

2 After the initial production at La Scala, a second production opened at the Emilia Romagna Teatro, Cesena, on 23 August 1913; this was seen by Toscanini. *L'Amore dei Tre Re* then quickly entered the Italian repertoire, and Krehbiel was wrong to conclude that these were the only two productions of the opera in 1913. William J. Henderson's radically contradictory claim that 'in the autumn of the year 1913, no less than fifteen companies were spreading its [*L'Amore dei Tre Re*'s] music abroad in its native land' (see below, p. 95) may be exaggerated, but it is probably closer to the truth.

operas. For novelties in the lyric drama we were long accustomed to wait not only until they had been tested and approved abroad, but until they had become part of the repertory of some admired singer who had won an engagement in New York. In this respect they shared the fate of a number of familiar and admired works of what may be called the universal list, which, because of the pernicious system which grew up under past regimes, cannot be performed now, because, despite the splendid forces of the Metropolitan, there are no representatives among the popular favorites in the company of their principal roles. We can have no 'Faust,' forsooth, because the titular part is not sympathetic to Signor Caruso;[1] we have been deprived for years of 'Carmen' for want of artists familiar with it whose personal popularity would guarantee its financial success. Bizet's opera is promised to us now only because Miss Farrar has deigned to study a new role in which she thinks she may achieve a triumph.[2]

We must therefore, so far as the popular favorites are concerned, put up with a list which is growing fearfully hackneyed and threadbare, and depend for an outlook upon the creative activities of the day upon the minor members of the company. Thanks to them and Mr. Gatti, we have had two novelties of late which may be said to have laid a foundation for the education in taste of the public upon which the Metropolitan opera will have to depend when the inevitable end of the temporarily regnant stars shall come. These operas are Moussorgsky's 'Boris

---

[1] Gounod's *Faust*, one of the most frequently performed operas at the Met in the 1880s and '90s, was less frequently put on after 1900, but still staged almost every season, including four performances in the 1912–13 season. After that it did not appear at the Met again until the 1917–18 season, though, which may have something to do with many productions being built around Caruso in the intervening years.

[2] *Carmen*, very frequently staged at the Met in the 1890s and early 1900s, had been last heard on 17 February 1909. It was finally revived, with Geraldine Farrar in the title role, on 19 November 1914.

Manfredo (Amato) and Fiora (Bori) in Act 1

Godounow'[1] and the opera brought forward last night, which, let it be said at once as a fact singularly pertinent to the argument, is the fine fruit of the Russian work grafted on an Italian stem. It is upon operas like these, in combination with the standard German list, which has already become a necessary prop to the season, that the future of the Metropolitan Opera House depends.

The story of the new opera was told at length in this journal last Sunday,[2] and it is necessary for present purposes only to recall it in outline. It is a tragedy to which the author of the book has given a romantic setting which suggests an historical period and historical peoples without putting a clog upon the imagination of the hearers. In this he has been followed by the composer, who, though he uses the musical vehicle which is the characteristic glory of his own country and borrows a device of dramatic expression which is equally characteristic of a different country, yet speaks in the language proper to the proclamation of passions which know no distinction of time or peoples. The poet's name is Sem Benelli (could we write Shem, as well we might, his race would be more clearly disclosed[3]), and he wrote his play not as a drama to be sung but as a play to be spoken. To fit it for opera some elisions were made and a scene for chorus added. A fine, strong play it is, in fine, strong verse, picturesque but direct, with a splendid command of the elements which

---

1 *Boris Godunov* had received its American premiere at the Met on 19 March 1913.

2 Krehbiel had published a preliminary feature, '"L'Amore Dei Tre Re" Is Eagerly Awaited,' in the *Tribune*, 28 December 1913, section 3, p. 4.

3 On the basis of his name, Benelli was frequently characterized, both inside and outside Italy, as Jewish, and encountered discrimination as a result. In the 1930s he publicly denied being Jewish, stressed that his family had been Catholic for as long as records went back, and said that the name had come from his godfather, Sem Nardi. See Guido Bonsaver, *Censorship and Literature in Fascist Italy* (Toronto: U of Toronto P, 2007), 73–74.

make a drama effective in its appeal to eye, ear and emotions. It would be difficult to recall another opera in which there is a more puissant exhibition of the elements of contrast in character, of conflicting motives, of the devastating result of passions at war with each other, all of which, nevertheless, challenge sympathy in almost an equal degree. To the careless reader there is something a trifle misleading in the title. The error, indeed, crept into the story of the opera as it has been printed.[1] It is a story of the love of three royal personages, but not altogether of the passion which is the burden of mediæval as well as modern romance. A barbarian who has made himself king of an undefined territory in Italy kills the wife of his son because of her adultery.

This king's passion is love for his son and the honor of his family. He is old and blind; his reign began forty years before the opening of the story, and there is nothing in the likelihood of nature, his acts or his speeches which indicates the possibility of his harboring a carnal passion for the young native princess who

---

1 The 'error' is found in Krehbiel's own summary of the plot published on 28 December 1913: 'The object of their [the Three Kings'] love and the one for whom each has a different passion is the Princess Fiora ...'. Montemezzi himself regarded this interpretation as correct, however, as Robert Lawrence revealed when he reported a 1941 conversation with the composer in 'Figure on the Battlements,' *Opera News*, 4 January 1964, 6–7:

> I asked his [Montemezzi's] explanation of the opera's title. 'It is clear,' I proposed, 'that Avito and Manfredo are in love with Fiora, but what about Archibaldo? The old man is blind, proud, implacable. Fiora has been faithless to his son, and as the father of Manfredo he strangles her to avenge his family honor.'
>
> It was then that Montemezzi contradicted: 'When the old king catches Fiora on the terrace after her night with Avito and questions her, she denies everything. He lays hands on her and demands, "Perchè tremi, se dici il vero?" ("Why do you tremble, if you are telling the truth?"), to which she answers boldly, "Ed anche voi tremate ... e non mentite" ("You're trembling, too ... and you're not lying"). In short, Archibaldo has a repressed, gnawing love for his daughter-in-law, and she knows it.'

was given to him to be his son's wife by her people as the price of peace.[1] The son is a warrior whose love for his wife is so pure and strong that, confronted with proof of her guilty commerce with another, he can only pity her, pity her dying lover, and love her the more, even to the uttermost of his own undoing. To the old king this trait in the character of his son, whom he had trained in all the virtues of his people, is a weakness, and he takes it upon himself to avenge the wrong done to his son, his house, his race. Groping in the dark, left to his own devices and hampered by the treachery of his servant, he yet discovers the unfaithfulness of his son's wife, and though he cannot know who is the partner of her guilt, he throttles her. The lover is of the people of the princess, and was betrothed to her before she became, perforce, a hostage and a loveless wife. His passion is like that of Tristan, Romeo and all their fellows who have lived since the race began. There is pathos in its fierceness and in the fatality which enshrouds it from its first disclosure. There is a greater pathos in the struggle which takes place in the heart of the young wife when she feels the first movings of a love for her husband, awakened by recognition of the overwhelming tenderness of his affection, and a still greater pathos in the conduct of the outraged husband, who cannot take revenge upon the man upon whom his wife had bestowed the boon for which he felt an infinite longing, and who follows him into death beside the body of the one who had been so dear to both. And when, at the last, the old man is left alone in a darkness made trebly dense by the triple destruction which he had wrought (for lover and husband had both sucked death in kissing the mouth of the woman whom he had killed and whose lips he had smeared with poison in the last despairing hope of thus discovering who had wronged his son and his house), there is infinite pathos in his impotent desolation and mute despair.

---

[1] But see previous note.

In this story, but more especially in its presentation, there are many dramatic motivi which have done service in other dramas. Involuntarily we think of Wagner's setting of the tale of Tristram and Iseult, of 'Romeo and Juliet,' of 'Francesca da Rimini,' of 'Pelléas et Mélisande.'[1] There are moments when a cursory glimpse might almost make one think one of these plays was occupying the stage, as when Fiora (the princess) is seen waving her scarf from the castle terrace and when Avito (the lover) comes into the crypt of the castle to say farewell to his dead love. But there is a large difference between Benelli's treatment of these episodes and the apparent sources which we have cited. Isolde waves her scarf wildly to call her lover to her side; Fiora waves hers with a breaking heart and heavy arms to speed her parting husband, though she cannot but know that his going is only a preface to the coming of Avito. The struggle between love and duty has begun. Here it may be said of the poet, as it must also be said of the composer, that he is so strong and self-reliant in his command of his theme and all its agencies of expression that the parallels only serve to illustrate the aphorism of Fuseli – 'Genius may adopt, but never steals.'[2]

The remark is indeed more significant as applied to Signor Italo Montemezzi, the composer of the music, than to the author of the play. Not only the scene of the scarf, but other episodes, must have called up memories in his mind of masterpieces which can scarcely be thought of without tempting the creative musician to imitation. The imitation may be unconscious, but is seldom missing. Echoes of the night of love in the Tristram tragedy have floated down from the stage of the Metropolitan Opera House several times since Wagner's great music first became domiciled

---

1 See above, pp. 55–56 and notes.
2 No. 50 in the posthumously published *Aphorisms, Chiefly Relative to the Fine Arts* by the Swiss painter Henry Fuseli (1741–1825).

there.[1] There were no echoes last night of either the love duet or of the music which brings her lover to Iseult's feet. Neither (and for this there might be a special expression of gratitude) were there pallid reflections of Debussy or reverberations of Puccini. Montemezzi is proof against temptation. This young composer speaks a speech all his own, and his score, we fancy, would have delighted the soul of Verdi, when, seeing the aberrations of his young confreres, he sat himself down in his old age to show them an example of devotion to the genius of their country's art.[2]

What, then, is meant by the remark made above that 'L'Amore dei tre Re' is the fine fruit of 'Boris Godounow' grafted on an Italian stem? Only this: That Signor Montemezzi has borrowed from Moussorgsky a constructive feature, which, though it has a national value in Russian music, which it lacks in Italian, is still of fine dramatic effectiveness. Melodically he is all Italian and a legitimate artistic grandson of Verdi. But his melodies, which flow onward like a river, now tumultuously as they carry the passion of the lovers upon their current, now gently with wooing murmurs as they float the emotions of the loving and magnanimous Manfredo, and anon interruptedly when they are broken into fragments by the dialogue, are as a rule superimposed on persistently reiterated rhythmical and melodic figures. Sometimes this *ostinato* accompaniment has a

---

1 'Several times' is a playful understatement; *Tristan und Isolde* had first been staged at the Met in 1886 and thereafter become a regular part of the repertoire, being revived almost every season. It had last been heard on 24 December 1913.

2 Verdi hesitantly started work on *Otello* in 1880, at the end of a decade in which he had frequently expressed criticisms of Italian theatre and music, and especially the Germanic influences being embraced by young composers. This judgment of Krehbiel, an ardent Wagnerian, on how Verdi at his most self-consciously 'Italian' is likely to have viewed *L'Amore dei Tre Re* is fascinating, given that so many other critics have regarded Montemezzi's opera as heavily, even excessively, influenced by Wagner.

Avito (Ferrari-Fontana) and
Fiora (Bori) in Act 2

delineative purpose, as when we hear in it the coming and going of Manfredo and his warriors; but as a rule the purpose of its employment is purely constructive, and the composer's splendid command of the stage and of musical expression enables him to give the figures a dramatic potency which at times reaches the marvellous and approaches his model. He shows equal mastery of the potentialities of harmony and orchestral color by means of which he not only puts a glow into his sustained melody, but also greatly heightens the emotional power of that portion of his dialogue which hovers between speech and song.

Though he occasionally makes use of reminiscent phrases, he does not employ musical symbols in the Wagnerian manner. His genius is of the inspirational-creative, not of the reflective order, which fact makes his successful blending of the Russian device (a folksong element in Muscovite music) with Italian melody all the more admirable.

Poet and composer have left us without clew as to even the approximate period in which the drama plays; but the scene painter, in three fine pictures, seems to invite the imagination to fix the time at about the tenth century. There is a suggestion, again, of the opera's Russian prototype in the semi-barbaric decorations which ornament the walls of the last scene, and of an earlier period than that mentioned in the architecture of the first scene. But the question of time does not obtrude itself because of the eloquent manner in which poet and composer have given voice to a tale which might be told of any time and any people.

The burden of the representation of 'L'Amore dei tre Re' falls upon four persons – the representatives of the old King (Archibaldo), his son (Manfredo), the faithless wife (Fiora) and her lover (Avito). There is but little ensemble singing, and that is confined to the last act, where the poet, to fit his play for operatic treatment, has introduced a hymn and a species of choral dialogue[1]

---

1 See above, p. 55 and n. 1.

which, like the *ostinato* accompaniment figures spoken of, has a prototype in Moussorgsky's opera. In this choral dialogue there is a brief irruption of the political element, which also plays its part in evoking sympathy for the lovers and saving their conduct from utter condemnation. Like all the other ethical and psychological factors, it is introduced into the drama with great deftness and achieves its purposes without attracting attention to itself or asking for accentuation through local color.[1]

One of the performers in this first representation outside of Italy was the original creator of the part of Avito in Milan – Signor Ferrari-Fontana, the husband of Mme. Matzenauer,[2] who this season, as last, is a member of the Boston Opera Company. He was a chance impersonator of the part on its first production, chosen because the tenor of the La Scala company who had been selected took ill a week before the opera was given its first hearing. He is a singer of heroic mould, and won his way to the admiration of a Metropolitan audience last night by dint of sincere and impassioned singing and acting and the disclosure of a voice of noble quality. One thing only militated against a complete artistic triumph on his part, and that was an unfortunate tendency to depart from just intonation. In the beautifully conceived and executed love scene of the second act, however, he swayed the audience like an elemental force, and

---

[1] As printed, this paragraph continues with the sentence: 'If it has a symbol it is haunting music of flute and horn, which, like the lark's song in "Romeo and Juliet," is the herald of the morn and the sign of parting, which comes back like a haunting memory in some of the climaxes of the second act.' This is clearly part of an analysis of the love music in Act 1, and its placement here an error resulting from some late abridgement or reorganization of the review, perhaps at the printing stage. (In Act 3, Scene 5 of *Romeo and Juliet* the sound of the lark signals the end of the lovers' one night together. Romeo says: 'It was the lark, the herald of the morn ... / I must be gone and live, or stay and die.')

[2] See above, p. 53, n. 2.

must have set many of the Metropolitan's patrons to wondering why his services were not commanded by Mr. Gatti instead of Mr. Russell.[1] Nobility of voice and style marked the performance of Signor Amato, and in a large degree also the singing and acting of Mr. Didur, who impersonated the old king.

The part of the heroine fell to Miss Bori, to watch whose growth toward a beautiful artistic maturity is a delight. In song and action she was an entirely convincing and sympathetic figure. Sincerity was the keynote of her impersonation, as it was of the entire performance, which enjoyed the uplifting influence of Signor Toscanini's direction – an influence always fairly entitled to be called an inspiration for performers and listeners alike.

The enthusiastic reception of the opera by the audience was unequivocal. The applause was loud after the first act, and tumultuous after the second, applause that was not the evocation of any claque, but arose spontaneously from all parts of the house. Seventeen curtain calls were counted after the second act, and the artists were showered with flowers. Between the acts the audience poured out into the foyers and brought its enthusiasm with it. In short, it was abundantly evident that the Metropolitan had secured an opera by a new composer which is a complete success, both with the cognoscenti and with the general public. Signor Montemezzi has come to New York, and New York is his.

Mr. Gatti-Casazza expressed himself as most happy over the outcome.

'"L'Amore Dei Tre Re" is a remarkable work, a work sincere in spirit, original in expression and admirably constructed,' said Mr. Gatti. 'Signor Montemezzi is a young man of great talent, which deserves to be encouraged. I am indeed happy that tonight's audience has taken to the work.'

---

[1] Henry Russell (1871–1937), director of the Boston Opera Company from its foundation in 1909 to its bankruptcy in 1915.

3. Richard Aldrich, *New York Times*, 3 January 1914.

Montemezzi Opera Warmly Received

'L'Amore dei Tre Re,' by Italian Composer, Makes a Deep Impression

Ferrari-Fontana's Debut

New Tenor of Metropolitan is a Beautiful Singer and Fervid Actor – Lucrezia Bori as Heroine

QUITE UNHERALDED by proclamations of European fame, a new opera by an unknown Italian composer was presented last evening for the first time in the United States at the Metropolitan Opera House, producing a deep impression upon lovers of dramatic music, wholly unprepared for such a sensation. The opera was 'L'Amore dei Tre Re,' the composer Italo Montemezzi. Another incident in this evening of surprises was the first appearance of a tenor known here hitherto only by name – Edoardo Ferrari-Fontana, of unusual gifts and accomplishments.

The audience, which was somewhat apathetic after the first act, was aroused to real enthusiasm after the second, which contains the finest material and the most powerful climax of the opera. The principal singers were recalled many times, and there was every evidence that both the work itself and the performance had been received with marked favor. The new tenor, Mr. Fontana, though he was apparently suffering somewhat from nervousness that affected somewhat the steadiness of his voice, and at certain moments the accuracy of his intonation, showed himself an artist to be reckoned with as a force in operatic art, an actor of grace and manliness as well as of force, a singer of unusual power and beauty of voice.

Its Composer a Master

Probably very few even of those who follow the course of musical history in the making had an intimation of the existence of the new opera before it appeared in the announcements of the Metropolitan Opera House; or knew more than the name of the composer. Yet the work disclosed its maker as already a master, of a power and originality rare in this present age of music. It disclosed, too, a true gift of musical creativeness, an instinctive feeling for the stage and an unusual command of the resources of the lyric drama in dramatic construction as well as in purely musical technique, the upbuilding of a musical fabric, the art of writing for the orchestra and for the voice.

'L'Amore dei Tre Re' has reached New York soon after its first appearance in Italy, and before it has appeared elsewhere outside of its native land. It was first produced a year ago last April in a provincial theatre;[1] was then given at La Scala in Milan, and is repeated there this season; and it is said to have been taken into the repertory of many other opera companies in Italy.[2] Montemezzi is still young, and his fame has not yet penetrated beyond the Alps. The author of the libretto, Sem Benelli, is also a young man, and though he is regarded as one of the most promising of Italian dramatists, his name too is little known outside of Italy except to students of Italian literature. In Italy, indeed, his admirers speak his name with that of d'Annunzio. His tragedy 'La Cena delli [sic] Beffe' has attracted much attention and has been played in Paris.[3] 'L'Amore dei Tre

---

[1] An obvious error: the premiere was at La Scala.

[2] See above, p. 63 and n. 2.

[3] *La Cena Delle Beffe* (The Supper of the Jests), described by Benelli as a 'dramatic poem,' is not a tragedy according to conventional definitions. Its premiere at the Teatro Argentina, Rome, on 16 April 1909 was an immense success, and established Benelli's fame. In 1910 a production in French, starring Sarah Bernhardt, was staged at the Théâtre Sarah-Bernhardt, Paris.

Re,' which has served as the basis for this opera, is an acting tragedy, and what Montemezzi has set to music is a considerable portion of the whole, taken over with very few abbreviations and alterations. Some of these as well as a few additions better to adapt the poem to musical treatment the poet himself has made.[1]

A Tragedy of Emotions

The course of this sombre tragedy was detailed in last SUNDAY'S TIMES. It is needless to add more now, except to say that the libretto is a work of literary art, a deeply felt exposition of conflicting passions, of the fate that entangles a royal lover and a princess betrothed to another of an alien race, of the emotional struggle in which her love finally overcomes an imposed duty, and the tragic outcome of an old father's jealous suspicions, and his revenge, which finally kills not only the guilty pair but also the son whose interests he had thought to guard. It is a tragedy of emotions, wrought with insight into the deeper springs of human conduct, rather than of action, and a knowledge of the text is hence especially necessary to its understanding. The verse is cast in a finely poetic diction, and of its kind this text is one of unusual distinction as an operatic libretto.

The characters are types rather than strongly marked individualities; they are the expression of ideas. They move in a world of legend, not of historical verity. There is a suggestion in the characters and their surroundings of Maeterlinck – a Maeterlinck of a clearer vision and a more sharply defined objective.[2] Their Italy is an Italy remote and undefined. Upon this dim and shadowy background are projected feelings, passions, emotions, with a glowing and burning light.

---

[1] The additions were the mourning choruses which replaced the opening episodes in Act 3: see above, p. 55 and n. 1.

[2] See above, p. 55 and n. 3.

There are many qualities in this book to tempt a musician of poetic impulses and imagination, and in setting it Montemezzi has shown himself to be such a musician. His music is well adapted to the expression of what the poet offers him. He is unusually self-contained in his inspiration, deriving little from his predecessors. It is rare to come upon one whose artistic lineage is so difficult to trace. He has escaped from the pervading influence of Puccini and of his artistic forbear Ponchielli that has so dominated the more recent operatic production of Italy. There is as little as may be of Wagner in this score – little of direct suggestion, little but what is in the general musical atmosphere of the modern world and from which none may hope to escape entirely. There is little of Verdi, unless some may find a fleeting turn of phrase, a harmonic connection, such as might lead the listener back to 'Otello.' Nor is there more than a trace of what is generally accounted the influence of modern France. And the music gives the impression of freshness and modernity, in the composer's own way.

Music Is Richly Colored

Montemezzi's score is not thematic in the sense in which Wagner's are and those of his followers. The orchestra has a preponderating part in the musical substance and the dramatic exposition, but there are only a comparatively few recurrent or reminiscent themes, and the score is written freely rather than by incessant utilization and combination of such themes. Montemezzi makes frequent use of short melodic figures repeated in the manner called 'ostinato,' often as a sort of accompaniment, and thereby gains a sort of plangent intensity of expression. There are a few, but only a few, touches of musical realism, as the agitated figure of pizzicatos in triplets suggesting the uncertain steps of the old blind King, and the rushing figure denoting the cavalcade with which Archibaldo invaded Italy, as he tells it, and again that other cavalcade with which Manfredo is about to depart in the second act. Otherwise the music is a constant interpreter of emotions, the exponent of moods, and has little concern with externals.

Montemezzi is a master of orchestration. The music is finely scored, richly colored with the intuitive sense of one who sees varied emotional expression in varying orchestral timbres. It is full, but not overcharged, and has a transparency that is grateful to the singers. And one of its admirable qualities is the sympathy with which it is composed for them. The vocal parts are in the manner of arioso, shapely and melodious, often with a superb sweep of line and breadth of phrase, finely modeled for declamation in the most musical sense, which is heightened and intensified speech.

There are beautiful specimens of this refined yet powerful art in the opera, as the speech of the old King Archibaldo, in the first act, describing his coming as a conqueror to Italy and his proud remembrance of it; Manfredo's air when he returns in the first act, and the two addresses to Fiora in the second act by Manfredo and Avito, successively, so finely differentiated in expression, and developed to so different an issue.

The climax and culmination of the opera is this second act, when Manfredo going to the wars, takes leave of Fiora and her 'secret grief';[1] when his tender gentleness of love overcomes her coldness into a kind of compassion, and when Avito then steals in, longing and pleading for her love. She waves her promised fare well to Manfredo from the battlement with the scarf he has sent her; but her hand fails her and falls heavy, her head drops, as Avito continues his importunities, kissing her robe, clinging to her knees: and she is conquered and yields to him. The composer

---

[1] The expression occurs in a direction in Act 2: Fiora says 'Volete la mia vita!' (You want my life!) to Manfredo '*con arcano dolore traboccante,*' or, in R. H. Elkin's translation, '*overflowing with secret grief.*'

Manfredo (Amato), Archibaldo (Didur) and Fiora (Bori) at the end of Act 2

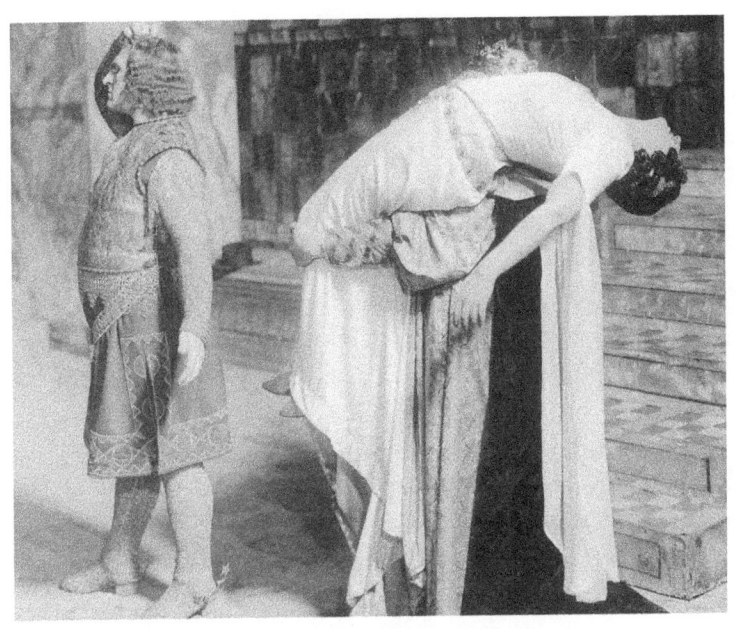

Another view of the same scene
Didur apparently experimented with different ways of carrying Bori

has found for this poignant play of emotional forces music deeply expressive, first, of the elegiac tenderness and knightly consideration of Manfredo's leave-taking, of Fiora's heavy-hearted waving of the scarf; then of the mounting passion of Avito's appeal, in music of burning eloquence kindling the desolation of Fiora's soul finally to an answering flame of rapture.

Hardly less moving is the last act. Effects of exquisite contrast and impressive solemnity are gained by the use of the funeral choir in the distance of the church, contrasted with the dolorous lamenting of the mourning throng around Fiora's bier in the crypt, the broken song of Avito and Manfredo as they successively enter and succumb to the poison placed on Fiora's lips by the old King; and finally the staggering blow that is dealt him as he gropes his way in to rejoice at the death of Avito, and stumbles upon his dying son, also fallen a victim to his trap.[1]

The first hearing of this work prompts the opinion that it is one of the strongest and most original operatic productions that have come out of Italy since Verdi laid down his pen. And one of its most valuable qualities is to be seen in the fact that the composer has attained his effects, even the most powerful, without finding it necessary to break with all that has been hitherto prized in music as euphony and an appeal to a sense of the beautiful. At the summit of his sonorities Montemezzi has not thought it necessary to wreck his listeners' ears, and yet he has not failed in his effects.

A Notable Performance

The performance of the new opera was notably fine. Its most conspicuous feature was the first appearance in the Metropolitan Opera House of Edoardo Ferrari-Fontana, who took the part of

---

[1] Aldrich's phrasing is misleading: Manfredo knows there is poison on Fiora's lips and deliberately kisses her.

Avito. Mr. Fontana, it is understood, had sung the part in some of the earliest performances of it in Milan. He made an immediate success, not only by his fine and impassioned acting – acting of genuine tragic temperament and of finished skill – but still more on account of his remarkably beautiful tenor voice. He is a true 'tenore robusto,' with not only power but also fullness, richness, and warmth of tone, splendid resonance and penetration, especially in his upper ranges. Mr. Fontana sings with admirable art, with style, in a manner that makes his voice count for its utmost. He would seem to be a valuable acquisition for the Metropolitan Opera House. If Mr. Fontana's future appearances bear out the promise he offered in his first one, his work in New York will be watched with interest and pleasure.

Miss Lucrezia Bori was the Fiora, and by her impersonation added measurably to the esteem in which she is held here. Her voice has never sounded more beautiful, and it is indeed a beautiful voice when she does not feel, or imagine, a necessity for forcing it beyond its normal power. Montemezzi's music is well adapted to her, and gives her voice its best opportunity. Miss Bori also disclosed unexpected power in the enactment of tragedy. Her impersonation of Fiora was sympathetic and convincing, suffused with tender grace and sadness. There was a dominating power in the way Mr. Didur enacted the blind King Archibaldo, a conception of the part wholly appropriate; and his singing, especially of his long apostrophe in the first act, was of his best. Mr. Amato was one of the mainstays of the performance as Manfredo, in which he was nobly dignified and tender, singing and acting with much skill. It is a part that he may well count among his most excellent.

The playing under Mr. Toscanini's direction was extremely fine. The orchestra does not often sound more beautiful in tone or more dramatically potent than he made it sound; and the choruses in the last act, especially the hymning of the distant choir, were exquisitely sung.

Some excellent scenery has been provided. In the second act there looms a building that has resemblance to the tomb of Theodoric at Ravenna, and the last shows the crypt of the Basilica of San Apollinare in the same ancient city.[1] But there is nothing in the text that places the action there, or that dates it with any reference to either of these structures. The castle parapet in the second act may be architecturally correct, but seems to lack something of verisimilitude.

---

[1] Aldrich appears to be in error here. The staging for Act 3, as Peyser noted (see above, p. 49), was loosely inspired by the church interior (not the crypt) of San Vitale in Ravenna.

4. Unsigned review attributed to Leonard Liebling, *Musical Courier*, 7 January 1914.

American Premiere of 'L'Amore Dei Tre Re'

Montemezzi's Opera Produced by the Metropolitan Opera Company in New York – Teutonic Note Strongly in Evidence – The Book Is Melodramatic in the Extreme

A BLIND MAN, Archibaldo, manages to secure the beautiful Fiora for his son, Manfredo. Fiora and Manfredo are man and wife at the opening of the drama. But Fiora loves Avito, her lover, and is entirely without interest in her husband. When Manfredo goes off to the wars Fiora and Avito have many stolen joys together and are occasionally interrupted by the entrance of the blind Archibaldo, who suspects Fiora, but cannot discover the name of her lover. In desperation the old man throttles his daughter-in-law because she refuses to disclose her lover. Manfredo returns just as his wife has been strangled. In order to discover the lover the enraged father-in-law puts poison on Fiora's lips as she lies on her bier in the crypt of the castle. Avito, the lover, kisses Fiora's lips and dies slowly while the husband, Manfredo, enters the crypt, kisses the same poisoned lips which destroyed Avito, and likewise dies just as his blind father seizes him, thinking him to be the lover whose name he seeks to discover.

Such is the story of 'L'Amore dei tre re,' which received its first performance in America on Friday evening, January 2, 1914, at the Metropolitan Opera House, New York.

It is full to overflowing with the lava of Italian passion – love, anger, jealousy, revenge, burning kisses, murder, poisoning. To an Anglo-Saxon or a Teuton such a story is needlessly fierce. It is devoid of any possible trace of that ideality and romantic beauty which appeal to the more imaginative nations of the north, and it abounds in the breathless and nervous abandon of that race whose passions have been fed for centuries by the wines and scorching sun of Italy.

We must commend the book, therefore, because it is so true to the national temperament of the Italians. It has the convincing appeal of truth to nature, and the drama moves and breathes with elemental fire. The real human appeal is fundamentally the same the world over, however much the details of expression and degrees of passion may vary. For this reason, therefore, 'L'Amore dei tre re' has the essentials of a fine drama for operatic treatment and it is evident from the first note that the composer, Italo Montemezzi, was profoundly affected by the story. But it was hardly to be expected that a young man of twenty-eight[1] could free himself from the influence of his predecessors and stand forth as a composer with a style of his own. He has not yet developed an individual style. Unfortunately, too, his tendencies seem to take him too far afield into the foreign lands of Germany and France. The first act has an unusually small measure of pure Italian music in it. There are pages by the dozen which might have been written by German composers half a century ago, though Montemezzi cannot be charged with any direct plagiarism of recognizable themes.

We know that this present opera has created no stir in the operatic world in Italy. It has been performed a number of times and accepted. So it is probable that its mild German flavor is enough to give it a certain piquancy to those Italians in Italy who are not too familiar with German music at its best. But we believe the work will hardly please those foreign nations that look to Italy for Italian works and leave to Germany that honor of supplying German works. We have been referring to the texture of the musical fabric, so to speak – the harmonies and melodic phraseology.

---

[1] Like other reviewers, Liebling makes Montemezzi ten years younger than he really was.

Montemezzi is true to his national style in that he invariably keeps his accompaniments subservient to the voices. And he also writes extremely well for the singers. No vocalist who has a voice to show off could possibly find fault with 'L'Amore dei re re,' as a means of vocal display, as a vehicle for the expression of passion. The composer seems invariably to have hit upon the right pitch for the dramatic expression of the rising and diminishing passion. In fact, we were often led to suspect that the young composer has more talent and brains than real genius. It is of course unfair to the yet undeveloped Montemezzi to compare or contrast his youthful work with that monumental product of Wagner's old age, 'Parsifal.' But with the sound of that choral writing still in our ears from Thursday's performance,[1] it was only too plain how much the young Italian has yet to expand before he can take his place among the really great composers of stage music. Let him not imitate Wagner, however. Verdi was unquestionably influenced by Wagner's genius, though he remained truly Italian to the end of his career. Yet in this choral scene in the crypt, where the dead Fiora lay in state, we could not help noticing several hints from the Holy Grail scene in 'Parsifal' – not pronounced, it is true, but as if the composer had flashed a few glances at Wagner in the same way that the singers on the stage look furtively to the conductor for their rhythm. The chimes, the chorus behind the stage, the general trend of the scene were 'Parsifal' efforts in miniature. They were undoubtedly due to the dominating influence of Wagner over the young composer's feelings, and could in no sense be called plagiarisms. We could not pick out certain passages and say 'This and this are Wagner.'

In the second act the composer shows his ability to express strong passions. The entire scene between Fiora and Avito is

---

1 *Parsifal* had been given a matinee performance on 1 January: a day before the premiere of *L'Amore dei Tre Re.*

at boiling point, and the drama as well as the music give the performers ample scope for all their powers. No doubt this opera enjoys the success it has had entirely to the opportunities it offers for a beautiful girl and an impassioned lover to display emotional frenzy. The stage picture of Fiora strangled and lying limp on the stony bench is very affecting.

But the drama is a gloomy affair at best. Archibaldo gropes his way about the stage blind, suspicious, enraged, finally throttling his daughter-in-law. Fiora is in tears, contortions, misery all the time. She lies to her father-in-law and deceives her husband. Avito sobs, groans, clasps his head, staggers under his load of woe and passion, and finally dies of poison. Manfredo goes away to the wars with a sad heart because he sees his wife does not love him.

Our sympathies were entirely with Fiora, first, because she was a pretty girl, and secondly, because she had been compelled to marry Manfredo against her will. She was true to her instincts in loving Avito. The crafty Archibaldo had no justification in scheming to get Fiora for his son Manfredo. If Avito had taken the old man by his abominable whiskers and thrown him over the parapet instead of slinking off after a great flourish of dagger and stabbing of atmosphere we should have been highly delighted. Fathers-in-law on the stage are as unattractive as the notorious mothers-in-law of domestic renown. All the world loves a lover, says the poet.[1] We should like to know who in the world loves a jealous, interfering, blind and outrageously bewhiskered father-in-law who keeps prowling around the castle and growling on all possible occasions?

No; 'L'Amore dei tre re' is a gruesome drama in which the only object of beauty, Fiora, suffers continually until she is murdered.

---

1 The phrase had become proverbial, but seems to have been derived from Ralph Waldo Emerson's 'All mankind love a lover' in his essay 'Love' (1841).

The injustice of the play is that everybody dies but father. The last curtain falls with Fiora on her bier ready for burial, while Avito lies on his back under the bier, and Manfredo on his side at the feet of his father, who stands, as usual, flourishing his goat-like chin ornament and mumbling his regrets. No one has any sympathy for him, however. If he had felt any manhood in him at all he would also have kissed the lips that he had poisoned and which had already killed his son and his daughter's lover. Not he; he continued to subsist on recitative, and groped his way to syncopated chords in the orchestra.

The performance of the work was admirable. Archibaldo was true to life in blindness and old age as acted and sung by Adamo Didur, who made the part vocally pleasant and dramatically unpleasant – which, of course, he was called on to do by the exigencies of the role.

Pasquale Amato, as Manfredo, had a part to play and music to sing which gave him unlimited scope for his unusual powers. Only a baritone with such a wealth of brilliant high notes could make this music so dramatic and effective. As an actor, too, Pasquale Amato is extraordinary on the operatic stage, and it was a foregone conclusion that his Manfredo would be a creature of flesh and blood and human passion, and not a mere stage puppet.

Edoardo Ferrari-Fontana, a newcomer who made his initial bow to the audience of the Metropolitan Opera House on this occasion, is a welcome addition to the tenor forces of our operatic stage. His acting was honest and carried conviction. His voice is agreeable and robust, and he uses it well. As an experienced and accomplished artist he will give pleasure in any part, even though the supreme note of pathos is not very much in evidence in the tone quality of his voice.

What shall we say of Lucrezia Bori? She was lovely to look upon, notwithstanding the anguish she was obliged to express throughout the drama. But she looked so sweet and innocent as she lay at rest on the catafalque enshrined in flowers that we felt

Avito might be envied for the favors which cost him his life. And she made a pathetic picture when she fell back dead from the villainous fingers of her father-in-law. Her matrimonial career was as chequered as that of the other Lucrezia – Lucrezia Borgia, the infamous daughter of Pope Alexander VI.[1]

But this Lucrezia can sing, and it is to be hoped that so sweet a singer and fascinating an actress will have no tragedy except upon the operatic stage where she is able to break hearts and to die with so much joy to her beholders.

With such a superb quartet of performers for the principal parts, and with the unrivaled Arturo Toscanini at the conductor's desk, it is small wonder the new opera was vociferously applauded.

Mozart, Weber, Wagner had no such opportunity at the age of twenty-eight as this young Montemezzi was given at the Metropolitan Opera House, New York, on Friday evening, January 2, 1914, with all the magnificent accessories of scenery, costumes and lighting for which this opera house is noted. The smaller parts, too, were excellently filled. In no way could the performance and representation be bettered. If the opera is eventually shelved, as it probably will be in a few seasons, the cause will lie in its lack of original good music and haunting melodies. It has no airs to linger in the memory. The composer uses the elaborate recitative of Wagner without having an individuality of his own in his harmonies and rhythms. It will fail, in other words, because it cannot influence musical thinkers, however effective and entertaining the work may prove when performed by artists as superb as those who first presented 'L'Amore dei tre re' in America.

[Cast details.]

---

[1] Lucrezia Borgia (1480–1519), forced into three political marriages by her father and brothers, also had several love affairs. Her second husband is thought to have been murdered by her brother Cesare.

5. Henry E. Krehbiel, *New-York Tribune*, 22 January 1914.

'I Tre Re' In Ascension

Third Performance Indicates Big Future for Opera

WITH THE third performance last night of Montemezzi's 'L'Amore dei Tre Re' it became more than ever evident that a new comet has swum into view upon the operatic firmament,[1] and that Italy has at last found a genius of whom it may well be proud. Italo Montemezzi owns no allegiance to the Veritists; the idiom of Puccini is not his; if he has drunk it is from the spring opened by the Verdi of 'Otello.' For Montemezzi is a worshipper of beauty, and never once does he violate its sacred canons.

And, happier than have been some composers, Signor Montemezzi has in America found worthy exponents of his ideas. Signor Toscanini directs the orchestra with a vigor that is as splendid as it is restrained; Miss Lucrezia Bori, both in song and action, gives a performance informed with exquisite pathos and uplifted by rare poetic feeling; Signor Ferrari-Fontana has brought back to us a real romantic tenor, a race supposedly passed beyond our shores with the departure of Jean de Reszke;[2] Mr. Amato has done no more skilful singing than in the part of Manfredo, and Mr. Didur as the blind barbarian chieftain is nearly all that can be desired.

Of good omen of better times in opera have been the large houses which have greeted each performance of Signor

---

[1] An echo of John Keats' celebrated account of how he discovered Homer: 'Then felt I like some watcher of the skies / When a new planet swims into his ken' ('On First Looking into Chapman's Homer').

[2] Jean de Reszke (1850–1925), the most celebrated operatic tenor of his time, sung regularly at the Met in the 1890s; his last performance there was on 29 April 1901. He retired in 1904.

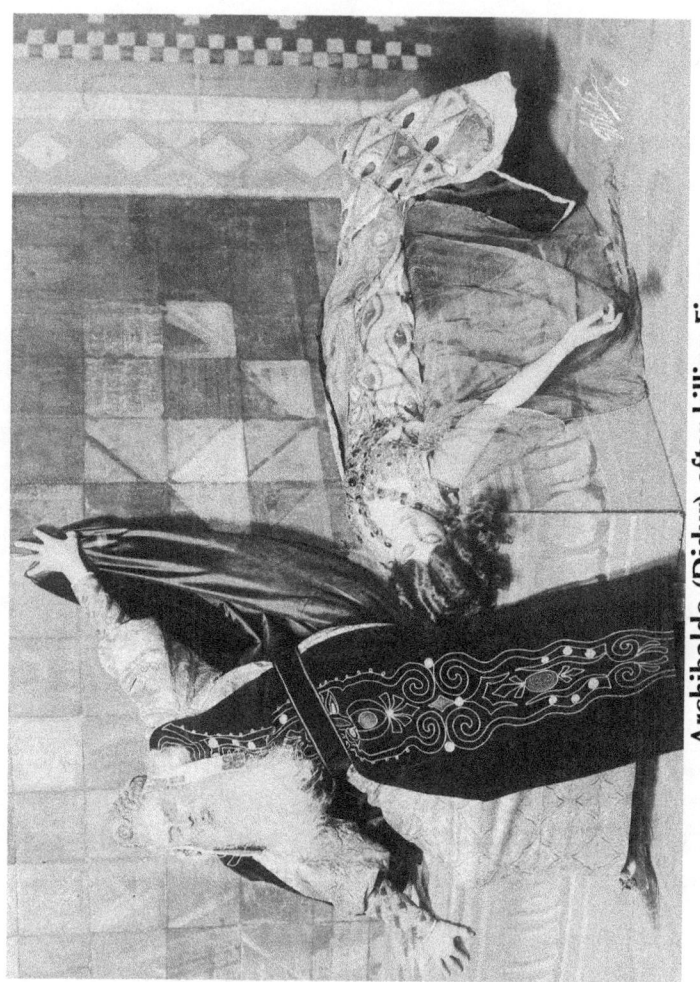

Archibaldo (Didur) after killing Fiora

Montemezzi's work. Last night the house was completely sold out. When the public comes to hear the work, and not to see the singer, then will come the operatic millennium. Let us hope that 'Boris Godounov' and 'L'Amore dei Tre Re' are the opening trumpets heralding this day.

William J. Henderson, early 1910s
A central figure in Montemezzi's American reception

6. William J. Henderson, *Opera Magazine*, February 1914.

Montemezzi's Opera a Success

THE HISTORY of opera in English-speaking countries in the years 1913 and 1914 will have to contain records of three surprises. The first was the production of Moussorgsky's opera, 'Boris Godunov,' in New York, and the second, the introduction of the same work to London in the summer season of Thomas Beecham.[1] The third was the production of Montemezzi's 'L'Amore dei Tre Re.' Much was known about the Russian opera, and the surprise was caused by the public reception of it. Most experienced observers of operatic affairs feared that it would not reach the popular heart, whereas, the people embraced it with avidity.

In the case of 'L'Amore dei Tre Re,' almost nothing was known here about the work. It had been brought out in Italy and had been treated with great respect and even warmth by the critics, but with some marked reservations. With the Italian public it had better fortune, and in the autumn of the year 1913, no less than fifteen companies were spreading its music abroad in its native land.[2] But great caution was observed in the preliminary announcements of the Metropolitan Opera House, and it can be said now that the authorities of that institution seemed to be not fully awake to their possession of a treasure.

---

1 *Boris Godunov* received its American premiere at the Met on 19 March 1913 and its British premiere at Drury Lane on 24 June the same year. The British production, with Chaliapin in the title role, was part of a 'Grand Season of Russian Opera and Ballet' mounted by Joseph Beecham, Thomas Beecham's father, with Sergei Diaghilev as artistic advisor. Thomas Beecham, who was part of the syndicate running the rival Covent Garden theatre, actually had comparatively little to do with it, and the London *Boris* was conducted by Emil Cooper.

2 See above, p. 63, n. 2.

One of the thrilling sensations of this writer's experience was his hearing of the first orchestral and stage rehearsal of the work, which he had already been studying in the score. His expectations had been thus excited, but the full disclosure of the new work by voices, action and orchestra was something to remember. 'They have made a great find!' was the mental exclamation of this one hearer. When the final full dress rehearsal was reached, everyone connected with the opera house was in a state of exaltation. It remained only to see what this uncertain public would do. But that faithful old jury failed not to find a true verdict. It convicted Montemezzi of having perpetrated a new art work. And let it be added that the swiftness and enthusiasm of the public appreciation of this opera is one of the encouraging evidences of the soundness of our taste.

Sem Benelli, one of the young generation of Italian poets, wrote a tragedy which his countrymen accepted as a creation of high literary and imaginative quality.[1] This is the play from which the libretto of 'L'Amore dei Tre Re' was made by a process of condensation. The book is indeed fine. It has all the essentials of a poetic tragedy – atmosphere, sinister power, splendid emotional climax and passionate lyric speech. These are inspiring materials for the operatic composer. Nevertheless, an inventor of commonplace melodies, whose appeal was addressed to the superficial ear rather than to the understanding, would have made a failure of this thing. Montemezzi succeeded by rejecting the latest methods of building Italian opera, and his compatriots have acclaimed what they call the 'rehabilitation' of their lyric drama.

Italian opera began with a lofty endeavor to unite speech and song in a new form of dramatic expression, which was called the

---

[1] It is not clear on what grounds Henderson advances this assertion. *L'Amore dei Tre Re* as a spoken play had been a failure.

'stile parlante.'[1] This product was overbalanced on the literary side. The result was that music soon claimed that recognition which the first efforts awarded her too stingily. Claudio Monteverde (1567–1643), the first real genius of opera, endeavored to preserve the direct and beautiful dramatic utterance of the first composers, but to impart also to his scores a larger measure of musical design. The ineffably beautiful arioso of his 'Lasciatemi morire,' the only number of his 'Arianna' that has come down to us, seems to have been the spring at which Montemezzi drank his first inspiration.[2] At any rate, he has accomplished the noteworthy task of fashioning an opera in the purest and most flexible arioso style, while at the same time utilizing every element of declamatory device, orchestral delineation and modern harmony which lay ready to the hand of a twentieth century composer.

The most striking characteristics of this opera are its dramatic expressiveness, its fluency of melodic line, and its clear embodiment of character. Next to these may be placed the opulence and transparency of the orchestration. The dramatic expressiveness of the work arises from the exquisite adaptation of the music to the moods of the text and the fine mastery of the genius of the Italian language shown in the construction of the musical declamation. The utterances of the persons in the play have all the directness of actual speech, while at the same time they float in a river of captivating melody.

---

1 Henderson discusses this in his book *How Music Developed: A Critical and Explanatory Account of the Growth of Modern Music* (New York, 1898): 'the composer sought to impart dramatic significance to his music by imitating the inflections of the voice in speech. ... The new style of music, the recitative, was called *Stile rappresentativo* or *Stile parlante*' (249, 252). *Stile rappresentativo* is the term more commonly used today.

2 *Arianna*, Monteverdi's second opera, was first performed at the Ducal Palace, Mantua, on 28 May 1608. It enjoyed considerable success in Monteverdi's lifetime, but sometime after 1640 the music was lost, apart from the famous lament, which Monteverdi had published.

In regard to this matter of melody perhaps a pertinent word may be said. There are many people who discern melody only in what musicians call a simple song form. For these there is no melody in a melodic phrase, but only in a finished 'tune.' Hence, when they go to the opera, they never hear any melody except in a fully developed aria. Now it ought to be understood that opera is a form of the poetic drama based on compromise. If the poetic text is permitted to be the dictator, then music becomes nothing more than recitative and usually that of the earliest kind. If music reigns supreme, then opera becomes a series of separate songs, each perhaps enchanting in itself, but without dramatic connection and generally with little or no dramatic expressiveness.

The ideal art of the opera is that which finds the happy mean between these two. This happy mean is what the greatest creative masters have sought, and it is the product which the most indolent part of the public dislikes. Montemezzi has elected to stand with the masters, and his score contains no tunes which can be lifted out and sung at the Sunday night concerts, as in the case of 'Vissi d'arte,' or 'Che gelida manina.'[1] The whole lyric play is carried forward in melodic speech, for every phrase is beautifully singable and musically eloquent; but there is nowhere that marshalling of phrases in stanza form which constitutes a 'tune.'

Those who go to future performances, therefore, will do well to bend their minds to a consideration of the beautiful poetic significance of the musical investiture of the text, and note well the wonderful atmospheric effects. The brooding of the tremendous tragedy is painted in the most skillful manner and by simple means. The first act is, as first acts should be, a perfect preparation. The second lets loose the mighty passions. In it there are two duets, one between the husband and wife, the other between the wife and the lover. The contrast between them

---

1 Celebrated arias from *Tosca* and *La Bohème* respectively.

is perfectly made. The nobility and tenderness of the husband strike in vain against the coldness of the wife. When the lover comes, the world suddenly blazes with passionate utterance. Then enters the aged father, making sure of the infidelity which he suspected in the first act. His elemental wrath sweeps him away and he strangles the wife of his beloved son.

All through this powerful act the music surges in great waves of expression, rising and falling in tumultuous pulses of feeling. The devices employed in creating the musical climaxes are not new, for there are no new devices in sight; but how admirably Montemezzi uses them! He has succeeded in making old things over, in rejuvenating methods which seemed to have outlived their usefulness. There is much modernism in the score, but, to our comfort, the composer has not been afraid to use the common idioms of musical speech. His instrumentation includes all the latest methods and makes as much of the Russian celesta as any recent composer has. Here, however, it can be said that Montemezzi has been ingenious in treating this tinkling instrument not continually as a special voice, but mostly as a blend in the color of many of his chords.

The production of the opera at the Metropolitan has been one of the triumphs of Mr. Gatti-Casazza's direction. Scenery artistically planned to accord with the moods of the drama, costumes well designed and accessories carefully prepared, furnish the correct background for four admirable impersonations and for orchestral support which could not be surpassed, if equalled, in any other opera house in the world. Miss Bori astonishes her warmest admirers by her good acting and her really beautiful singing in the role of *Fiora*. Edoardo Ferrari-Fontana, a tenor borrowed from Boston, is the representative of *Avito*, the lover, and his warm voice, dramatic singing and generally satisfying impersonation stamp him at once as one of the best operatic artists recently heard in this city. Mr. Amato has a role well suited to the exhibition of the finer qualities of his art, which are too often relegated to the background by reason of the robust style of music allotted to him. Adamo Didur, whose success as *Boris Godunov*, revealed histrionic abilities previously unsuspected, acts the father *Archibaldo* with dignity and pathos. The musical direction of the opera is in the hands of Mr. Toscanini and it can be said, unhesitatingly, that he has not of late shown in any other work such fine and searching appreciation of the possibilities of a score. The orchestra has played this music with real affection, with tenderness and with opalescent color. In short, the entire production has been a noteworthy artistic achievement.

7. John van Broekhoven, *Musical Observer*, February 1914.

L'Amore Dei Tre Re

A new opera by the young Italian composer, Italo Montemezzi

ON FRIDAY evening, January 2d, the Metropolitan Opera Institute presented its second novelty of the season to the New York opera public, a new Italian opera by the young composer, Italo Montemezzi, entitled *L'Amore dei Tre Re* (the Love of Three Kings). This new opera, which was given for the first time last April in an Italian provincial opera house,[1] has been produced nowhere else outside of Italy. Hence it is the more surprising that the New York public and critics were so unanimous in expressing their conviction that here was a new work of extraordinary musical dramatic vitality, the interest in it increasing with every repetition of the opera. So much so in fact that this second operatic novelty of the season seems destined to overshadow in interest the first novelty, viz., Richard Strauss' *Rosenkavalier*.

These two new operas from the two sources of antipodal musical temperament – the German and the Italian – call forth comparisons. For anyone inclined to study or observe the national art tendencies of nations must be impressed with the dissimilarity between the methods, conceptions, intentions and emotional directions of the two composers as conveyed in their works. The German is nothing if not thoughtful and profound. And the Italian cannot conceive anything human unless it is expressed in emotions – in passions. Germany is philosophic; Italy is poetic. The artworks of both nations prove this. German art has much to do with formulas, Italian art with sensuousness.

---

1 Broekhoven was probably misled by Richard Aldrich on this. See above, p. 76 and n. 1.

And these national characteristics prevail in the two operas – *The Love of Three Kings* of the Italian composer, and the *Rosenkavalier* of the German composer.

The composer of *L'Amore dei Tre Re* lacks naught of the technical musical equipment of a Richard Strauss; but in the manner of the judicious employment of his musical medium in expressing poetic conception, and delineating emotional subtleties, Montemezzi is the master. It must have been noticed, for instance, by those who have a disposition for observation, that in no instance did Montemezzi need the whole orchestral forces, the mere power of instrumental tone to give expression to some of the most forceful dramatic situations in the action. He obtained this in most cases with a few instruments and a moderate degree of dynamic power. The voice of the actor or actress was never submerged in the orchestral tonal mass. And this extraordinary moderation in the employment of the instrumental volume in highly dramatic moments is one of the most convincing proofs of Montemezzi's dramatic genius. He handles his material – although still young – like an experienced veteran. He seems to conceive the dramatic expression to lie more in the intensely emotional quality of the voice, or the melodic phrase in the orchestra, than in the forceful vehemence of the orchestral mass. Nowhere in the whole opera, which embraces extremely strong emotional situations, does he make use of such an orchestral chaos as we find in the third act of the *Rosenkavalier*, where the action depicts the comic undoing of Baron Ochs. Nor does this young maestro feel the necessity to invent excruciating harmonic combinations and resolutions to enable him to give adequate expression to dramatic points. The admirers of Richard Strauss have in this opera an excellent example of the dramatic effectiveness of moderation and restraint in the use of orchestral material in comparison to the obvious effort to achieve strong dramatic expression by forceful and boisterous contrapuntal construction and orchestration, as found in *Salome* and *Elektra*. If Richard Strauss had composed the music to the libretto of the *Love of the* [sic] *Three Kings*, he would have torn passion to tatters[1] and exhausted every instrumentalist in the orchestra with the effort to conform the tonal power of the orchestra to the portrayal of intense passion by the singers. None of this is found in this successful opera of this young Italian.

A New Style

Italo Montemezzi is not an extremist, nor is he a conservatist. He is in the best meaning of the term 'a modernist,' or rather 'an opportunist.' For he has as clear a vision of the modern operatic methods and tendency as he has of lyric-dramatic expression. In this opera he has distinctly made an attempt – which is most successful – of combining some of the old and well-established methods of orchestral treatment with modern requirements. The old and well-worn orchestral figures serving as accompaniment, which are still in use in Verdi's *Aida*, as we have example in Fig. 1,[2] giving merely a form of broken chord or arpeggio, Montemezzi retains in principle, but varies them melodically and rhythmically, so as to suggest almost a leitmotiv character and significance.

---

1 A pointed allusion to Hamlet's advice to the players: 'O, it offends me to the soul to hear a robustious periwig-pated fellow tear a passion to tatters, to very rags, to split the ears of the groundlings, who for the most part are capable of nothing but inexplicable dumb-shows and noise' (*Hamlet* Act 3, Scene 2).

2 From the accompaniment to Radamès' 'Forse l'arcano amore' in his first scene with Amneris.

In Fig. 2 we have a few measures from the love scene between Fiora and her lover, Avito, from Montemezzi's opera. From this example, we observe his object to make the harmonic accompaniment more serviceable dramatically and emotionally. Against the long-drawn tones in the upper voice, the triplets in the accompaniment add an extraordinary value as a musical, emotional and dramatic element of far greater significance and importance than the figure of the accompaniment in Verdi's *Aida*, Fig.1.

This method of constructing his harmonic groundwork in the form of a mobile, rhythmical, melodic, dramatic adjunct to the melody, or melodic theme, Montemezzi makes into a system which is new in operatic technic. It is found in the orchestral and chamber music of the classic and more modern composers, but it has not been used as a system in opera. He uses it with extreme good judgment to give body to the harmonic construction, movement to the rhythm, thematic significance to this reiteration of his accompaniment, and finally makes with its use the impression of a counterpointic independence of the instrumental voices which approaches the Wagnerian polyphonic style.

What effective dramatic use these accompaniment figurations may be put to is seen in Fig. 3, which is based on the B flat minor triad, and which, in this form, Montemezzi uses as a leitmotiv associated with the blind king's character as an avenger of his son's wrongs.

And again in Fig. 4, he breaks up the D major chord into rhythmical accompaniment, which serves as a solid harmonic basis, and at the same time adds in giving the scene a touch of the martial character called for in the narrative of the blind king, Archibaldo. This rhythmical phrase is made musically interesting by assigning to it two oboes and English horn.

In the love scene in the second act between Fiora and Avito, he employs a reiteration by the muted violins of a rhythmical phrase in a melodic form of the E flat major chord alternating with the dominant. And to enhance this almost bare construction, he introduces a poetic phase by having a single voice behind the scenes to sing a melancholy long-drawn phrase on the vowel 'Ah,' as shown in Fig. 5. The dramatic effect is exquisite, by far transcending the simplicity of the means employed to obtain it. It is a fine illustration of the composer's genius for dramatic composition.

In another instance he enhances the hackneyed repetition of a single chord by the addition of a melodic phrase, as in Fig. 6.

This particular phase of Montemezzi's method of composition is dictated by a spirit of submission to Italian custom; it is a concession to popular expectation and practice. But in that he has imbued the old-fashioned humdrum accompaniment with renewed life, motion, and dramatic significance, he has raised the possibility of Italian opera to a new prospect of life, which may be the source of the Italian opera regaining [the] supremacy it held before the advent of Richard Wagner.

That this young opportunist has also the counterpointic facility of the German school besides the Italian emotional warmth and poetry is clearly obvious from the many examples of counterpointic writing in his opera. In Fig. 7 we have an extract from the scene between Fiora and Avito in the first act, which is not unworthy of a Richard Wagner.

Another example of polyphonic writing taken from the scene between the two lovers is shown in Fig. 8, in which we have an evidence of Montemezzi's instinct for sustained melody and modern harmony which only can be compared to Wagner's best style.

Fig. 8.

[Brief account of Montemezzi from the *New York Times* and extended summary of the plot.]

Tragic Subject

The libretto of this tragic tale is an operatic adaptation of a tragedy by the Italian poet, Sem Benelli, who also wrote the book for the opera.[1] The characters in the operatic version seem to be a compound of Shakespeare's *Lear* and *Romeo and Juliet*, with a suggestion of *Elektra* to increase the tragic horrors. Yet, in spite of the many painful situations, Montemezzi has much alleviated the oppressive aspect of the play by his moderation in depicting the musical setting of the drama. The music, in no instance, aims to increase the horrors by a heaping up of orchestral forces. The chief object of the composer seems to have been to convey the tragic emotions of the inner voice more than the brutal vehemence of exterior action. This allows him to maintain an outline of aesthetic principles in conjunction with

---

1 This is misleading: the libretto is simply a shortened version of the play, with two brief episodes substituted by choruses. See above, p. 55 and n. 1.

a proper proportion of musical beauty of sound truly elevating to the normal individual; and certainly surprising in the modern tendency to startle, shock and stir the emotions by dynamic exaggeration. It was this demonstration of moderation in the employment of the modern musical medium of expression in so tragic a subject that impressed the public and critics. And as the musical setting left nothing to be desired as a truthful portrayal of the dramatic spirit of the play, and gave great pleasure in other directions – notably orchestration and treatment of the vocal parts – the opera as a whole met with a warm reception at its first performance.

The management of the Metropolitan Opera House may be congratulated on having presented their patrons with this latest work of young Italy before the European press had given its dictum. It gave the New York critics an opportunity to have a first opinion of a work which is bound to make its appearance on the operatic stage of the world. To the conductor, Arturo Toscanini, is due the thanks of the public for his admirable presentation of the work and the artistic rendition of the opera. And to the principals in the cast is due all the honor which can be conferred on painstaking artists.

8. Lawrence Gilman, *North American Review*, February 1914.

A Remarkable New Opera from Italy: Montemezzi's 'L'Amore dei Tre Re'

[Reprinted with minor changes as 'A Note on Montemezzi' in *Nature in Music and Other Studies in the Tone-Poetry of Today* (New York: John Lane, 1914)]

TO AN observer of the musical heavens the discovery of a new composer is as thrilling an event as the discovery of a new star must be to those who watch the more fruitful heavens of actuality. By 'a new composer' we mean, of course, a new composer of parts – one who speaks with a voice that is arresting by reason of its beauty, or its volume, or its singularity. To have lived in the day of, say, Wagner's emergence must have been a stupefying experience indeed – though there is the hideous possibility that even the most liberal, the most unimpeded, among us might have reacted to him as did Ruskin to 'Die Meistersinger,' which he dismissed, with delightful vehemence, as an 'affected, sapless, soulless, tuneless doggerel of sounds; ... as for the great *Lied*, I never made out where it began or where it ended, except by the fellow's coming off the horse-block.'[1] But if we cannot all have been present on that occasion when

---

1 *Die Meistersinger* received its British premiere at Drury Lane, London, on 30 May 1882. John Ruskin (1819–1900), the great British art critic and social theorist, denounced it in a letter of 30 June to Lady Burne-Jones. The first part quoted by Gilman reads, in full, 'of all the affected, sapless, soulless, beginningless, endless, topless, bottomless, topsitierviest, tuneless, scrannelpipiest – tongs and boniest – doggerel of sounds I ever endured the deadliest of, that eternity of nothing was the deadliest.' See *The Works of John Ruskin*, ed. E. T. Cook and Alexander Wedderburn, 39 vols (London: George Allen, 1903–12), 37:402.

the Quintet must (let us hope) have fallen upon our ears like the voice of all the angels singing out of heaven, there are many of us who have had the immeasurable privilege of watching the wonder and loveliness of a 'Pelléas' flush the tonal skies with a beauty as magical and melancholy as an autumn sunset,[1] or have seen an 'Elektra' flame in those self-same skies like the terrible, burning star of the Apocalypse, the name of which was wormwood, and which embittered the waters into which it fell; 'and many men died of the waters, because they were made bitter.'[2] And there, perhaps, is the fitting motto for what we are about to say.

How is one to know whether the new light in the esthetic sky is an enduring radiance or a false dawn? Whether the flaming star is a fact or an hallucination? How, that is to say, are we to know whether our new composer is worthy of our liking or not? We fancy the candid pessimist would tell us that we may know the authentic from the delusive by remembering the words of the Scriptural narrative that we have just quoted. Are the waters embittered by the burning star? If they are, then (says our candid pessimist) you may know that Genius has come upon the earth. Has any genius – has any genuinely creative composer (to stick closely to our muttons) – ever failed to embitter the waters? When Ruskin called the music of 'Meistersinger' a 'soulless,

---

1 *Pelléas et Mélisande* received its American premiere at the Manhattan Opera House on 19 February 1908. It was not put on at the Met until 1925.

2 *Elektra*, sung in French, received its American premiere at the Manhattan Opera House on 1 February 1910. It was not staged at the Met until 1932, to Gilman's annoyance: see below, p. 303 and n. 1. Gilman's quotation is from Revelation 8:10–11: 'And the third angel sounded, and there fell a great star from heaven, burning as it were a lamp, and it fell upon the third part of the rivers, and upon the fountains of the waters; [11] And the name of the star is called Wormwood: and the third part of the waters became wormwood; and many men died of the waters, because they were made bitter.'

The final scene with Manfredo (Amato) dying in his father's arms

tuneless, doggerel of sounds' he merely echoed the opinion of most of the critics and many of the public of his time. We all remember how the most important music composed since the death of Wagner – the music of Debussy and Richard Strauss – was greeted by those who should have been the first to announce and extol it. So that it might almost be stated as a critical axiom that you may know a masterpiece by the bitterness it precipitates; and that a work which is hailed upon its appearance as a masterpiece is – something quite different.[1] The new work of an innovating genius will always taste bitter in the mouth to all save a few. If it does not – if its flavor delights the palate at once – let the heedful beware!

All of which is prefatory to a consideration of a new opera, by a new composer, which has made more noise in New York than any lyric novelty of recent years. We refer, of course, to Italo Montemezzi's 'L'Amore dei Tre Re,' which was produced at the Metropolitan in the first week of the new year amid general and indisputably sincere rejoicings – rejoicings which would have been a fit greeting, indeed, for a new 'Tristan und Isolde,' and which awoke, in the memories of some, ironic recollections of the quite different reception that marked the disclosure of 'Pelléas et Mélisande' and 'Elektra.'

Montemezzi is a wholly new apparition in the operatic field, so far as the world at large is concerned. He is young – in the early

---

1 The argument here is obviously not acceptable as a transhistorical truth; it is, rather, an attitude which emerged in the Romantic period, with the supposed alienation of the modern artist in society. In English, the first creedal statement of the case is perhaps that found in William Wordsworth's 'Preface' and 'Essay, Supplementary to the Preface' of 1815 where Wordsworth argued that the quantity of 'insults' he had received showed that his poetry was original and important and that 'posterity' would judge it favourably. The argument was widely ridiculed at the time, demonstrating how absurd it seemed a century before Gilman used it to extol Debussy and Strauss (both of whom had enjoyed plenty of success by 1914) at Montemezzi's expense.

thirties;[1] and his native Italy saw the production of 'L'Amore dei Tre Re' only a year ago. His two previous operas had made no fame for him, and to-day, save in Italy and in New York, he is virtually unknown. Nor is the dramatist who has supplied the literary basis of his opera much better known. Sem Benelli is a contemporary Italian poet, whose name is often bracketed by his countrymen with that of Gabriele D'Annunzio; but few non-Latin readers are familiar with his work. His 'L'Amore dei Tre Re' is a 'tragic poem' in three acts. It is a play that might have been written for musical enlargement, so ideally suited is it to the purposes of the lyric stage. This drama is almost as spare, as free from accessory elements, as is Wagner's 'Tristan.'

Fiora, wife of Manfredo, is a young princess who has been wedded against her will to the son of the conqueror of her people. She loves Avito, and, in her husband's absence, gives herself to him. The blind and aged Archibaldo, jealous of his son's honor, surprises her in the arms of her lover and strangles her. As she lies dead he smears her lips with poison, thinking to entrap her lover when he shall come to kiss her. But it is not Avito alone whom he entraps; Manfredo, too, kisses desperately the poisoned lips of Fiora; and Archibaldo, entering then, and thinking he has caught the lover, wraps his arms about the body of his dying son. It is a heart-shaking utterance of the sightless old king upon which the curtain closes:

> Ah! Manfredo! Manfredo! Anche tu, dunque,
> Senza rimedio sei con me nell'ombra![2]

It is said by those who best know Italian that Signor Benelli has accomplished in this play a dramatic poem of conspicuous

---

[1] A figure closer to the truth (38) than the statements of other American critics, though still tending to make Montemezzi younger than he really was.

[2] In R. H. Elkin's translation the lines read: 'Manfredo! Manfredo! Thou also, then / Art with me past salvation in the shadows!'

excellence as literature. Upon that point we have no right to an opinion. But, quite aside from its literary quality, the play, as a drama for the lyric stage, is beyond question admirable. It is very simple, very powerful, very moving. It has passion and pathos. It is eloquent of

> Earth's old and weary cry.[1]

Would that we could honestly avoid saying that it is worthy a more gifted composer than Signor Montemezzi! Let it be admitted at once, with all heartiness, that Montemezzi is a musician who commands respect. He is a composer of evident scholarship, of indubitable feeling, of deep seriousness and sincerity. It is certain that he has been profoundly moved by the drama he has undertaken to set, and that he is quite single-minded in his endeavor to heighten and intensify it in his music. He is obviously not concerned about wooing the ears of the groundlings. He has given us a score in which, from beginning to end, there is not a measure that can justly be called meretricious; a score that makes no *ad captandum* appeal whatsoever. He has applied himself with undivided earnestness and devotion to the task of setting forth his dramatic theme with all the enhancing power of which he is capable. There is here no defect of intention, but only a defect of capacity. If dramatic music of the highest order could be achieved without inspiration, then Montemezzi would have given us a masterpiece to which we all, without exception, could offer homage. But for our part, we see no profit in judging a work of art save by the criterion of the best. To extol a new work because it is not so bad as some, or because its composer is very young and may do better, or because he might have done worse, seems, to say the least, beside the point. We have a stubborn conviction that there is no such thing as a second-rate masterpiece. The supreme obligation of music is to be eloquent: if it is not eloquent, it has failed.

---

1 From W. B. Yeats' poem, 'The Sorrow of Love.'

It has been intimated that Montemezzi is entitled to some kind of credit because he is different from Puccini. Now it is certain that Signor Puccini has many faults, and has committed many esthetic indiscretions. His place is assuredly not with the high gods of music. But he *can* be eloquent; and he has unescapable individuality – the two cardinal virtues which Signor Montemezzi has not. Montemezzi's ideas lack distinction; but, what is worse, they lack character. His music is wanting in profile; it has no marked personality. It has feeling, it is rhetorically impressive; but of true imagination it has little. We should not think of denying that the scene in 'L'Amore dei Tre Re' which arouses the greatest enthusiasm in its hearers – the love scene of the second act – is extremely effective and exciting; Montemezzi has written music for this scene which is an excellent imitation of the real thing – music which the incautious and the non-exigent would assuredly defend as eloquent beyond question. But it is not a difficult thing for the resourceful composer of to-day so to manipulate the marvelous expressional resources that modern music has acquired from the masters of the past that all but the most wary are beguiled into thinking that they are listening to the authentic speech of inspiration. Plagiarism is not implied, for plagiarism is unnecessary. A commonplace melody, if it be large-molded and passionate in accent, and uttered in an ascending *crescendo* by the wonderful myriad-voiced orchestra that is now at the disposal of any accomplished craftsman, can suggest with extraordinary similitude the veritable tongue of genius. But that is not what we mean by eloquence in music. We mean the kind of eloquence that stabs the spirit like a flaming sword; that strikes the mind with an instant conviction that an immortal saying has been uttered; that floods the heart with something that is part exquisite ecstasy and part exquisite pain; that opens to the inward eye, for a brief moment, a vision of the heights where eternal Loveliness dreams its eternal dream, and makes us know that we have seen

Beauty itself amid
Beautiful things.[1]

It is no pleasure to disparage so earnest, so dignified, so scrupulous a musician as Signor Montemezzi, especially as it is possible for the most exacting to listen with true pleasure to many pages of his opera, wherein are to be found a persuasive expression of feeling that is always sincere and deep. But to say or to imply that he has produced a score which is worthy to be named in the same breath with a work of essential genius like 'Pelléas et Mélisande,' or like 'Elektra,' or even like 'Der Rosenkavalier,' is merely to darken counsel.[2]

Of the production of 'L'Amore dei Tre Re' at the Metropolitan no praise could be too hearty. Miss Bori as the much-loved Fiora, Mr. Ferrari-Fontana as her lover Avito, Mr. Amato as Manfredo, the husband, and Mr. Didur as the blind avenging Archibaldo, are so completely satisfying in their several rôles that a sense of the excellence of their impersonations can best be conveyed by

---

[1] From 'I am Beauty itself among beautiful things,' George William Russell's once celebrated epigraph, loosely translated from the Bhagavad Gita, to his early poem 'Krishna.' The poem and its epigraph first appeared in America in Edmund Clarence Stedman (ed.), *A Victorian Anthology 1837–1895* (Boston and New York: Houghton Mifflin, 1895), 605.

[2] The expression 'darken counsel' can be traced back to the Authorized Version of Job 38:2: 'Who *is* this that darkeneth counsel by words without knowledge?' However, it seems to have been popularized by the *Exhortation to Peace and Unity* (1688) long attributed to John Bunyan and included in the many editions of his collected works:

> How many are there ... that instead of multiplying knowledge, multiply words without knowledge; and instead of making known God's counsel, darken counsel by words without knowledge?

After this supposed application of Bunyan's, the expression is found in many eighteenth- and nineteenth-century Christian texts. Gilman's using such vocabulary is characteristic of his very literate, allusive, pseudo-religious style of criticism, but in the present instance it registers the seriousness of the claims being advanced for Montemezzi's genius.

Jules Speck, 1916
Director of the First Met Production of
L'Amore dei Tre Re

saying that they are as nearly ideal as human fallibility can ever permit. As for the achievement of the prodigious Toscanini, who learned the score in a few weeks and conducted from memory a performance of superb impressiveness – but why enlarge upon a miracle? If Mr. Toscanini were dead, the story of his deeds would read like a fable.[1]

---

1 The final paragraph is omitted in *Nature in Music*, and replaced with:

> When all is said, however, one is far from being insensible to a certain pathos that is implicit in this noble and sincere, yet disappointing expression of the indisputable talent of this true artist – the pathos that envelops all those who love with passion beautiful things: who try to speak, however haltingly, however brokenly, of those mysteries which, after all, are beyond speech: who are dreamers of dreams: who have seen, and cannot forget; yet who are not without consolation: for they know that 'there will come a time when it shall be light, and man shall awaken from his lofty dreams, and find his dreams still there, and that nothing has gone save his sleep.' (165–66)

The quotation, a favourite of Gilman's, is from the preface to *Hesperus oder 45 Hundposttage* (1795) by Jean Paul (1763–1825), the German Romantic writer. Gilman slightly adapts Thomas Carlyle's translation.

Boston Premiere

Boston Opera House, 9 February 1914

3 performances

Cast:

Fiora .... Lucrezia Bori[1]
Avito .... Edoardo Ferrari-Fontana
Manfredo .... Pasquale Amato[2]
Archibaldo .... Pavel Ludikar[3]

Director: Louis P. Verande
Stage and Costume Design: Joseph Urban
Conductor: Roberto Moranzoni

---

1 In the final performance she was substituted by Luisa Villani.
2 After the first performance he was substituted by Mario Ancona.
3 In the final performance he was substituted by Jean Vanni-Marcoux.

BOSTON OPERA HOUSE
BOSTON OPERA COMPANY
LESSEES
GRAND OPERA Season of 1913-1914

WEDNESDAY EVENING, FEBRUARY 18, 1914

L'Amore dei Tre Re

Cast

ARCHIBALDO	VANNI MARCOUX
MANFREDO	MARIO ANCONA
AVITO	EDOARDO FERRARI-FONTANA
FLAMINIO	ERNESTO GIACCONE
UN GIOVANETTO	LORENZO FUSCO
FIORA	LUISA VILLANI
ANCELLA	KRISTINA HELIANE
UNA GIOVANETTA	MYRNA SHARLOW
UNA VECCHIA	ELVIRA LEVERONI

Synopsis of Scenery

Period: In the middle ages, forty years after a barbaric invasion.
Act I. A spacious hall in a medieval castle.
Act II. Terrace on the castle wall.
Act III. Crypt in the castle chapel.

MASON & HAMLIN PIANOS USED

Programme for the final performance, with three of the principals changed

1. Philip Hale, *Boston Herald*, 10 February 1914.

'Love Of The Three Kings' Is Seen Here

Production Proves Great Event of the Season at Boston Opera House – An Engrossing Performance – Miss Bori Admirable as Fiora – Fontana Plays Avito with Authority

MONTEMEZZI WAS fortunate in his libretto. It is said that he at first wrote incidental music to Benelli's tragedy from which the libretto was arranged.[1] Whether this report is true or false is now immaterial. The libretto even in the English version by R. H. Elkim [sic] is out of the common. The original is 'writ in choice Italian,'[2] so those thoroughly acquainted with that language say, and in the English there is still a poetic flavor.

The story told by Benelli is simple, frank and short. It is noble, not sensual. The maiden, betrothed to Avito but given in marriage for political reasons to Manfredo, was not a light o' love. Her legal mate, unlike Francesca's,[3] was a man whom she could respect and might have loved if he had been the first comer. Faithful to Manfredo, she would have been unfaithful to Avito, for she was ingenuous, not given to deceit, and although through pity for Manfredo she attempted to put Avito from her, at last she could not lie and she gloried in her confession though she knew death was then giving eyes to the blind old baron.

Was the Baron also in love with her, or did he love her because his son was her husband? Here is a delicate point that admits of academic discussion, an interesting subject for those

---

1 There is no evidence for this.

2 From Hamlet's description of *The Mousetrap*: 'the story is extant and writ in choice Italian' (*Hamlet* Act 3, Scene 2, Folio text).

3 The eponymous heroine of the *Francesca da Rimini* story. See above, p. 56 and n. 3.

giving preparatory lectures on the music drama.[1] This is certain: Archibaldo was sinister in his vengeance, a righteous vengeance as he thought, by reason of his blindness, as Stevenson's blind man in 'Treasure Island' is peculiarly terrible.[2] But Archibaldo is one of the wise old men of the operatic stage; he would have been of close kin to Maeterlinck's Arkel and Marco[3] if he had only been a little more of a philosopher and not a man of action.

The snare prepared by Archibaldo and Manfredo to catch the lover by putting poison on the lips of Fiora as she lay in state after having been throttled by the old Baron would have pleased the Elizabethans. It takes us back to the tragedies of Webster and Tourneur.[4] Yet in this tragedy it does not seem extravagant, or too melodramatic. The trick was an Italian one, and the Italians were masters in the art of poisoning. A helmet donned by an adversary, a torch held before an honored guest, the pommel of a

---

[1] Montemezzi believed that Archibaldo was in love with Fiora. See above, p. 67, n. 1.

[2] Pew in Robert Louis Stevenson's *Treasure Island* (1883). There are no similarities between the stories: Hale simply means the blindness of both men makes them all the more sinister.

[3] Characters in *Pelléas et Mélisande* (1893) and *Monna Vanna* (1902). See below, p. 132, for Hale's view of Arkel.

[4] A shrewd recognition that demonstrates the great breadth of Hale's reading. In *The Revenger's Tragedy* (1606), attributed to Cyril Tourneur (1575–1626), the Duke is killed by being tricked into kissing a poisoned skull attached to a mannequin – believing it a country girl ripe for seduction. In *The White Devil* (1612), by John Webster (*c.*1580–1638?), Isabella, wife of the Duke of Brachiano, is murdered with poison applied to the lips of her husband's portrait. Another Jacobean play, *The Second Maiden's Tragedy* (1611), first published in 1824 and now attributed to Thomas Middleton (1580–1627), comes even closer to Benelli's concept: there the necrophilic Tyrant is killed when he kisses the poisoned lips of a corpse. Middleton's plot device was reused by Philip Massinger (1583–1640) in *The Duke of Milan* (1623). The English dramatists favoured Italian settings for such stories.

saddle, riding boots, a bouquet or fan, the lips of a portrait – all these were sure instruments of death, and there were even more ingenious devices that the murderer in Marlowe's 'Edward II.' boasted of having learned in Italy.[1]

Throughout the libretto there is the poetic expression that gives nobility to what might otherwise be a common story of illicit love and mediaeval retribution.

Montemezzi's opera is literally a drama with music, and no one can justly appreciate the talent shown by this composer until he is familiar with the text: not only the story in detail, but the dialogue, with its expression and its subtle suggestion. At the very beginning there is a remarkably beautiful passage for the orchestra, exquisitely lyrical, that illustrates the lines in which Fiora is described as sleeping, and Archibaldo exclaims: 'Well, let her sleep; since youth is but a dream, naught else.' So in the same act the orchestra is pictorially eloquent in Archibaldo's magnificent account of how he and his comrades came into Italy, the land they love.

The music of Montemezzi is singularly original. It does not follow the scheme of Wagner or of Debussy. The influence of the later Verdi is not felt. It is wholly free from any taint of Puccinism. While there is no aria, while there is no ensemble – except the

---

1 Lightborne, the assassin in Christopher Marlowe's *Edward II* (*c*.1592), says:

> 'Tis not the first time I have kill'd a man:
> I learn'd in Naples how to poison flowers;
> To strangle with a lawn thrust down the throat;
> To pierce the windpipe with a needle's point;
> Or, whilst one is asleep, to take a quill
> And blow a little powder in his ears;
> Or open his mouth, and pour quick-silver down.
> (Act 5, Scene 4, 29–36)

The text is from Osborne William Tancock's edition of *Edward II* for the Clarendon Press Series (1879).

little but impressive funeral chant at the beginning of the third act and the duets when examined are not duets in the conventional meaning of the word – there is no copying of the formulas of heightened speech invented by Wagner and later by Debussy. On the other hand, there is no falling into barren recitative.

How pathetic by their simplicity are the replies of Fiora to Manfredo in the second act! Here are the accents of a perturbed soul that feels at its heart its innocence, though the world might proclaim it guilty. And in this opera there is no sensuous love music; there is the ecstasy of kindred souls. Archibaldo and Manfredo both know of this ecstatic love. For this reason the latter cannot live after he learns that Avito was loved in this manner. When Archibaldo rails against Fiora after the murder Manfredo does not bellow for revenge. 'Of such great love that child-heart, then, was capable, and not for me.' If Fiora could have heard this cry, she might have rushed to her husband's arms in loving adoration, and from a child suddenly become a woman.

Thus we go back to the tragic poem itself, and this is the highest tribute to Montemezzi's music. It is impossible to separate the music and the poem. The Italian has done in an Italian way for an Italian drama what Debussy did in a subtly French way for the Belgian symbolist.[1] The effect is the same, though the means procuring it are very different. It would be idle now to speak of technical matters, of the composer's harmonic system, his use or avoidance of ultra-modern scales, his employment of instruments, his invention of timbres. All this would now seem pedantic. Let us speak only of the result obtained by this richly endowed composer with a rare instinct for dramatic effects. This result was overwhelming.

Nor is it too much to say that the production of this opera, hitherto unknown here, is the great event so far of this operatic

---

1 Maurice Maeterlinck (1862–1949), whose *Pelléas et Mélisande* (1893) served, in shortened form, as the libretto of Debussy's opera.

The Boston Opera House, c. 1910

season. The performance was an engrossing one. Miss Bori, by her beauty, her voice and vocal art, her free and natural acting, portrayed the charming simplicity and child-like character of Fiora. Mr. Fontana, although his make-up was to many disillusionizing, sang and acted with irresistible authority. Mr. Amato gave full expression to the love of Manfredo, hoping almost against hope. Mr. Ludikar gave an impressive performance of Archibaldo, defining sharply and powerfully the various phases of the baron's nature.

Mr. Moranzoni deserves the highest credit for preparing the orchestral performance with necessarily few rehearsals.[1] Under his leadership the orchestral narration was varied and always eloquent.

Mr. Urban's settings were effective in design and color, beautiful to the eye, romantic in spirit. If only he had given more stage room for the action! The librettist calls for a 'spacious hall in the castle.' But Mr. Urban is not fond of space and he forgets that he thus sometimes cramps the actors.

There was a large and brilliant audience. There were many curtain calls.

---

1 This is presumably because *L'Amore dei Tre Re* was a late addition to the season. See below, p. 135 and n. 2.

2. Olin Downes, *Boston Post*, 10 February 1914.

'Love Of Three Kings' Sung For First Time In Boston Opera

Newest and Interesting Work From Twentieth Century Italy Artistically and Effectively Presented Before Representative Audience

Italo Montemezzi's 'Love of Three Kings,' opera in three acts, after the drama of Sem Benelli, was performed last night for the first time by the Boston Opera Company with complete success. The work is in several respects one of the most interesting which have come from modern Italy. It was mounted artistically and effectively presented by nearly the same cast as that which interpreted Montemezzi's music when 'The Love of Three Kings' was heard for the first time in America on Jan. 2, at the Metropolitan Opera House in New York.

A certain number of curtain calls may be expected on any first night, but if the recalls of yesterday evening were a manifestation of politeness on the part of the audience courtesy was strained to a breaking point. This audience was numerous and representative.

[Details of the cast and the plot.]

This opera is remarkable, first of all, for the beauty and conciseness of the libretto. Then, too, the composer has met the dramatist half way. With uncommon resource as regards invention as well as technique, he supplements the text.

Rarely is such an admirable balance of musical and dramatic elements of an opera met with. The libretto is so beautifully adapted that the composer may write freely without delaying or distorting his drama; and he may write real music – not music which is merely subservient to conversation or incident on the stage, but music which does, indeed, apotheosize the big moods of the drama, and permit the characters to express in tones more than they could possibly express by means of speech. That is a true province of music, and such a relation between Montemezzi and his librettist offers the most encouraging sign that has come from modern Italy in many years, so far as music-drama is concerned.

Climax in Second Act

The composer reached his climax in the second act. Here his invention is unforced and unflagging, and his dramatic instinct wholly equal to the situation. The love duet of Fiora and Avito is music to be ranked among the best that contemporary Italy has produced. It has been said that in earlier operas Montemezzi suffers from a lack of experience in writing for the stage. Such a deficiency was not in evidence last night. In fact, if there was a fear it would be that he appreciated too well some of the telling theatrical devices of his contemporaries. His orchestration is of extraordinary beauty and brilliancy, his style always refined and melodic.

For the present it must be enough to conclude with a word about the performance. Mr. Ferrari-Fontana sang with all his wonted intelligence and fervor the ardent music of Avito. Mr. Amato was far more in his element as a singer than when he sang here a few days ago as the Barber of Rossini,[1] for this is modern Italian music: it demands a big tone and a dramatic style. Both of these things, it is hardly necessary to say, are Mr. Amato's in a superlative degree.

Miss Bori was a beautiful and gifted interpreter, although her upper tones have too much edge. The middle register of her voice is of a haunting quality. Mr. Ludikar's Archibaldo is a competent impersonation, although a bigger tone would have served him

---

[1] Amato's first performance of Rossini's Figaro in Boston was on 31 January.

Designs for the First and Third Acts
Joseph Urban

well. The smaller parts were admirably taken, and the singing of the beautiful choruses in the last act deserves especial praise. Mr. Moranzoni conducted with what appeared, at a first hearing, to be a deep appreciation of the score and its innumerable beauties, and he obtained the effects he desired. The curtain calls after each act were innumerable.

3. Philip Hale, *Boston Herald*, 15 February 1914.

'L'Amore Dei Tre Re' Again Performed

Opera on Repetition Makes Deep Impression by Its Strength and Beauty

MONTEMEZZI'S OPERA was performed yesterday afternoon for the second time. It again made a deep impression by the dramatic strength and poetic beauty of the libretto and by the singularly original and eloquent music, which faithfully, but not slavishly, heightens constantly the effect of dialogue and situation.

As we said last Tuesday morning, Montemezzi has done in an Italian way for an Italian drama what Debussy in an ultra-modern French way did for the Belgian Maeterlinck. Each composer worked adroitly in his own manner; each showed an unerring instinct for the stage. To say, however, that Montemezzi imitated the methods of Debussy would be absurd. Maeterlinck's play is based on the idea of fatality, of death. This, as Bruneau said of the Belgian's dramas, and [']the atmosphere of sorrowful legend which enwraps them as in a great veil of crape, that which is distinct and enigmatical in them, their vague personages, poor kings, poor people, poor inhabitants of unnamed lands whom fate leads by the hand in the mist of the irreparable, the resigned, naive, gentle or solemn conversation of these passive unfortunates – all this suited in a most exact manner the temperament of Claude Debussy.'[1]

---

1 Alfred Bruneau (1857–1934) discussed Debussy in his *Musique de Russie et Musiciens de France* (1903). Hale knew the relevant passage from the preface to *Twelve Songs by Claude Debussy*, ed. Charles Fonteyn Manney (Boston, 1913), which he quotes. Hale's text is confused here. The Bruneau passage, as translated by Manney, starts 'The idea of fatality, of death, on which all the pieces of Maeterlinck are based, the atmosphere of sorrowful legend …' Hale has 'enwraps' instead of 'envelops,' 'distinct' instead of 'distant' and 'mist' instead of 'midst,' probably as a result of careless transcription.

In Debussy's opera the men and women are wanderers and wonderers in a dream. Pelleas is a lover in tapestry. Melisande is passive, a plaything of Fate. Golaud alone stands out from the mist, the perplexed and tortured Golaud, who anxiously questions Melisande even when she is dying. Arkel is the old man of experience, the contemplative, sympathetic observer. And these beings move and suffer to music that was heard only in dreams before Debussy fixed it in notation: music of bodement; music that whispers of hopeless love and inevitable death; music for hands folded in resignation; music of mystery that will never be explained.

In Benelli's drama there are men of action. Manfredo is a warrior, chivalric towards his wife, Fiora, even when he knows her guilty of love for the one to whom she had been betrothed. Avito, the lover, is a gallant prince of flesh and blood. Fiora is not at all mysterious. She glories in her love, and confessing it mocks at death. The old baron is not given to philosophizing. He avenges literally with his own hands the honor of his son and house. The passion of the lovers in 'Pelleas and Melisande' is expressed for the most part as on a window of stained glass. In Benelli's drama the passion is glowing and ecstatic. And so in Montemezzi's opera we hear the sound of horses' hoofs rushing to battle, trumpets calling a retreat, the music of deeds, the praise of Italy won in contest, the exultation of frenzied lovers, the harsh notes of suspicion, jealousy, rage, the more terrible because they come from sightless old age that should be calm and trustful.

The music of Debussy might have been written for the orchestra of ivory instruments that played 'a little unanimous overture' for the Tetrarch Emeraude Archetypas of the White Esoteric Isles.[1] The music of Montemezzi is for a tale of heroic passion. But the

---

[1] References to the short story 'Salomé' (1887), a parody of Flaubert, by the French writer Jules LaForgue (1860–87). Hale included an account of LaForgue's story in the Boston Symphony Programme book of 27 April 1912, with the quotation concerning the 'unanimous overture.' The story had not been translated into English.

Louis P. Verande, c. 1912
Director of the Boston Production
of *L'Amore dei Tre Re*

two operas are alike in the inseparable connection of text and situation with music. Each opera in its own way is lovely and incomparable. As Debussy had no predecessor, so Montemezzi has been uninfluenced in thought and expression. There is no trace of Wagner, Verdi, Debussy, Puccini, in 'L'Amore dei Tre Re.'

The performance was brilliant and impassive [sic]. Miss Bori was again charming to the eye and the ear, emotional as singer and actress, portraying the character of Fiora with fine touches, placing her securely in the gallery of operatic heroines. Mr. Fontana, a manly and passionate lover, sang and acted with authority.

Mr. Ancona, who took the part of Manfredo for the first time, gave a creditable performance and was well within the picture. The dominating figure in this opera is the blind old man, the avenger, and Mr. Ludikar in this role has established himself as an actor of rare intelligence and dramatic power. Perhaps the highest tribute to his art is the fact that there was no thought of Mr. Ludikar in the role. There was the man Archibaldo himself, terrible in his suspicions, sinister in blindness that sharpened other senses and gave him mental vision. Mr. Ludikar in other parts has shown skill in characterization. As Archibaldo he is a creative tragedian.

Mr. Moranzoni gave a still more eloquent reading of the score than on the first night. In view of the fact that he necessarily had few rehearsals, his command of the orchestra and the manner in which the players responded to his poetically dramatic wishes were remarkable.

4. Roger Sessions, *Harvard Musical Review*, February 1914.

New Boston Opera House Productions

THE BOSTON OPERA COMPANY has this year added three new works to its repertoire: Fevrier's *Monna Vanna*, Montemezzi's *L'Amore dei Tre Re*, and, last but not least, *Die Meistersinger*. *Monna Vanna* has already been reviewed in these pages, so it is necessary only to recall that its reception was rather luke-warm.¹ [...]

L'Amore dei Tre Re was performed first on Monday, February 9. This work was substituted for Zandonai's *Francesca da Rimini*, which was withdrawn on account of Mme. Cavalieri's indisposition.² *L'Amore dei Tre Re* is distinguished for its beautiful libretto, which offers a decided contrast to the average contemporary Italian libretto. The music, however, was disappointing in view of the praise accredited it by the New York critics, who hailed it as something quite extraordinary. So many of us were disappointed at the facile, very smooth treatment of the music! It is not music which is calculated to arouse moral indignation; nor does it seem likely that many

---

1 *Monna Vanna* (1909) by Henry Février (1875–1957), based on Maeterlinck's play of the same title, was given its American premiere by the Boston Company on 5 December 1913.

2 Henry Russell, the director of the Boston Opera Company, had secured the world premiere of *Francesca da Rimini*, and advertised a production for the 1913–14 season. Lina Cavalieri (1874–1944) arrived in Boston in November 1913 with a view to singing the title role, but in January 1914 Russell had to announce that Cavalieri's illness meant he had lost the opportunity of a world premiere, and Zandonai's opera premiered at the Teatro Regio, Turin, on 19 February instead. See Konrad Dryden, *Riccardo Zandonai: A Biography* (Frankfurt: Peter Lang, 1999), 145. It seems clear that Montemezzi's opera was substituted for Zandonai's, for advance prospectuses for the Boston season make no mention of *L'Amore dei Tre Re*.

are very deeply moved by it. One is tempted on hearing *L'Amore dei Tre Re* to think of Mendelssohn, or Goldmark.[1]

One hates to think that so beautiful a libretto has received such insignificant musical treatment. Sig. Montemezzi shows great promise, it is true; but to imply that *L'Amore dei Tre Re* would be worthy of the composer of an *Elektra*, an *Ariadne in Naxos*, a *Pelleas*, or even a *Louise*, seems pure folly.

---

1 Karl Goldmark (1830–1915), who as an opera composer was mainly known for *Die Köningin von Saba* (1875).

5. H. T. Parker, *Boston Evening Transcript*,
19 February 1914.[1]

Moranzoni And Marcoux

New Eloquence And Old At The Opera

The Conductor's Remarkable Work with 'The Three Kings' – The Singing Actor as the Blind Old Archibaldo – An Individual Design Largely Accomplished – Mr. Ferrari-Fontana's Leave-Taking

TO THE AVITO – Mr. Ferrari-Fontana – of the original performance of 'L'Amore dei Tre Re' in Milan was joined last evening at the Opera House the Fiora, Mme. Villani, now of the Montreal company.[2] Furthermore, Mr. Marcoux took the part of the old blind king for the first time on any stage;[3] Mr. Urban bettered the play of his lights, especially in the coming of the clouded dawn of the beginning; and

---

1 Parker had reviewed the first Boston performance of *L'Amore dei Tre Re* with great enthusiasm, hailing it as a 'masterpiece,' the greatest Italian opera since Verdi, 'a living musico-dramatic unity that sweeps the hearer into it, that bears him along its course, that leaves him no sensations except those that spring from it. Of such is Verdi's "Otello"; of such is Montemezzi's "L'Amore dei Tre Re."' See 'Montemezzi's Masterpiece of Opera,' *Boston Evening Transcript*, 10 February 1914, 13. Parker avidly attended all three Boston performances of Montemezzi's opera, and had clearly travelled to New York to see the Met's production, too.

2 Luisa Villani (1884–1961) was a member of the National Opera Company of Canada, based in Montreal, which managed a single brief season between November 1913 and February 1914. By the time she arrived in Boston, the company had in fact been disbanded, hence Villani's availability.

3 Jean Vanni-Marcoux (1877–1962) was a member of the Boston Company between 1912 and 1914. He sang Archibaldo with them again when they gave the French premiere of *L'Amore dei Tre Re*, but it did not become one of his regular roles.

Mr. Ancona was more at ease in the music of Manfredo, though his version of the part, beside Mr. Amato's is pale and tame indeed.[1] Yet, as heretofore, the chief glory of the performance remained Mr. Moranzoni's conducting and the response of the orchestra to him.[2] [A general statement about improving orchestral standards.]

Last evening, for example, the orchestra achieved sonorities that were large and eloquent, yet neither hard nor coarse. It phrased expressively and euphoniously, like human voices feeling and uttering the thought or the emotion of the moment. It heeded the low, ominous, rhythmic underbeat that Montemezzi likes to use in moments of suspense; it wrought the shimmering traceries of tone that he weaves as background to the voices on the stage pouring out their ecstasies, and it was plastic and eloquent in those vivid passages of transition in which the passions of the drama ebb like some receding wave, only to flow forward in another wave newly shaped and colored. An operatic orchestra rises high when it plays with beauty and power of tone in themselves and uses both as though the band were actors in the drama and were creating the music out of it. The orchestra at the Opera House did these things yesterday as it has seldom done them. [...]

Mr. Moranzoni's Crown

[More on the way Moranzoni and the orchestra have improved.] In a word Mr. Moranzoni has sharpened, refined and

---

[1] Pasquale Amato, who had sung Manfredo in New York, only appeared in the first Boston performance.

[2] Roberto Moranzoni (1880–1959) had been the musical director of the recently founded Boston Opera Company since 1910, and continued with its successor, the Boston Grand Opera Company, until 1917. In 1914 he conducted the first British production of *L'Amore dei Tre Re*, and, with the Boston Company, the French premiere in Paris. In 1917 he moved to the Met for seven years, in which time he conducted *L'Amore dei Tre Re* on twenty-eight occasions.

deepened his imagination. He no longer receives and imparts relatively crude and superficial impressions of his music and his dramas. He penetrates and conveys their inner substance and spirit. Eloquent by temperament he always was. Now he goes deeper into the sources of such eloquence in music and play and better commands the means to transmit it.

Montemezzi's opera is rich in such springs; in it the orchestra gives back to Mr. Moranzoni what he asks, while the play, the music, the opportunity and by this time the outcome have all kindled him. Not even under Mr. Weingartner has the orchestral part of an opera been more fully and thrillingly the voice of music and drama than Mr. Moranzoni made it last evening in 'The Love of Three Kings.'[1] The significant melodies stood out in their intrinsic beauty and at each return they had the diverse voice and power that the moment in the drama and the music bade. Mr. Moranzoni was passionate indeed in the music of Fiora and Avito, but he felt also the tenderness of their longing, and surrender. As imaginatively he divined the music of Manfredo – the high hope that fills it in the beginning; the saddened hopelessness that has settled upon it in the parting. His vivid modulations of pace and accent seemed of the very gropings, bodily and spiritual, of the blind king, and the fierce and latent power in the proud old prince sprang out of his climaxes. The 'atmospheric' music like that of the chanting in the crypt rose from the orchestra and the voices under Mr. Moranzoni's leading until it filled not merely the stage but the whole theatre. When the music merely delineated, as in the comings and the goings of Manfredo's cavalcade, the conductor caught its true quality of instant and passing suggestion. Finest eloquence of all, he carried Montemezzi's music in its long sweeps of songful and glowing tone, wherein is half the power of the music,

---

[1] Felix Weingartner (1863–1942), a leading Austrian conductor, conducted for the Boston Opera Company between 1912 and 1914.

while out of them, but not breaking them, flashed the phrase that was the musical essence of the moment; while around them played the harmonic and the instrumental color in endless light and shadow. Not before has Mr. Moranzoni been so supple and various of imagination and voice; or so mingled feeling for the beauty of music and for its imparting force; or so been master of himself and all his means. His young fire is well mated to Montemezzi's and Benelli's, to Fiora's and Avito's.

Mr. Marcoux in a New Part

Mr. Marcoux's impersonation of the blind old king, awaited expectantly and applauded deservedly, differs materially from the other two versions of the part known to our stage – Mr. Didur's at the Metropolitan and Mr. Ludikar's here in Boston. So far as in a single performance it was possible to catch Mr. Marcoux's design he has felt the kinship of Montemezzi's and Benelli's opera to classic tragedy and he has taken imaginative thought of Archibaldo's Roman environment. (For forty years had the old prince dwelt in Italy.) Mr. Didur and Mr. Ludikar imagined him as the white-bearded, shaggy-haired Northern 'barbarian,' still of rude outer semblance, a Maeterlinckian figure without the Maeterlinckian gentleness and wisdom. Mr. Marcoux conceives him changed by two score years of new environment. His Archibaldo with filletted head, scanty white locks, aquiline and shaven profile, erect and august figure, clad in a flowing mantle of steely and changeful blue with deep red and simply broidered underdress, looks the Roman rather than the barbarian prince and father. His blindness has seemingly altered the poise of his head, so that it is thrown up alert as one who is ever searching the darkness about him for the sensations of things rather than for the things themselves. When he must grope across the castle terrace, it is as though spirit as well as body alike returned to the material world. He lives among the other dwellers in it in

Jean Vanni-Marcoux as Archibaldo

an august solitude that he has peopled with them as he divines them and that he peoples also with memories and anticipations. It is a restless solitude, too, and out of it in the first act this Archibaldo pours those sensations of Italy that haunt him with the intensity of age.

In this solitude, the old king has nursed his tenderness for Fiora, which gives meaning to the title of play and opera and which Mr. Didur and Mr. Ludikar both overlook. Mr. Marcoux denotes it in the quality of tone that he gives to Archibaldo's first reproaches to Fiora and in the gentle hand that he lays upon her shoulder. Her young pride evades and opposes him; yet he chides with longing pity.[1] Out of the world of sensations again, Mr. Marcoux's Archibaldo listens to the dialogue between Fiora and Manfredo in the dawn. By the telepathy of acting of which he is master, the spectator feels them entering into him. They coalesce in his sharpened and solitary spirit into a single sensation of foreboding. He turns away as one who would avert his face from destiny when he utters it. Mr. Marcoux's voice is not a voice for the intrinsic songfulness of Montemezzi's declamation; he cannot give it the pervading Italian warmth; but its power made the old king's memories like a great panorama of great deeds and rich living remembered. Dry and hard as Mr. Marcoux's voice sometimes seems, he can fill it with masculine tenderness as in his words to Fiora, and it can be, as it was at the end, the moving speech of a great foreboding.

In the days in which Manfredo lingered vainly by Fiora and she was unsoftened, the old king dwelt beside them, but most in the solitude of his brooding sensations. Surely and yet more surely he knew that his son could not touch the girl's heart; deeply and yet more deeply his foreboding filled him. Then out

---

[1] Parker's understanding that Archibaldo has 'longing' feelings of love for Fiora agrees with Montemezzi's interpretation of his opera. See above, p. 67, n. 1.

of these depths rose the pride of his race, of his house, of his conquest and his kingship. It is an emotion that comes quickly to birth in a solitude of sensations and foreboding. It played in him with Roman austerity and with barbarian fierceness. So, as Mr. Marcoux seemed to impersonate him, he came upon Fiora, knew her to be foresworn and slew her, as an old Roman might have slain one who had dishonored his house and hers; as a barbarian might have seized and killed the object of his vengeance.

Mr. Didur's and Mr. Ludikar's Archibaldo rises out of the shadows to the slaying as the instrument of a fate as blind as he. Mr. Marcoux's gropes across the battlement alternately rigid and tremulous, to do the deed of long-nursed and still rage. In body and spirit he shakes and almost falls in the recoil from his fury accomplished. The design and the execution praise the force and the individuality of Mr. Marcoux's imagination. He would have Archibaldo the smouldering instrument of fate, as Benelli and Montemezzi surely intended, but he would heat him also with the brooding frenzy of the old king, half-Roman, half-barbarian, and stricken in the honor of his house. In like passion, Mr. Marcoux's Archibaldo bears a naked sword into the crypt wherewith he may finish his vengeance and slay Fiora's lover. It drops from his hand when he hears Manfredo's voice and then in Mr. Marcoux's tones a great desolation floods Archibaldo. Hitherto in the darkness he has felt and moved. Now it has engulfed and imprisoned him. In voice and in sensation, it is Mr. Marcoux's most vivid moment – as yet – with the part.

The Departing Fontana

Mme. Villani came and went, making the performance possible – since there was no other Fiora in America except the unavailable Miss Bori – but contributing nothing to it beyond a conventionally 'capable' operatic impersonation. In turn, Mr. Ferrari-Fontana took leave for the year of the Opera House in

America in which he has first disclosed his signal abilities and its public as signally appreciated them. In all the parts that he has taken here – Tristan, Gennaro in 'The Jewels,'[1] Samson, Canio in 'Pagliacci' and finally Avito – his voice has spoken for itself in the full body, the large power, the running sweep, the impassioned depths and the glowing heights of his tones. He is an 'heroic tenor' in the fine sense of a much-abused label – endowed with magnificence of voice, with largely and wisely ordered eloquence of song, with a speech of music and a speech of passion, with vivid, tense and masculine emotion of many kinds, with romantic aspect and romantic bearing. As he sings, so he acts – with large intensities, with long sweeps of unfolding emotion or with a swift blow of feeling concentrated. He has his idiosyncrasies and his shortcomings. Sometimes he drives his voice until it shakes, not with feeling, but with the beginning of something close to a tremolo. Italian-wise he will sob. Now and again he exalts force of tone to the detriment of beauty. He does all things in broad lines and with broad strokes. It is the virtue of 'heroic tenors' so to do, and as such for the time, Mr. Ferrari-Fontana has not his equal or hardly his like on the American operatic stage. And with Mr. Marcoux he is the discovery of our opera house.[2]

---

1 *I Gioielli della Madonna* (1911) by Ermanno Wolf-Ferrari.

2 On 19 February, a day after his final Boston appearance, Ferrari-Fontana sang in the Met's last performance of *L'Amore dei Tre Re* for the season, then set sail for Europe the same night.

Later Criticism, 1915–1962

MUSICAL AMERICA'S GALLERY OF CELEBRITIES—No. 43

Montemezzi, the Distinguished Italian Composer of "L'Amore dei Tre Re," which Made Such a Success at the Metropolitan Two Years Ago, and Other Operas. Viafora, the Cartoonist, Says of Him: "Effery time he hav' three King he draw a fulla house—you know—just lika poker!"

Cartoon of Montemezzi

Musical America, 7 October 1916

1. Richard Aldrich, *New York Times*, 14 February 1915.

The Reappearance of Montemezzi's Opera, 'L'Amore dei Tre Re' – Some Merits of Its Originality

THE REAPPEARANCE of Montemezzi's opera, 'L'Amore dei Tre Re,' in the repertory of the Metropolitan Opera House last Thursday was a source of great satisfaction to many lovers of the finer things in opera. The work had created a profound impression at its first production last season, and apparently had done so without any expectation of it on the part of anybody connected with the production. So far as the general public was concerned the name of Montemezzi or of his opera had never been seen or heard. It came as a surprise; all the more since it came after many echoes, more or less feeble, of prevailing styles, as the original utterance of a man who has apparently provided himself with his own mode of expression. Montemezzi stands by himself on his own feet. His opera does not contain any strong reminiscence of any of the popularly accepted musical modes, nor show any direct influence of even the greatest personalities who have influenced modern musical art.

This is not to say that 'L'Amore dei Tre Re' is an epoch-making work, or that it is likely to found a school or control the course of dramatic music in Italy or outside of it. But originality is a rare and unusual thing, and is something to be prized. In this connection it is amusing to see how one rash critic, reviewing what was said about the originality of 'L'Amore dei Tre Re,' wrote, in what was expected to be a permanent form, for the edification of posterity.[1] 'It has been intimated,' we read, 'that Montemezzi

---

1 The 'rash critic' was Lawrence Gilman, who had, uniquely among the 1914 reviewers, published his account of *L'Amore dei Tre Re* in a book. For the passage in question, see above, p. 115.

is entitled to some kind of credit because he is different from Puccini.' It may not only be intimated, but affirmed, that he is. How much credit would he be entitled to if he were not different from Puccini? If he were a replica, a copy, an imitation of Puccini; if he adopted Puccini's style, Puccini's mannerisms – which even that great man possesses? Or how much if he were the same sort of reflection of Verdi, or Ponchielli, or Wagner, or Debussy? One of the misfortunes of some of the contemporary Italians is that they cannot be different, or different enough, from Puccini. We have heard operas within the last few years by Cilea, by Giordano, by Leoni, by others of their school, that suffer from such a misfortune, and that have thereby declared their impotence.[1] Even a man like Wolf-Ferrari, who has an individual style and method of his own, undertook to show that he could 'write Puccini' too, and did it very competently in 'The Jewels of the Madonna'; but he is entitled to less credit for this than for his own charming works.[2] Any composer of German opera in these days who can free himself from the direct and overpowering influence of Wagner, and produce something with some trace of originality in it is entitled to 'some kind of credit,' and the satisfaction of being told that he is not an 'epigone.'

It is one of the great merits of Montemezzi's setting of Sem Benelli's beautiful drama that it is singularly successful in the evocation of the mood, the poetic atmosphere, that so remarkably envelops that drama. It is a drama of emotion, wrought with

---

[1] *Adriana Lecouvreur* (1902) by Francesco Cilea (1866–1950) was staged at the Met in the 1907–08 season; *Fedora* (1898) by Umberto Giordano (1867–1948) in the 1906–07 season; *Madame Sans-Gêne* by the same composer had just received its world premiere at the Met on 25 January 1915; *L'Oraclo* (1905) by Franco Leoni (1864–1949) had been heard even more recently, on 4 February 1915.

[2] *I Gioielli della Madonna* (1911) by Ermanno Wolf-Ferrari (1876–1948) was introduced to New York by the Chicago Opera Association in 1912; though very successful, it was not mounted at the Met until 1925.

insight into the deeper springs of human conduct rather than of action. The characters are types rather than strongly marked individualities. They are the expression of ideas. They move in a world of legend, not of historical verity. There is a suggestion in them and in their surroundings of Maeterlinck – a Maeterlinck of a clearer vision and more sharply defined objective. Their Italy is an Italy remote and undefined; 'in the Middle Ages, in a remote castle; forty years after a barbarian invasion,' says the book. Upon this dim and shadowy background are projected feelings, passions, emotions, in an expression at once poetic and noble, and vivified in a poignant simplicity and subtle suggestiveness.

It is not often that a musician is so successful in conveying through music the essential quality of a dramatic poem as Montemezzi has done in his score. His music is not to be imagined divorced from the poem. He has made it of the very fibre and texture of Sem Benelli's verse. It is a true interpretation of it, raising it to a higher power of eloquence, and so doing it fulfils the high function of music in the lyric drama.

Montemezzi has obtained his ends without finding it necessary to embrace all the most venturesome of modern experiments in melody, harmony, tonality, or style. In so far he is a conservative, and all the originality and fertility of resource that he has displayed within these limits avail him nothing in the estimation of the high priests of the newest styles in music. These are insensible to anything but what comes upon their ears with the cachet of the latest 'development,' the 'ultra-modern,' and hence it is that 'L'Amore dei Tre Re' is for them a work of impotent mediocrity, and has been written down as such.[1] Fortunately the finer taste of the public at the Metropolitan Opera House is able

---

[1] The criticism still seems to be mainly aimed at Gilman, though given Aldrich's plural 'high priests' it is possible he also knew Roger Sessions' review. The criticism could also apply to Leonard Liebling's concluding remarks (see above, p. 90), though Liebling was no champion of modernism.

to grasp and to submit to the beauty, the charm, the impressiveness of Montemezzi's music.

It is not an opera likely to become widely popular. In this respect its composer has undoubtedly something to learn of Puccini. But it was found desirable to give 'L'Amore dei Tre Re' five times last season, and though its production this season has been postponed till the thirteenth week there is a likelihood that it will find a renewed response in the sympathies of the music-lovers at the Metropolitan.

2. Unsigned review attributed to Gilbert Seldes, *Evening Ledger* (Philadelphia), 24 March 1915.[1]

Music

PHILADELPHIA'S SECOND operatic premiere of the season,[2] 'L'Amore dei Tre Re,' a musical setting by Italo Montemezzi of Sem Benelli's poetic tragedy of the same name, was given last night at the Metropolitan. [Cast details.]

Settings and Singers

There was only one unhappy feature of this splendid occasion, and it was one to which, by long use, most patrons of the Metropolitan have accustomed themselves – the settings. Just when the Metropolitan will discover that an entirely new and wonderful art of stage picturing has been developed within recent years is something no one may dare to predict. So far the New York company is as innocent of 'inscenierung' as it is ignorant of 'stylization' in production.[3] It is using scenery which would

---

1 A review of the first performance in Philadelphia.

2 The first premiere was Giordano's *Madame Sans-Gêne* (23 February).

3 A reference primarily to the revolutionary theatrical ideas set out in *Die Musik und die Inscenierung* (1899) by Adolphe Appia (1862–1928). This book was first published in a German translation by Princess Elsa Cantacuzène, who used 'Inscenierung' as an equivalent term to mise en scène. Appia's ideas concerning stylized, non-realistic presentation of opera were just starting to influence theatrical practice in the early 1910s, though it was not until the 1920s that they enjoyed much currency. According to Patrick Carnegy, 'America had had a first taste of Appian principles in the severely simplified staging of *Tristan* designed in 1912 for the Boston Opera by Joseph Urban.' See *Wagner and the Art of the Theatre* (New Haven, CT: Yale UP, 2006), 197. It seems probable that Seldes had become aware of Urban's designs – possibly including those for *L'Amore dei Tre Re* – while at Harvard, and that they had brought Appia's ideas to his attention.

not pass in a third-rate Continental house. And all the while the talents of Josef Urban are being spent on Edward Sheldon and the Follies.[1] It is absurd.

But when that reservation has been made, nothing but praise remains. In the order of importance one can praise the singing-actors, the music and its conductor, and the overpowering drama to which all were devoted. Of the singers, Mr. Ferrari-Fontana alone is unfamiliar to this city. In Boston and later in New York he has earned an excellent repute. His voice is robust and pleasing, not always clear in production, but sturdy and colorful and rich with dramatic expression. In the lyric passion of the second act he sang with restrained and persuasive emotion the throbbing appeals of Avito, and through the play made of the Prince a credible, skilfully imagined personage. So close a parallel to this was the work of Mr. Amato as Manfredo that the two characters seemed to merge in the end, as they properly should in the meaning of the play, and to stand together in a strange and tragic unity. Against them stood the Fiora of Miss Bori, done with such bitter justness, such beauty as to be heartbreaking, and the great Archibaldo of Adamo Didur, done with such art as to be appalling and finally exalting. For singing and acting the cast

---

[1] Josef Urban (1872–1933) moved to America in 1911 to become the artistic director of the Boston Opera Company. He introduced American audiences to some of the ideas of Adolphe Appia (see previous note) and designed the Boston *L'Amore dei Tre Re* (see above, p. 129). In 1914 he designed Edward Sheldon's Broadway show, *Garden of Paradise*, and his innovative sets won such acclaim that in 1915 he was hired to design the lavish Broadway revues mounted by Florenz Ziegfeld as the *Ziegfeld Follies*. Seldes's mention of these entertainments here strikes a disdainful note, but it is symptomatic of his wider development as a critic that in the 1920s he expressed great enthusiasm for the Ziegfeld revues, comparing them favourably to the Met's productions. See Michael Kammen, *The Lively Arts: Gilbert Seldes and the Transformation of Cultural Criticism in the United States* (New York: Oxford UP, 1996), 86, 95. Urban began working for the Met in the 1917–18 season.

Pasquale Amato as Manfredo

of 'Pagliacci' alone stands with this one;[1] for impressiveness of characterization, Mr. Didur's own Boris must be brought into comparison.

The Music

As the brilliant Toscanini revealed the score of Montemezzi's opera last night, with all the intuitive power always at his command, the auditors (those who really listened) were given a passing glimpse into the future of Italian opera. That in this future Montemezzi will share largely may pass without doubt. Almost as scornful as Moussorgsky of the 'set pieces' demanded by the older convention, Montemezzi can achieve lyric intensity in his brief and nervous melodic line, and can build drama into his music as Puccini never ventured to build it. The three brief acts of this opera are fulfilled of thought and emotion; the climaxes of passion are reared one on the other, and the music which serves now as their substructure, now as their very material, unfolds and progresses with astounding fertility of imagination and invention. In the first act it seems that the composer has abolished the artist, and the exuberant orchestration makes of that act a symphonic poem into which an opera has been unhappily fused. The two later acts are more just.

Strange harmonies there are, and orchestral accompaniments which seem to disperse, rather than concentrate, feeling at the moment. But they are eventually synthesized, and the music, maugre its defects, is almost a miracle, a score in which not one bar is without its proper interest and effect.

---

[1] *Pagliacci* had been last heard in Philadelphia on 12 January 1915, with Lucrezia Bori as Nedda, Enrico Caruso as Canio, Pasquale Amato as Tonio, Riccardo Tegani as Silvio and Pietro Audisio as Beppe. Seldes, presuming he was the reviewer on that occasion too, had praised it as 'a perfect cast' and particularly lauded Bori and Caruso. See 'The Opera,' *Evening Ledger*, 13 January 1915, 11.

The Play

Of 'The Love of the Three Kings,' as Benelli wrote it, something was said in these columns before this production. The unusual quality of the plot and the rare beauty of the poetry have been noted. But nothing could have prepared one for the majestic and dazzling effect of the play as it was produced. The lovers and the beloved, and beyond them the dominant figure of pride and frailty, of the aged King, torn with the last vestige of passion, were such as to daze the imagination, to make the tragedy seem not of the stage, but somehow of the eternal essence of tragedy itself. It left those who followed it bewildered with its cruel beauty, mournful, almost inconsolable, yet strengthened and made clean of smaller passions and of smaller fears.

Lucrezia Bori as Fiora

3. Karleton Hackett, *Chicago Evening Post*,
7 October 1915.[1]

Montemezzi's 'Love of Three Kings' Given

Novelties by Boston Opera

'L'Amore Dei Tre Re' with one performance takes its place with the big works of the modern repertoire. The production by the Boston Opera Company at the Auditorium last night was magnificent, one of the occasions that will be remembered. It was one of complete satisfaction, a poetic drama illumined by music which revealed its inmost spirit with a sustained power that flowed in one glorious stream from the first note to the last and with artists upon the stage who made the thing live in their every word.

It is Italian music fed from that upwelling fountain of melody, yet with all the richness of orchestral color which modern art has placed at the disposal of the man with the power to use it. It was a deep gratification to realize that a man can still say a big thing within the bounds of what we have always considered the art of music. If a man has the genuine creative force which can think a new thought he will be content to say it to us in direct and comprehensible form; it is only when a man distrusts his creative powers that he has to resort to the limitless possibilities of concealment which lie in the superabundance of decoration.

Montemezzi is one more name we shall have to learn. He has something to say, as one hearing of his work proves in the most convincing manner. He chose a drama of poetic beauty and of the kind of dramatic force which reveals itself to the eye. The salient points one can grasp, even tho he may

---

[1] A review of the first performance in Chicago.

Luisa Villani and Edoardo Ferrari-Fontana as Fiora and Avito

The 1915 Boston cast restored the partnership that had sung in the 1913 premiere of *L'Amore dei Tre Re* at La Scala, as drawn here by an Italian artist

not have read the story nor understood the language, and Montemezzi has illustrated it with music which shows forth the very soul of the tragedy. Yet thru it all is the feeling of the beauty of it. Melodic expression of thought, not tunes of pretty triviality, but broad and sweeping lines that were pregnant with meaning. Not piling Ossa on Pelion or cacophonous counterpoint or seeking for power thru the impressive confusion of complexity, but with something vital to be told that could gain dignity from directness.

Adamo Didur as the 'tremendous old man'[1] and George Baklanoff as the husband of misfortune were tragic figures of the heroic mold. One felt that they might indeed be termed 'kings,' for they were men of might who did what to them seemed good and gave the law to their fellows. One is a little at a loss to know what to say of such performances within the narrow space allotted. Either there should be a detailed account, which is not possible, or just a bare statement that both of them gave characterizations which both histrionically and vocally take their places with the big things that our Auditorium stage has known during the long series of years.

Mme. Luisa Villani and Eduardo Ferrari-Fontana were both of them in the original cast at La Scala and gave fine performances. Mme. Villani lacked something of the illusive quality of charm which wrought the spell. There was not quite the inner flame of the spirit which is the mystery of woman, that subtile essence which draws all the heroes of Greece to the Plains of Troy and has ruled the kings of the earth from that day until now. What she did was well done, but not in the exalted spirit of tragedy. Mr. Ferrari-Fontana was not in the best of condition, tho no trace of it appeared to the audience save that he,

---

[1] This description is not applied to Archibaldo in the opera, or in Benelli's play. Perhaps Hackett was recalling Mary Johnston's use of the term to describe Tolstoy in *Hagar* (1913).

perhaps, did not feel perfectly free to give himself – and he wore an unfortunate wig. His was a fine performance, but he has more in him.

The orchestra was an instrument of wonderful beauty in the masterly hands of Roberto Moranzoni. The final honor of the performance must go to him, and the audience amply testified to their appreciation by the applause. There were a great many recalls for all the artists, for it was an event.

4. Otheman Stevens, *Los Angeles Examiner*, 7 March 1916.[1]

Grand Opera 'Three Kings' An Artistic Triumph

Singers Of Very Best And Orchestra Excellent

Crowded House Captured by Vocal Stars, While Pavlowa Ballet Is Entrancing[2]

'L'AMORE DEI TRE RE' is real grand opera; not so very grand as to price, for five dollars is a bagatelle – if you have it – compared with the exquisite completeness of the production, but grand in every detail, as given last night at the Mason by the Boston Grand Opera Company.

Singers are of the best; orchestra flowing out into the auditorium in size, and as directed by Roberto Moranzoni, competent in every essential, to interpret the Montemezzi music, a score that is almost futurist in its advanced type; a base of Wagnerian method and a superstructure of Debussyian phrasing; Urban scenery such as we have never had before, thoroughly artistic and massive, painted with suggestions of symbolism; and the opera itself all picturing sorrow and death, forming a manner of mortuary symphonic beauty; the wealth of sorrow of 'Lucia'[3] is as a smile to this beautifully ponderous symphonic rhythm of grief.

And an audience that completely filled the house, that was understandingly appreciative, and apt with its applause; a decidedly limousine audience; something of a fashion show; more of a display of culture.

---

1 A review of the first performance in Los Angeles.

2 The Russian Ballet Company, headed by Anna Pavlova (her name then often written as Pavlowa), was touring with the Boston Grand Opera Company. For the programme, see above, pp. 15-16.

3 Donizetti's *Lucia di Lammermoor* (1835).

Mr. Behymer[1] always gives us good grand opera; this time he has placed before us a musical menu that might be served at the Metropolitan or at Covent Garden.

Ultimate in Modern Music

In composition 'The Three Kings' seems to be the ultimate in modern music. It is consumingly interesting to the ordinary observer of music and of intense value to the erudite. There is much of the massive majesty of Wagner, and a lot of suggestion that is found in Strauss with those detached, seemingly incomplete phrases which mark Debussy. In a way it may be termed emotionally interpretative and more, for every sentiment being sung is often presaged and always expressed in tonal picturing of feeling; even action, such as approaching footsteps, is given form by the orchestra.

Montemezzi departed from the usual order in making the basso King Archibaldo quite as important as the tenor or soprano. Signor Mardones[2] in that role had almost the entire first act, including the final aria, which he gave with such perfection of both tone and expression as to arouse the house to gratitude.

Quickly Wins Admiration

Maggie Teyte, the Fiora, wife of Archibaldo's son, Manfredo, but loving Prince Avito, played and sang with consummate perception. Her role was cold, and as the faithless wife lacking in natural sympathy, but she drove her way straight into the admiration of the audience by the beauty of her tones and quite as

---

1 Lyndon Ellsworth Behymer (1862–1947), a noted Los Angeles impresario. He had also served as a literary editor for the *Los Angeles Herald*, a paper with which Stevens had been much involved; the two men were almost certainly acquainted.

2 José Mardones (1869–1932).

much by her remarkably adept acting. Miss Teyte would make a movie queen at first trial. She 'registers' as the phrase goes, 'making every move a picture,' all with the dignity of the highest form of histrionic art. Even an absurdly long kiss in the second act – it had to last fully five minutes to meet the demands of the score – was carried through with such accuracy of passion as to keep the most aggressive gallery god from giggling. Miss Teyte proved that a prima donna can also be something of a Duse.[1]

Zenatello,[2] the tenor who sang Avito, has a robustly beautiful voice and is thoroughly masculine in temperament; his tones are both exact in pitch and control, resounding with power and answering eloquently to every phase of emotion. He is in every detail a great artist.

Thomas Chalmers, the Manfredo, husband of Fiora, has a captivating baritone voice, soaring well into tenor qualities in its higher notes, potently male in others. He, like the others, combines in a rare degree most capable acting skill, and pleasingly avoids the traditional operatic poses and gestures.

The minor roles were all in the hands of artists.

In joyous contrast to the somber beauty of the opera must have been the Pavlowa ballet, 'Snowflakes,' from Tschaikowsky's 'Nut Cracker' ballet. [More on the ballet.]

In the opera itself, in the principals, in the orchestra and director, in scenic beauty the whole affair is of the highest order, quite beyond any measurement of price, because it is in all ways more than satisfying all demands.

Honest advice is that everyone should see all of the productions of this grand opera and Pavlowa company. Everyone who takes delight in music must hear 'The Love of Three Kings.' You cannot know what must be known unless you do.

---

1 Eleonora Duse (1858–1924), with Sarah Bernhardt one of the two most celebrated actresses of the time.

2 Giovanni Zenatello (1876–1949).

Claudia Muzio as Fiora, 1918

5. Unsigned review attributed to Henry E. Krehbiel, *New York Tribune*, 15 March 1918.[1]

Revival of Leon [sic] Benelli Work at Metropolitan Is Auspicious

ITALO MONTEMEZZI's opera 'L'Amore dei tre Re,' which since the departure of Miss Lucrezia Bori has been absent from the repertory of the Metropolitan Opera Company,[2] was revived last night, with Enrico Caruso as Avito, Claudia Muzio as Fiora, Pasquale Amato as Manfredo and José Mardones as Archibaldo. Of these, only Mr. Amato had been heard previously in the opera at the Metropolitan, though Mr. Mardones appeared in it with the Boston Opera Company at the Manhattan.[3]

The revival of 'L'Amore dei tre Re' is a cause for congratulation, for it is a sincere, a beautiful, a moving work, which for dramatic power surpasses anything that has come out of Italy since the death of Giuseppe Verdi. The drama of Sem Benelli is a poem of rare beauty, purity and imaginative fire, and to it

---

1 There is no reason to doubt that this review is substantially Krehbiel's, but the odd mistakes in the title and the first paragraph (see note 3, below) suggest it was tampered with by some other hand.

2 Bori sung in the Met's production of *L'Amore dei Tre Re* at Atlanta, Georgia, on 30 April 1915. After this she developed nodes on her vocal chords which required several operations and prevented her performing for nearly six years.

3 Mardones had taken the role of Archibaldo for the Boston Company in their 1915–16 season (see above, p. 162), which included two performances at the Manhattan Opera House, New York, on 26 October and 5 November 1915. In fact, as Krehbiel notes below, it was not Mardones but Adamo Didur who sang in this first performance. The basses alternated the role this season, a fact which caused William J. Henderson to quip: 'It is well that there are two basses to alternate in this role, for the new Fiora is no rose leaf to carry off at the end of the second act.' See 'Caruso As Avito At Metropolitan,' *Sun*, 23 March 1918, 8.

Signor Montemezzi has set music of supreme fitness. It is music which, while somewhat Wagnerian in its treatment, is yet completely Latin in its insistence on classic grace and beauty of line. It characterizes without ever calling on the assistance of discords; it is forceful without ugliness.

Signor Montemezzi and Signor Benelli have in their work that nobility of spirit which is the touchstone of all great art. Theirs is an art free from the brutality of Mascagni and the miasma of D'Annunzio. Both musician and poet have returned to the great tradition, confident that even in a democratic world tradition can live and bring forth fruit. They believe in the beauty of virtue, the poignancy of tenderness, the nobility of death. Theirs is as perfect a wedlock as has been accomplished in the field of art.

Last night's performance had both its virtues and its weaknesses. It was unfortunate that Mr. Caruso was in far from good voice, with the result that the exquisite love duet became an exceedingly one-sided affair. And as the great tenor was never born to be a hero of romance, the histrionic side of the part fell by the wayside.

Miss Muzio was a beautiful figure as Fiora, and she sang the music with passion and yet with restraint. She has as yet much to learn in the finer shadings of the character, as it lacks yet the pathos and the poetry of which it is capable.

Mr. Amato was in far from good voice, yet he lent a great dignity and nobility to Manfredo, and Mr. Didur was superb as the blind king.

Mr. Moranzoni gave a vigorous – at times, perhaps, a too vigorous – orchestral reading. With Mr. Caruso vocally himself again, and with a general polishing and coördination of the performance, the present revival ought to go far toward equalling the memorable performances of the past.

No performance but the best is worthy of 'L'Amore dei tre Re.'

6. James Gibbons Huneker, *New York Times*, 23 March 1919.[1]

'L'Amore dei tre Re'

'L'AMORE DEI TRE RE' was sung for the first time this season yesterday afternoon at the Metropolitan Opera House. It is stained-glass opera. Not that it lacks incident or vivid action – there is plenty to spare of the latter – but that its dominant atmosphere is psychological. Its characters are like figures in a dream tapestry. Without the haunting magic of 'Pelléas and Mélisande,' it is none the less poetic, as poetry is understood on the lyric stage today. The book by Sem Benelli is admirable, a better one seldom has been written. In it there are echoes of D'Annunzio – the muted melancholy of his 'Virgins of the Rocks;'[2] not forgetting Maeterlinck in one of his early plays, for example, 'La Princesse Maleine.'[3] Concise, swift, tragic

---

1 This appears to be Huneker's first full account of *L'Amore dei Tre Re*, a work he had not dealt with in his previous position as critic for the *Philadelphia Press*. He had first seen Montemezzi's opera on 10 April 1915, and wrote a brief notice for his 'Seven Arts' column in *Puck* (week ending 15 May 1915, pp. 14, 20) stating that he agreed with Lawrence Gilman's estimate of the work (see above, pp. 109–18). The 1915 notice was the germ of this much fuller 1919 review, and Huneker repeats several phrases from it.

2 The novel *Le Vergini delle Rocce* (1896). A successful English translation by Annetta Halliday-Antona and Giuseppe Antona, *The Maidens of the Rocks*, had been published in Boston in 1898; a second translation by Agatha Hughes, *The Virgins of the Rocks*, appeared in London the following year.

3 *La princesse Maleine* (1889) was Maeterlinck's first play. As with the reference to D'Annunzio's *Vergini delle Rocce*, Huneker seems to be mainly gesturing at 'echoes' of mood, atmosphere and possibly poetry, but there are parallels in the plots that explain his association of this particular play with Benelli's tragedy. These include the strangulation of the heroine, the princess, with the connivance of old King Hjalmar, the father of her lover; the suicide of the prince; and the old king's isolation at the end.

is the story of the Three Kings, father, husband, lover. If you wish you may read symbolism into the moving narrative, yet its symbolism does not fly like a flag as in some theatrical breezes. Montemezzi's music is a mosaic of Wagner – always the fly in the ointment of modern composers – and, of course, Verdi, also Puccini, Dukas, Moussorgsky, and Richard Strauss. However, the composer has assimilated his foreign material, and if Tristan or the Valkyrs do at times peep through his bars they are welcome attired as they are in his brave orchestral garb.

'The Loves [sic] of Three Kings' was produced at Milan nearly seven years ago,[1] and here during the season of 1913–1914. The original cast comprised: Lucrezia Bori as Fiora, (it is good news to learn that Bori will return to opera,[2]) Didur as the blind King Archibaldo, Amato as Manfredo, and Ferrara-Fontana [sic] as Avito. Caruso sang Avito last season;[3] yesterday the rôle was assumed and sung by Martinelli.[4] Claudia Muzio, who followed Bori, was again the too-much beloved Fiora, a woman literally slain because of love. Chalmers replaced Amato as Manfredo.[5]

To tell the truth, this work has never proved a magnet for the public, which prefers 'Cavalleria' and 'Pagliacci,' yet, it is musically and dramatically superior to 'Lodeletta [sic],' 'Isabeau,' 'Francesca,' 'Marouf,' 'Fiammetta,' 'Gismonda' and the rest of the thin, tasteless pastry manufactured by deft enough cooks,

---

1 In fact, nearly six years earlier, the premiere having been on 10 April 1913.

2 For Bori's enforced break from singing see above, p. 165, n. 2.

3 Caruso sang the part of Avito on five occasions between 14 March and 17 April 1918; he never returned to the role.

4 Giovanni Martinelli (1885–1969), who had been singing at the Met since 1913.

5 Thomas Chalmers (1884–1966) had previously sung the role of Manfredo with the Boston Grand Opera Company (see above, p. 163). He joined the Met company in the 1917–18 season, and sang the role of Manfredo with them twice.

James Gibbons Huneker, 1918
The most celebrated American music critic of the early 1900s

but containing little that is nourishing.[1] Meyerbeer, despite his stodginess and pompousness, has more genuine music in some of his operas than all these artificial kickshaws lumped together. We eat the air promise-crammed.[2] Wind-pudding and sawdust pie reward us. We leave stuffed, but not satisfied. 'The Three Kings,' even if it does not boast a marked individual profile, at least produces a poetic impression because of its libretto and artfully evoked musical atmosphere. There are moments when you forget the stained-glass mysticism; Archibaldo's narration in Act I., wherein he boasts of his deeds as a conqueror; Avito's entrance song and declamation in the death scene; Manfredo's aria in his return, the various duos, and the terrible scene in Act II., with its climax – the blind King staggering under the load of Fiora's body. The last act is dolorous. There are, strictly speaking, no leading motives, though there are a few ingeniously developed musical figures in Act II. A broad arioso flows throughout and is subtly interwoven with the pattern of the drama. A happy balance between voice and orchestra is achieved. The orchestration of Montemezzi is rich, sombre, ductile, dynamic. Best of all, the voices are not drowned by the orchestra.

---

1 *Lodoletta* (1917), Mascagni's opera, performed at the Met on 12 January 1918; *Isabeau* (1911), by the same composer, performed by the Chicago Company in 1917, and then staged by them in New York on 13 February 1918; *Francesca da Rimini* (1914), Zandonai's opera, performed at the Met on 22 December 1916; *Mârouf, savetier du Caire* (*Marouf, Cobbler of Cairo*) (1914), by Henri Rabaud, performed at the Met on 19 December 1917; *La reine Fiamette* (1903), by Xavier Leroux, performed at the Met on 24 January 1919; *Gismonda* (1919) by Henry Février, performed by the Chicago Company, who gave the first New York performance on 27 January 1919. Most of these productions were American, or at least United States, premieres, and *Gismonda* was a world premiere. Huneker's comment amounts to a sweeping and up-to-date attack on the contemporary Italian and French operas selected for American performance.

2 An allusion to Hamlet's statement, 'I eat the air, promise-crammed' (*Hamlet*, Act 3, Scene 2).

The tale might have been transposed from one of Dante's impassioned pages. Love, jealousy, hatred, followed by poisoning and death – here is fit material for any tragic poet. D'Annunzio would have buried the plot beneath an avalanche of his gorgeous rhetoric. Sem Benelli commits no such error. His story scuds under bare poles, without one incident, attitude, gesture, or phrase too many. An accomplished playwright is this Italian. Gilbert wrote plays before he made the best light opera books in the English language. Much scurrilous wit has been wasted on Scribe's librettos for the Meyerbeer operas, nevertheless they have never been bettered, not even by Richard Wagner and his inchoate plots wedded to supremely beautiful music. You may follow Benelli's action without the aid of the words, as the classic Triangle is exposed with perfect clarity; the husband who goes to war, the lover, the 'erring' wife – only wives 'err,' never husbands – whose excuse is that her husband is an 'alien enemy,' that her lover is of her own people. Always an excuse. Isolde was married to an amiable, elderly gentleman, and, perhaps, she, like Anna Karenina, didn't like the shape of his ears.[1] Always an excuse. Charles Bovary fell asleep after dinner and snored. A wonderful excuse for the immortal Emma, his spouse.[2] Aïda loved Radames as a man, though, incidentally, she found it profitable to tempt him from his duty for the benefit of her father and country. Truly an excuse. We think Carmen the frankest sinner of the lot. Since Eve coquetted with Satan, disguised as a cobra di capella, or hooded snake, in Paradise Alley,[3] Carmen is the

---

1 In Tolstoy's *Anna Karenina* (1873–77), Anna, on starting to experience desire for Vronsky, feels, for the first time, that her husband's ears are unpleasantly large.

2 In Flaubert's *Madame Bovary* (1856) Charles Bovary's snoring is represented as part of his provincial simplicity and coarseness.

3 Various streets in America have been informally named Paradise Alley for their association with prostitution.

most convincing of legendary coquettes. Her excuse was caprice and passion. None better. As for poor Fiora, she was a woman killed by kindness.[1] It was not a pleasant death in her case.

Mr. Martinelli sang with so much fire and force in the first act that he seemed a bit fatigued in the trying second act. But he is an intelligent artist and his voice is of natural beauty. No doubt he will later get into the skin of the character. Didur, too, shows the wear and tear of a strenuous season, but his Archibaldo is a finely thought out rôle. Mr. Chalmers found a congenial part, and, like Mr. Martinelli, will work it out more elaborately. Miss Muzio was a passionate Fiora, more robust than subtle, and always interesting. The cast was competent. Roberto Moranzoni conducted.

---

1 An allusion to the title of Thomas Heywood's tragedy, *A Woman Killed with Kindness* (1603).

7. Reginald de Koven, *New York Herald*, 23 March 1919.

Montemezzi Opera Impressively Sung at Metropolitan

'L'Amore dei Tre Re' Is Produced for First Time This Season

THERE ARE, I know, many musicians and operatic amateurs who feel that Montemezzi's opera, or music drama, 'L'Amore dei Tre Re,' which was sung at the Metropolitan for the first time this season yesterday afternoon, is the best operatic product that has come out of Italy since the great early vogue of Puccini.

If I do not subscribe unreservedly to this dictum it is not because I do not recognize and appreciate Montemezzi's many and admirable qualities, both as musician and composer, but because I ask myself, Is this opera in the direction of operatic progress and development?

Since the Puccini vogue aforesaid only two operatic names of any real note or import have come out of Italy to reach these shores – Montemezzi and Zandonai. Of the two, I much prefer the former as the more sincere and inspired musician.

Montemezzi has a purposeful, flexible, forceful and pictorial touch in orchestral expression, and thereby aptly limns and delineates the varied mood and emotion in scene and situation of the drama he would illustrate in music. I find his vein of melodic invention quite restricted; he therefore writes drama with music rather than opera of the Puccini type, like 'Tosca,' which has both drama and music, and so – and often with success – makes his keen dramatic appreciation and power of dramatic expression atone for his lack of real melodic invention.

Montemezzi's score certainly at times lacks both contrast and variety; the emotional strain of the tortured tragedy is never relaxed, the eternal shock of the basses at poignant moments becomes monotonous. And, oh, for one strain, only one – which even the impassioned illicit love duo does not supply – of pure, unforced lyric melody!

Personally I am strongly of opinion that modern opera to continue to obtain must be more lyric and less of the stage, stagy; more sung and less acted.

The presentation yesterday, with much the same cast as last season – save for Caruso – was most finished, artistic and impressive. As the old blind king, the central figure of the horrid drama, the instrument of relentless fate, both pathetically and vengefully dramatic, intense and commanding, Didur in voice and action was superb. I never heard Martinelli as Avito sing better, while Muzio as Fiora struck the right note in her impersonation of the fair and frail woman tossed about between duty and desire, and sang with much charm and clarity of tone.

As Manfredo Mr. Chalmers sang with both power and distinction but was dramatically a little pale and unconvincing. Bada as Flaminio was fervent but vocally somewhat thin. The smaller rôles were all adequately filled, and Mr. Moranzoni conducted with all possible dramatic feeling and effect.

I suppose that grand opera and poignant tragedy are so indissolubly connected in the public operatic mind that it would be futile for any composer to try to separate them.[1] Yet, why not? The tragedy of 'L'Amore dei Tre Re' is often frankly unpleasant; and surely there is enough tragedy with us ever, without going to the opera or elsewhere to have our souls harrowed or our emotions and sentiments tortured and mangled. Why always, operatically, sup full of horrors?[2]

---

1 De Koven, however, *had* tried to separate them in *The Canterbury Pilgrims*, billed as a 'Grand Opera' and given seven performances at the Met in March and April 1917. His comment here suggests he was disappointed with the limited success of his opera.

2 Shakespeare's Macbeth says 'I have supped full with horrors' (*Macbeth*, Act 5, Scene 5). The quotation was often corrupted into the form given by De Koven.

8. Carl Van Vechten, extract from *Interpreters and Interpretation*, 2nd edition (New York: Knopf, 1920).

[On Mary Garden as Fiora]

On the whole I feel that the most enthusiastic of Miss Garden's admirers have so far done the woman scant justice. Most of us are beginning to realize that she is the greatest of living lyric artists, that she has done more to revive the original intention of the Florentines in inventing the opera to recapture the theatre of the Greeks, than any one else. She has made opera, indeed, sublimated speech. And she is certainly the contemporary queen of lyric sigaldry.

[...] Mary Garden is probably the greatest living singer. It is, indeed, with her voice, and with her *singing* voice that she does her most consummate acting. Indeed her capacity for colouring her voice to suit the emergencies not only of a phrase but of an entire rôle, might give a hint to future interpreters, were there any capable of taking advantage of such a valuable hint. But, good God, in such matters as phrasing, *portamento*,[1] *messa di voce*,[2] and other paraphernalia of the singing teacher's laboratory, she is past-mistress, and if any one has any complaints to make about the quality and quantity of tone she used in the second act of *l'Amore dei Tre Re* I feel that he did not listen with unprejudiced ears.

[...] But Fiora! What a triumph! What a volcano! I have never been able to find any pleasure in listening to the music of Montemezzi's *l'Amore dei Tre Re*, although it has a certain pulse,

---

[1] From the Italian expression *portamento della voce* (carrying of the voice), which refers to the smooth 'carrying' of the voice from one pitch to another (in preference to abrupt shifts of pitch).

[2] 'Placing the voice': the technique of controlling a gradual crescendo and decrescendo while sustaining a single pitch.

a rhythmic beat, especially in the second act, which gives it a factitious air of being better than it really is. The play, however, is interesting, and subtle enough to furnish material for quibble and discussion not only among critics, but among interpreters themselves. Miss Bori, who originally sang Fiora in New York, was a pathetic flower, torn and twisted by the winds of fate, blown hither and thither without effort or resistance on her part. It was probably a possible interpretation, and it found admirers. Miss Muzio, the next local incumbent of the rôle, fortified with a letter from Sem Benelli, or at least his spoken wishes, found it convenient to alter this impersonation in most particulars, but she was not, is not, very convincing.[1] Her intentions are undoubtedly good but she is no instrument for the mystic gods to play upon.

But Miss Garden's Fiora burned through the play like a flame. She visualized a strong-minded mediæval woman, torn by the conflicting emotions of pity and love, but once she had abandoned herself to her passion she became a living altar consecrated to the worship of Aphrodite and Eros. Such a hurricane of fiery, tempestuous love has seldom if ever before swept the stage. Miss Garden herself has never equalled this performance, save in Mélisande and Monna Vanna,[2] which would lead one to the conclusion that she is at her best in parts of the middle ages, until one reflects that in early Greek courtesans, in French cocottes of several periods, in American Indians, and Spanish gipsies she is equally atmospheric.[3] Other Fioras have been content to allow

---

[1] I have found no other reference to Muzio being advised by Benelli. Other reports do not suggest that she departed radically from Bori's interpretation.

[2] The eponymous heroine of *Monna Vanna* (1909) by Henry Février (1875–1957).

[3] References to the eponymous heroines of Massenet's *Thaïs* and *Manon* (among other 'cocottes'), Victor Herbert's *Natoma*, and *Carmen*.

Mary Garden as Fiora

the hand of death to smite them without a struggle. Not this one. When Archibaldo attempts to strangle her she tries to escape; her efforts are horrible and pathetic because they are fruitless. And the final clutch of the fingers behind his back leave the most horrible blood-stains of tragic beauty in the memory.[1]

---

[1] The blood was real, if Garden's own description of the scene is to be believed:

> Virgilio Lazzari was the blind old king, and what a fight we two used to have in the strangling scene!
> 'Mary, look at my hands!' he used to say to me after that scene.
> They were covered with scratches from my nails. How I used to fight for my life in that opera! Lazzari killed me, but what a struggle it was, and how I loved and adored it! I lived and died every minute of it.

See *Mary Garden's Story* (London: Michael Joseph, 1952), 153.

9. Henry T. Finck, *New York Evening Post*,
10 January 1924.[1]

Gala Performance Of Italian Opera

Montemezzi, Composer of 'Love of Three Kings,' Honored At Metropolitan

LAST NIGHT's gala performance at the Metropolitan Opera House recalled two of the most notable events in the history of that famous institution, the premieres of Puccini's 'Girl of the Golden West' and Humperdinck's 'Koenigskinder' in presence of their composers.[2] Last night the recipient of the ovations was Italo Montemezzi, the composer of 'L'Amore dei tre Re.' After the tragic and exciting second act, where the jealous and brutal old caveman, King Archibaldo, has strangled the lovely Fiora and carried out her body hanging limply over his shoulders, there were many enthusiastic recalls for Lucrezia Bori, Adamo Didur, Beniamino Gigli and Millo Picco.

Address by Paul D. Cravath

Then Signor Montemezzi was brought on and after the audience had enthusiastically brought him back again and again Paul D. Cravath[3] came out with him, as well as a man bearing a silver

---

1 Finck was one of the few American critics who initially had a mostly negative view of *L'Amore dei Tre Re*: see above, pp. 2–3. His opinion of the opera steadily improved over the years. This is his last review of Montemezzi's work.

2 Puccini's *La Fanciulla del West* was staged at the Met on 10 December 1910, and Engelbert Humperdinck's *Königskinder* eighteen days later, on 28 December 1910. Both performances were world premieres.

3 Paul Drennan Cravath (1861–1940), a very prominent lawyer, who served on the board of the Metropolitan Opera House and later (in 1931) became its president and chairman.

wreath. Turning to the composer, Mr. Cravath made this brief and appropriate address:

'Mr. Montemezzi: This is an important anniversary in the calendar of the Metropolitan Opera Company. Ten years ago your great opera 'L'Amore dei tre Re' received its first production in this house. It won instantaneous recognition and success, and has since held an honorable place in our annual repertoire. The performance this evening is the fortieth in this house.[1] The tragic story of love and death that you have told with such charm and eloquence still holds the Metropolitan audiences under its spell. You have earned high rank among the great masters of opera upon our roll of honor. The board of directors of the Metropolitan Opera Company ask you to accept this silver wreath as evidence of our recognition of your brilliant achievements and as a token of our gratitude and esteem.'[2]

Forty performances in ten years is a good record for any opera at the Metropolitan where the repertory has to be so large and varied. It is not so large a number as that which have been accorded to Puccini's 'Butterfly' or 'Tosca'[3] which are undoubtedly more original and meaty operas than 'The Love of Three Kings'; but apart from Puccini no other Italian composer since Verdi has created an opera superior to Montemezzi's. In Milan they call it the Italian Tristan, and no

---

1 This claim may be doubly misleading. Met records suggest that it was actually the thirty-ninth performance. More importantly, not all of these had taken place in the Metropolitan Opera House itself: performances had been given in Philadelphia, Atlanta and Brooklyn.

2 Finck's transcription of the speech is slightly different from that of Deems Taylor. See below, p. 183.

3 By this juncture the Met had given *Madama Butterfly* 168 times and *Tosca* 174 times. These operas had of course been in the repertoire much longer: a fairer guide to comparative popularity is that in the decade 1914–23 *Madama Butterfly* had 74 performances and *Tosca* 68.

doubt Montemezzi was strongly influenced by that greatest of musical love-tragedies, harmonically, orchestrally and in the use of leading motives. But most of the music reflects the composer's own individuality; it is music which improves on acquaintance. I cannot prove that assertion more eloquently than by stating that one of my colleagues, Herbert F. Peyser, told me last night he had heard thirty-six of the forty performances of this opera referred to by Mr. Cravath, not to speak of several others in which Mary Garden appeared.[1] And Herbert is hard to please – very.

Montemezzi had the advantage of an excellent libretto, made by Sem Benelli. It is tragedy from start to finish, relieved only by episodes of love making. If there had been a fourth act the composer would have had to follow the example of the juvenile Richard Wagner, who wrote a tragedy in which he killed off forty persons and then had to bring back some of them as ghosts to carry on the story.[2] But operagoers are used to tragedy and love it; and they certainly love lovers, especially when they sing so entrancingly and ardently as Lucrezia Bori and Beniamino Gigli did last night.

---

1 Peyser almost certainly saw *L'Amore dei Tre Re* more often than any other American critic. See below, p. 203.

2 The Shakespearean tragedy 'Leubald und Adelaide' that Wagner wrote around the age of fifteen. There is a full account of this in *Mein Leben*, but Finck did not know of this, and his information came from Wagner's 'Autobiographische Skizze' ('Autobiographic Sketch') of 1842. Finck gives a translation of the relevant passage in his *Wagner and His Works* (New York, 1893):

> I [Wagner] projected a grand drama, a sort of compound of *Hamlet* and *King Lear*; the plan was extremely grandiose: forty-two persons died in course of the piece, and in developing the plot I found myself compelled to make most of them reappear as ghosts, because otherwise there would have been no personages left for the last acts. (1:20)

Histrionically Mr. Gigli did not make so much of the part of Avito as Edward Johnson did. Where is he?[1] The ferocious, murderous King Archibaldo is Mr. Didur's best part in acting; too bad his voice is so rough and worn. Millo Picco appeared for the first time as the superfluous husband;[2] he seemed more affected by his wife's death than his predecessors were.

The Art of Lucrezia Bori

But the glory of this opera is Lucrezia Bori. She sang the part of Fiora at the very first performance, a decade ago when her impersonation was a delight to the eyes as well as ears. It has ripened since that time; her voice, no less lovely, is richer, deeper, more luscious, more laden with pent-up feeling; and her art as an actress has become more subtle and impressive even since last year. Her facial expression is becoming as eloquent as Farrar's and Calvé's.[3] There could be no more striking contrast than her features present when she holds her true love in her arms, when she evades the caresses of the husband who had been forced on her by convention, and the horror when she realizes that the King is bent on murder. Those who were so lucky as to see and hear Lucrezia Bori's Fiora last night, will place it in their memories in the front row of their portrait galleries of operatic celebrities.

---

1 Johnson had been singing the role of Avito with the Chicago company since 1920, and had sung it at his Met debut on 16 November 1922. He would sing the role regularly at the Met between 1927 and 1933.

2 In fact Millo Picco had made his debut at the Met in the role of Manfredo on 7 April 1919, and sung it a second time on 28 February 1920.

3 Geraldine Farrar (1882–1967), who sang regularly at the Met between 1906 and 1922, and Emma Calvé (1858–1942), who sang there regularly from 1893 to 1904.

10. Deems Taylor, *World*, 10 January 1924.[1]

At The Metropolitan

'Maestro Montemezzi: This is an important anniversary in the calendar of the Metropolitan Opera Company. Ten years ago this week, your great opera, 'L'Amore Dei Tre Re,' received its first production in this house. It was received with immediate approbation and acclaim and has since held an honorable place in our annual repertoire. The performance this evening is the fortieth in this house. The dramatic power of this story of love and death that you have told with such appealing beauty and dramatic power still holds Metropolitan audiences under its spell. You have earned high rank on the roll of honor of the great masters of opera. And now, sir, the Board of Directors, and the management, and Mr. Gatti Casazza of the Metropolitan Opera Company ask you to accept this silver wreath as evidence of our recognition of your magnificent contribution to operatic art, and as a token of our gratitude and esteem for you as an artist and as a man.'

So saying, Paul Cravath of the Metropolitan directorate,[2] standing before the curtain after the second act of last night's 'L'Amore Dei Tre Re,' turned to Italo Montemezzi and gave him a large silver wreath mounted on a purple velvet placque. The

---

1 In the course of his stint as music critic for the *World* (1921–25), Deems Taylor reviewed *L'Amore dei Tre Re* on several occasions; this is the most substantial of his reviews. In January 1922 he had reported that 'Montemezzi's brief masterpiece still retains its potency. Benelli's poetic and thrilling libretto, together with the music that throbbed and glowed in perfect and beautiful commentary upon every word and line, held the huge audience [at the Met] in absorbed silence.' See 'L'Amore Dei Tre Re,' *World*, 4 January 1922, 11 (reprinted from the previous day's late edition).

2 See above, p. 179 and n. 3.

audience applauded and some of it cheered. Even the orchestra players, most of them, gave up part of their entr'acte rest period to stand and applaud the composer of one of the twentieth century's lyric masterpieces. Mr. Montemezzi, spare, gray haired and smiling, made the best possible reply he could have made. He took the wreath and bowed low in silence.

Altogether a memorable occasion. It would have been even more memorable if the performance had been superlatively good. Unfortunately the Metropolitan Opera Company could not render Mr. Montemezzi this service, because it could not provide the proper cast.

Miss Bori, of course, is excepted. She was in good voice and gave a graceful and appealing performance, one that more nearly recalled her incomparable Fiora of former seasons than anything she has done recently.[1] Mr. Didur, too, although his voice is not what it was, made Archibaldo a tragic and powerful figure. This, and Klingsor, are the two best roles he plays, and in them he always maintains an impressive standard of excellence.

But there are three Kings in Montemezzi's opera, and all three of them must be nearly perfectly played if his artistic aims are not to be defeated.

They were not so played last night. Mr. Gigli sang ravishingly and acted with obvious sincerity, but he lacked both the romantic charm and tragic intensity that Avito must possess. Mr. Picco's appearance in the role of Manfredo can be explained only by the fact that he once made an emergency debut at the Metropolitan in the part.[2] His voice lacked expressiveness and

---

[1] In a review of November 1922, Taylor wrote: 'She [Bori] seems happily to have returned to her old conception of the part. Last year her Fiora was a little too mature, a little too sophisticated for Benelli's driven heroine. Last night she was again the helpless, tragic girl, fighting her love, and dying for it – the Fiora that she was at first, the one we all remember.' See 'At the Metropolitan,' *World*, 17 November 1922, 11.

[2] See above, p. 182, n. 2

power, and his acting was too much of the 'Lucia' school[1] to carry much conviction.

The orchestra sounded coarse upon occasion, but was generally good. Mr. Moranzoni's conducting was not inspired, although he acquitted himself creditably.

Incidentally, it is interesting to record that, despite the Metropolitan's sterling evidences of regard, 'L'Amore Dei Tre Re' was performed exactly once last season and had its initial performance of this season only last night. If the Metropolitan forces think so highly of Mr. Montemezzi's masterwork, why don't they give it more and better performances?

---

[1] I.e. in the style required for Donizetti's *Lucia di Lammermoor*, a staple of the Met's repertoire at this time.

Joseph Novak's set for the Second Act
In 1926 this replaced Sala's earlier design in Met productions

11. Olin Downes, *New York Times*, 28 October 1928.*

The Opera Season's Opening

Tomorrow's Gala Event to Be Marked by a Poetic Musical Drama of Italy[1]

IT IS good news for lovers of music, if not for those whose conception of an opening night of grand opera is scenic pomp, the diamond horseshoe and the gallery in frenzied salutation of the tenor and his sweet romanza, that the Metropolitan Opera Company will open its season of 1928–29 tomorrow night with the poetic and glamorous score of Italo Montemezzi, 'The Love of Three Kings.'

Miss Ponselle will take the part of Fiora, a part which has been given in the past to only three Metropolitan sopranos – Miss Bori, who created it for New York; the statuesque Miss Muzio, and the protagonist of tomorrow evening.[2] It is a great part, one that demands of the singer, in addition to vocal opulence and splendor, dramatic intensity and the projection of high

---

* © 1928 The New York Times. All rights reserved. Used by permission and protected by the Copyright Laws of the United States. The printing, copying, redistribution, or retransmission of this Content without express written permission is prohibited.

1 Downes wrote many very approving notices of *L'Amore dei Tre Re* for the *New York Times*. This one has a special interest, as parts of it were published, in Italian translation, in a pamphlet promoting Montemezzi's music that Ricordi issued in 1933. There is good reason to suppose that Montemezzi himself recommended this particular review for the purpose.

2 Rosa Ponselle had sung the role twice before, on 29 December 1926 and 26 April 1927. Downes forgets that Fiora had also been sung by Florence Easton on four occasions, 18 April 1919, 1 January 1921, 25 March 1922 and 21 February 1928. The remainder of the forty eight performances given to this date had been divided between Bori and Muzio. The latter had not won the same critical acclaim as the former.

tragedy. The opera is unique among the works of Montemezzi, who never approached it before or since it appeared in musical inspiration and emotional power, and it stands alone in the contemporaneous literature of music drama. It has no intimate relation to current tendencies in the musical art, dwelling in a place independent of 'schools' and 'periods,' following its own laws of beauty. It appears as one of those solitary flashes of genius that may from time to time illuminate an otherwise dark sky, for the past twenty years have not been fertile in great music, and 'The Love of Three Kings' has had neither predecessors nor successors. The art of the Italian realists has nothing to do with it. It stands nearer the late Verdi, but its great second act utilizes the orchestral if not the symphonic methods of the second act of Wagner's 'Tristan.'

We need not claim that the opera is an Italian 'Tristan.'[1] It cannot rank so high, but in his long melodic flight and in the noble purity and intensity of feeling that Montemezzi achieves in these pages he has once more vindicated the finest elements of the Italian musical genius and has placed himself in a niche in the temple of art which will remain secure through the passing of many years. His Italian lyricism is paired with a patrician sense of beauty. His technical methods are always appropriate to the situation and effective in the theatre. On occasion he writes stage music which derives from the most approved modern methods, but these passages are of a nature which is neither ephemeral nor banal. There is no commonplace character or moment in this piece, and there is no moment that composer and poet have failed to make beautiful. The libretto, made from Sem Benelli's play, which was deemed a complete impossibility

---

1 See Henry T. Finck's comment above, p. 180: 'In Milan they call it [*L'Amore dei Tre Re*] the Italian Tristan.'

for the opera house by the composer's friends,[1] proves ideally constructed for his purposes. Each rôle is poetically as well as dramatically significant. Each part adds to the beauty of the picture and is an essential feature of it. We have referred to the rôle of the heroine, but the greatest rôle, of course, is that of Archibaldo, the magnificent old barbarian, colossal in his pride of race and his love of the soil that he conquered and made his own, ruthless, terrible in the vindication of his possessions and his honor.

---

[1] Montemezzi later told Herbert F. Peyser that: 'When I first decided to construct an opera on the tragedy of Sem Benelli virtually nobody approved of the scheme. All my friends and even my publisher disapproved.' See Peyser's 'For Deeper Enjoyment of *L'Amore Dei Tre Re*,' *Opera News*, 10 January 1949, 4–6, 30–31, p. 6.

Rosa Ponselle as Fiora, 1926

12. Lawrence Gilman, *New York Herald Tribune*, 30 October 1928.

The Opera Season Opens: 'L'Amore dei Tre Re' at the Metropolitan, With Ponselle

IT IS SAID that Mr. Spurgeon, the eminent divine, proposed to his inamorata by the aid of a passage from Martin Tupper.[1] Mr. Gatti-Casazza[2] has resorted at times to expedients almost equally desperate, from the standpoint of the music lover, in wooing the favor of his opening-night opera audiences. But his choice of last evening's inaugural opera can surely have seemed desperate to no one – except, perhaps, to those few who resent the invasion of opera by beauty and gravity and sincerity.

If many such were on hand last night, they were deserving of commiseration. Montemezzi, in composing 'L'Amore dei Tre Re,' had no thought of the groundlings, of those for whom opera is a show or a diversion. 'L'Amore dei Tre Re' is neither. It is almost as spare, as free from accessory elements, as concentrated in its direct and passionate intentness as is 'Tristan und Isolde' (wide apart though the two works are in their musical quality). Montemezzi in this score inhabits a different world from the facile and shallow Puccini, in whose heart so many merchants trafficked.

---

1 Charles Haddon Spurgeon (1834–92), the leading British Baptist preacher and writer, suggested the possibility of marriage to Susannah Thompson, his future wife, by drawing her attention to a passage in Martin Tupper's *Proverbial Philosophy* which begins 'Seek a good wife from thy God.' See W. Y. Fullerton, *C. H. Spurgeon: A Biography* (London: Williams and Norgate, 1920), 162–63.

2 The sole director of the Met since 1910.

In 'L'Amore dei Tre Re' there is not a measure from beginning to end that is musically meretricious, that was written with a view to an ad captandum appeal. From beginning to end the music is the handmaid of the tragedy, plastic and devoted and inflammable – beautiful often, in its own right, but never asserting that right to the damage of the work's integrity and its noble unity of address.

Let us hope, therefore, that the majority of last night's audience were properly grateful to Mr. Gatti-Casazza for giving them so deep a pleasure upon an occasion that has often yielded no pleasure deeper than that to be extracted from the dreary, spectacular banalities of 'La Gioconda' or the perfumed pieties of 'Thais.'

There are cynics who declare that the tactful and astute director of the Metropolitan selected 'L'Amore dei Tre Re' for his opening bill not because it was good, but because it was short. Those who choose may feast to their heart's content upon such clammy disillusionment. We, being sealed of the clan of cheerfully determined illusionists, prefer to think that Montemezzi's opera was offered to us last night because it is not only a fine work but an effective one; because it is not only the noblest music drama that has come out of Italy since Verdi's 'Otello,' but because it is a flexible and responsive vehicle for the Metropolitan's performing forces.

Surely, there were many last night who found their major satisfaction in witnessing Montemezzi's swift and passionate fantasy upon the old Greek theme of the tangled feet of Destiny – in seeing the lovers, Fiora and Avito, awaiting the doom that is about to fall upon them; seeing Fiora cowering yet defiant before the blind, inexorable steps of the terrible old king, guiltless in her own view, but horribly guilty in his; or Avito drinking poison from the lips of the adored and slain woman, that 'sweet fruit upon the ancient tree of death';[1] and in hearing the eloquent music – music simple, sensuous, passionate – which Montemezzi has put in the mouths of these figures of tragic ecstasy, the ecstasy of love and hate.

For those who were not thus centrally engrossed and moved, there were the figures of the music-drama's pattern as limned by the sumptuous-toned Rosa Ponselle – a Fiora of warmth and sincerity, if not a Fiora of wholly capturing illusiveness; by Mr. Martinelli as Avito, ardent and forthright; by Mr. Pinza as the somber Archibaldo.

But, most influential of all, there was the superb conducting of Mr. Serafin, who, with due respect for every one else concerned, was the dominating star of last night's performance. The kindling, propulsive, immensely dramatic leadership of this remarkable Italian kept the music unceasingly aglow and alive.

If it was not, aside from the lustrous and duly applausive audience, a 'brilliant' opening, perhaps it was something better – an evening of rich artistic satisfaction in a lyric theater that can, at its best, deal worthily with great matters. We are still remembering high moments of communicative passion and sincerity in a performance that was worthier of a second night than of a first. We are still remembering the shadowed, sensuous beauty of Rosa Ponselle's voice in that loveliest passage of Montemezzi's score,

---

1 No exact source for this quotation has been traced, but Fiona Macleod includes an unreferenced quotation describing Jocasta as 'a silent fruit on the tree of death' in her preface to *The House of Usna* (1903).

Fiora's 'Dammi le labbra e tanta ti daro di questa pace,'[1] with its troubled ecstasy and sweetness. We are still hearing those urgent orchestral voices in contrary motion that give so passionate a life to the music of Montemezzi's poignant second act. We are still held by the pity and terror of the overwhelming finale of that great act, with its curtain falling upon the picture of the dreadful Archibaldo staggering beneath the burden of the dead body of the woman he has slain.

Above all, we are still happy over the realization that the most glittering and external occasion that the opera in America provides is able now and again to yield an evening of beauty and high illusion in the theater of the mind.

---

[1] 'Give me your lips, and I will give you of this peace': Fiora's words to Avito in Act I.

13. Oscar Thompson, *New York Evening Post*, 3 November 1928.

From the Strangulation of Fiora to the Vindication of Helen – An Opera Not for All-Conquering Stars

I<small>F</small> C<small>HALIAPIN</small> would only sing Archibaldo –[1]

A remark of tumultuous implications overheard at the opening of the opera season Monday night as the curtain fell, a little quicker than usual, on the blind old king of a nameless land staggering under the burden of the lifeless form that dangled over his right shoulder.

Atlas with the World on his back, Hercules hoisting Antæus aloft, scarcely fire the imagination more than the thought of the stalwart Russian bearing the limp Fiora across the stage in this most thrilling moment of Montemezzi's 'Love of the Three Kings.'

And this, irrespective of the Fiora. Ezio Pinza, be it remembered, is also a big man. Possibly there was no real need of a quick curtain Monday night, and if some member of the technical staff of the Metropolitan arises, watch in hand, to dispute the insinuation that this actually was a quicker curtain than usual, the point need be argued no further.

But if Chaliapin would only sing Archibaldo –

What a choking there might be in that scene of struggle and strangulation! What vividness in the anger and suspicion and the uncanny sensitiveness of the blind monarch! And does any flood

---

[1] Chaliapin had sung at the Met in the 1907–08 season, then returned triumphantly on 9 December 1921 in the role of Boris Godunov. He sang at the Met every season through the 1920s, his final appearance being on 20 March 1929.

of orchestral sound ever obscure the vocal line when Chaliapin sings, as the orchestra quite generally obscures the voice in the narrative of Archibaldo in the first act?

This implies no criticism of Mr. Pinza, whom the writer of these lines regards as the most generally satisfactory Archibaldo the Metropolitan has known, though Adamo Didur was at times more tragic and Jose Mardones sang the music more sonorously.[1] What Didur most possessed, Mardones lacked. And Mardones gloried in the orotund tone Didur did not command. Virgilio Lazzari of the Chicago company also was a very competent Archibaldo. It is a role that seems never to have been badly done.

But Chaliapin as Archibaldo –

Caruso once essayed Avito.[2] He was not happy. This thought of Caruso struggling with a part obviously uncongenial to his vocal style and his unromantic bearing may not at first blush seem to have any bearing on the suggestion that Chaliapin undertake Archibaldo.

Caruso was essentially an acting singer, Chaliapin is a singing actor. Caruso failed as Avito because he lacked just the qualities that might make Chaliapin a tremendous success as Archibaldo. But antithetical in many respects as the supreme gifts of these two artists appear, it is possible to see them in much the same

---

[1] Didur sang the role of Archibaldo on a total of thirty-three occasions for the Met, the last being on 15 January 1929. Until 1918 the part was exclusively his. José Mardones first sang Archibaldo for the Metropolitan Company in a Philadelphia performance on 19 March 1918, and went on to take the part on seven more occasions, the last being on 15 February 1924. Although Léon Rothier and Pavel Ludikar also sang the role on a handful of occasions, it belonged to Didur and Mardones until the advent of Pinza, who first sang Archibaldo on 28 February 1927 and performed the role fourteen times with the Met, the last being on 3 April 1941.

[2] See above, p. 166.

relation to 'L'Amore dei Tre Re.' The question with Chaliapin, as with Caruso, is whether he would not be too essentially a star to meet the requirements of an opera that has no stellar role.

As it is true that the listener ordinarily finds it possible to be equally sympathetic toward all four of the chief characters, though their sins against one another are of such serious description as infidelity and murder, so it is true that these four parts stand upon practically the same level of importance. Fiora is not the all-dominating person of the vermilion impersonation by Mary Garden, with its tempestuous outbursts and its frenetic writhings.[1] Miss Garden has a way of dominating the stage that is not unlike Chaliapin's, though the acting technique of the two artists has more points of difference than of similarity. The four Fioras of Metropolitan performances, Lucrezia Bori, Claudio Muzio, Florence Easton and Rosa Ponselle,[2] have been less highly colored and the ensemble has profited thereby.

This writer has personally regretted some recent changes in Miss Bori's characterization which have tended to make it more melodramatic after the fashion of Miss Garden's, less the fragile, idyllic creature torn by emotions beyond her power to resist.

To return to Avito. At the time Caruso undertook the part, in succession to Edoardo Ferrari-Fontana and Giovanni Martinelli,[3] he had been displaying no small interest in the role of Siegmund. Older attaches [sic] of the opera house recall how he frequently heard parts of 'Walkure,' and how he gave many small indications of being drawn to the heldentenor part.

'L'Amore,' purely Italian as it is, was his closest approximation to Wagner at the Metropolitan. It required him to sing music of

---

1 For Garden's interpretation of Fiora, see above, pp. 18–21, 175–78.
2 See above, p. 187, n. 2.
3 In fact, Caruso took the role before Martinelli.

the longer line that is not divided into arias and other set numbers. He had the breath control and the command of phrase as well as the staying power to have sung this music superbly. But he never really mastered the style. Uncomfortable, he plodded. The gold of his voice lacked something of its usual luster when poured into unfamiliar molds. So, discouraged, he gave it up, and after that he seemed to lose interest in Siegmund.[1]

Unable to employ his unmatched vocal resources to their best ends, Caruso by no means dominated 'L'Amore' as Avito. Perhaps he was the least successful in the part of any of the tenors who have sung it in New York. Ferrari-Fontana certainly is remembered in the role (though his appearances were comparatively few[2]) in a manner Caruso is not. Doubtless there are many opera-goers who have forgotten that the king of tenors even so much as undertook the part. Edward Johnson, who sang opposite Miss Garden in most of the Chicago company's representations of the opera in Manhattan and who has since been cast for it opposite Miss Bori at the Metropolitan,[3] has been far happier than was Caruso. Beniamino Gigli, too, has succeeded in accommodating the Caruso type of voice to this music better than Caruso himself did.[4]

---

[1] Caruso only sang in a Wagner opera once, when he starred in three performances of *Lohengrin* (in Italian) in Buenos Aires in 1901. It is worth setting Huneker's view of Caruso's Wagnerian potential beside Thompson's: 'It has often been a cause of critical wonderment why Caruso never sang the music of Richard Wagner. What a Lohengrin he would have been, what a Parsifal, yes, even a Tristan! He knew every note of these rôles.' See James Gibbons Huneker, *Variations* (New York: Charles Scribner's Sons, 1921), 276.

[2] Ferrari-Fontana sung Avito in the Met's first eleven performances of *L'Amore dei Tre Re*, making his final appearance in the role on 10 April 1915.

[3] Johnson first sang Avito with the Met company on 16 November 1922, and had sung it on five more occasions by the time Thompson wrote, the last being on 26 March 1928.

[4] Gigli first sang Avito at the Met on 1 January 1921; he sang the part on nine occasions altogether, the last being on 29 December 1926.

No one of these has been a dominating Avito. Clearly the role was never intended to stand forth in too prosilient relief. What Lucien Muratore might have made of it, if the Chicago company's internal ructions had not led to his withdrawal soon after he had learned the part, is conjectural, with a suspicion remaining that he probably would have been the most poetic and dramatic of Avitos.[1]

Manfredo is no secondary role. That admirable artist Pasquale Amato quite held his own with it in the first cast that included Bori, Ferrari-Fontana and Didur. That he later sang it less well was another matter.[2] With the Chicagoans, Georges Baklanoff and Carlo Galeffi also proved that the part had a blend of vocal and dramatic appeal which an artist of consequence could use to enlist no small sympathy for the big-hearted husband. Giuseppe Danise has sung the music better than he has acted

---

[1] Lucien Muratore (1876–1954) left the Chicago Company after the 1921–22 season, having clashed badly with Mary Garden, then acting as the company's director. But Thompson is wrong in suggesting that Muratore did not sing Avito, and in assuming a connection with his leaving the company. It was announced that Muratore would sing the role in New York in the course of the Chicago Company's 1922 visit, but this did not happen because he fell ill with acute appendicitis and had to cancel most of his performances. By March, however, he was sufficiently recovered to sing the role in Baltimore, and 'M. S. W.' in the Baltimore *Sun* reported that '… Muratore, almost out from sickbed, attained in the amorous duet with Garden a splendor of song which is unescapably the finest passage of the whole opera. This emphatically was the opinion of the great audience whose plaudits at the close, generous to all the artists, reached its highest enthusiasm for the tenor.' See 'Impressions of the Opening,' *Sun*, 7 March 1922, 5. Muratore repeated the role at subsequent stages of the Chicago Company's 1922 tour.

[2] Amato sang Manfredo in the first eighteen performances of *L'Amore dei Tre Re*, through to 17 April 1918. He returned to the role on four further occasions, the last being on 1 January 1921.

the role[1] – a criticism that has applied generally to a good many performances of 'L'Amore' at the Metropolitan. Lawrence Tibbett gave real promise in both directions when he appeared with Miss Bori and Johnson in a performance that had more than the usual amount of physical illusion.[2]

It is in this detail of physical illusion that Chaliapin as Archibaldo might be tremendous, individually, and in being just that throw the entire opera out of focus. That he would make the patriarch's blindness a palpable and palpitant thing beyond any and all suggestions of it in the impersonations familiar to this public seems inevitable. But with this and other details of a colossal impersonation to minify the other parts, Fiora and Avito and Manfredo might very well appear as if seen through the wrong end of a telescope – not a new charge with respect to Chaliapin's relation to other singers in the operas he has graced and galvanized. There is quite enough of this in works less sensitive, less exquisite than 'L'Amore.'

Essentially different as the two operas are, the thought inevitably flits to 'Pelleas et Melisande.' There is more to sing in 'L'Amore,' but it requires much the same type of cast. Cardinal requirements can be summed up in the words fitness and proportion, and among these is one which Mr. Gatti, in announcing why he had so long delayed undertaking the Debussy work, referred to as 'la physique du role.'[3]

---

[1] Danise first sang Manfredo on 3 February 1921, and returned to the role on eleven further occasions, the last being the performance Thompson had just seen.

[2] Tibbett first sang Manfredo in Philadelphia on 25 January 1927, alongside Bori and Jonson, with whom he sang the role on five further occasions. He took the part of Manfredo on ten occasions in all, the last being on 30 April 1929.

[3] Giulio Gatti-Casazza, the sole director of the Met since 1910, did not bring out *Pelléas et Mélisande* until the 1924–25 season.

So contemplated, an all-star performance of 'L'Amore dei Tre Re' is just the performance most sincere lovers of the lovely work which opened the Metropolitan season would be most thoroughly unhappy over. A cast, for instance, which included Mary Garden as Fiora, Chaliapin as Archibaldo, Caruso redivivus as Avito, and (why not?) the septuagenarian Mattia Battistini as Manfredo,[1] might cause such gnashing of teeth as has not been heard at the Metropolitan in many years; aside from affording those who interrupted the first act with applause on Monday night, many more instances in which to show how utterly tasteless operatic enthusiasm at times can be.

Probably there would be one consolation, however. A performance of 'L'Amore' designed along such lines would likely include Angelo Bada as Flaminio. It is not one of the best of his innumerable small parts, but it, at least, would be in perspective.[2]

It is from thoughts of 'L'Amore' and perspective that the attention must now be turned in quite another direction. There need be no fear of looking through the wrong end of the telescope at Tuesday night's first American performance of 'The Egyptian Helen.'[3]

---

[1] Mattia Battistini (1856–1928), the most celebrated baritone of his day, who never sung at the Met.

[2] Angelo Bada (1876–1941) probably holds the record for appearing in more performances of *L'Amore dei Tre Re* than any other singer. He sang Flaminio in every one of the Met's first twenty-seven performances, and appeared in the role on fifty occasions, the last being on 9 March 1933.

[3] Strauss's new opera, *Die Ägyptische Helena*, given seven performances at the Met in the 1928–29 season, but not revived there until 2007.

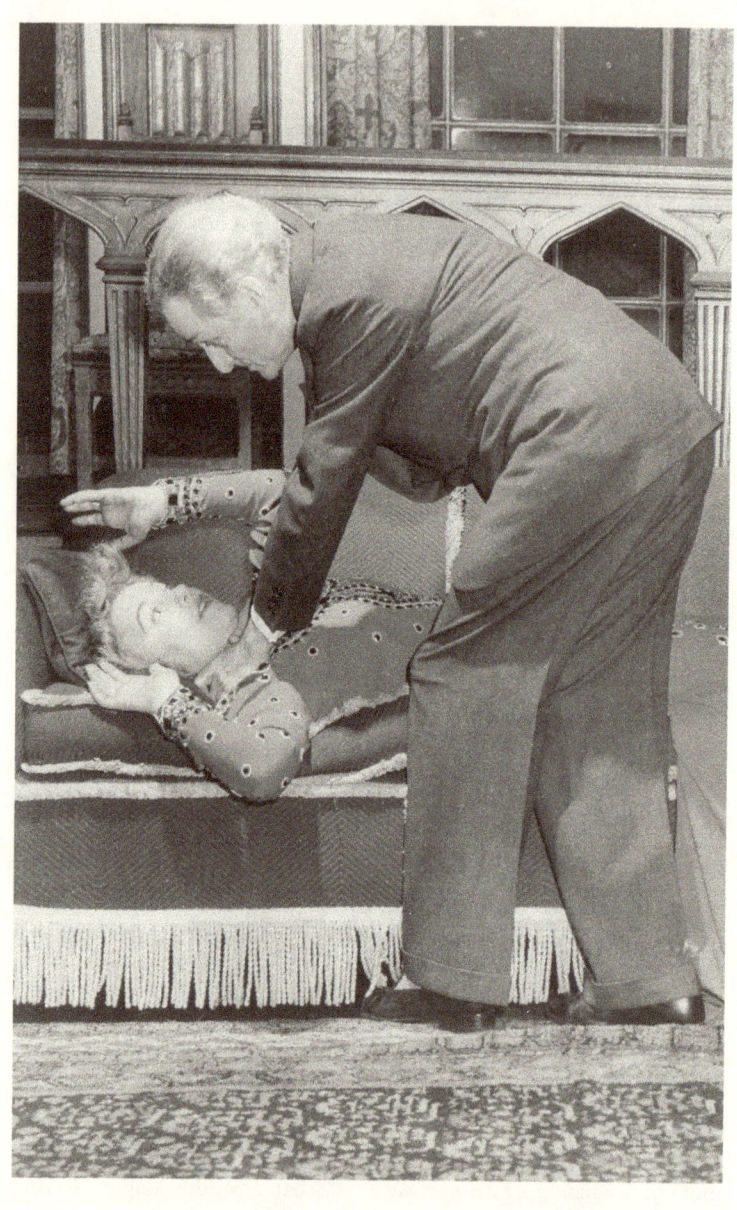

Montemezzi instructs Grace Moore in the strangulation scene, 1941

14. Herbert F. Peyser, *Opera News*, 10 January 1949.

For Deeper Enjoyment of *L'Amore Dei Tre Re*

SINCE 1914 *L'Amore dei tre Re* has been an article of faith with me. The work is my favorite opera next to *Otello* and *Aïda*. I consider it the greatest lyric drama that has come out of Italy since Verdi. I have never willingly missed a performance of it and have heard it over sixty times without ever wearying of it in the slightest.[1] To my thinking it wears perfectly and it never ages. It is to me as fresh and intensely moving as the first time I heard it. All the changes music has undergone in the intervening years have left it untouched.

[Peyser quotes a long letter from Montemezzi, written in summer 1948, explaining the circumstances in which he composed the opera.]

Strictly speaking, the opera is without a prelude. The twenty-one bars of music which precede the rise of the curtain establish with a few simple but telling strokes the noble and tragic mood of the work and emphasize certain elements which are woven into the texture of the score. These include sharply accented chords, powerful syncopations and *sforzandi* and *ostinato* figures, which play a vital role in the work and, together with vivid cross-rhythms, lend exciting movement and pictorial suggestion to the music. The first of these *ostinato* figures, which Montemezzi undoubtedly owed to his profitable studies of Mussorgsky in general and *Boris* in particular, is that figure in sixteenth and thirty-second notes introduced *poco piu mosso* in the fifth bar and suggesting the gallop of horses.

---

1 Peyser's figure reflects the fact that the opera was performed less often in the 1930s and '40s. By January 1924 he had already seen it around forty times: see above, p. 181.

It will be heard repeatedly in the first and, especially, the second act and acquires a significance of the most tragic poignancy.

The rising curtain to the accompaniment of a delicately mournful wisp of melody over nostalgic triplets presently acquaints us with the thematic label of the blind Archibaldo – a series of stumbling, detached chords, a true Wagnerian leading motive, a musical delineation of the hesitant gait of the sightless old king. By association the figure eventually acquires a dreadful significance of doom and terror.

The interchange between Archibaldo and his attendant, Flaminio, is marked not only by some of that lyrical melody which is one of the glories of this work but of those syncopations and *ostinato* figures just mentioned. When Flaminio says '*Ricordate la vostra giovinezza*'[1] Archibaldo launches on that indescribably noble and uplifting page, the narrative '*Son quarant' anni*,'[2] recounting his coming to Italy at the head of a barbarian horde forty years ago, of his love of the enchanted country and his desire, had he the power, to make Italy queen of the world. The

---

1 'You are remembering your youth.'

2 'It is forty years.'

Herbert F. Peyser (*L*) with his long-term partner, the singer Christopher Hayes

music moves with steadily increasing momentum and its pace is accentuated by its play of *ostinato* figures, notably that figure heard in the first bars of the opera and depicting the savage stamp of warlike steeds. At the end of this passage the orchestra, having gathered up its lyric impetus, bursts triumphantly into a sonorous full cadence – a device which under other circumstances might seem a trivial solicitation to applause but which here conveys an impression of absolute rightness and justification.

The exit of the blind king and the coming of Fiora and Avito are marked by the thin call of a flute in the distance. The first phrases of the lovers are characterized by a heart-shaking melancholy. Then, when Avito expresses his fear that something may endanger the inward peace Fiora claims to feel, we hear that supreme phrase of love music which, in the second act, furnishes the shattering climax of the opera:

Archibaldo's return and his menacing scene with Fiora is marked by the same elements which have characterized the earlier episodes. One thing the listener may note is the similarity of constructive methods utilized by Montemezzi and Wagner – not merely in the matter of leading motives and their disposition but the utilization of what Alfred Lorenz calls the 'Bar form'[1] and other symphonic aspects of constructive balance and harmonic relationship. And still another Wagnerian influence is the skill which Montemezzi exhibits in what Wagner called 'the art of transition.'[2] A little masterpiece of this transition from one mood to a totally different one are those brief thirteen bars beginning with the exit of Fiora and ending with the return of Manfredo.

The second act, the weightiest of the opera, begins with an energetic theme typifying Manfredo. The music is full of unrest, the sound of tramping horses, the warlike notes of fanfares. The colloquy between Fiora and Manfredo strikes a sorrowful note. It is hard to imagine more poignancy of expression with simpler means than Fiora's brief recitatives sustained by nothing more than simple harmonies with which she replies to her heart-broken husband.

---

[1] Alfred Lorenz (1868–1939), a German musicologist and conductor, published the four hugely influential volumes of his *Das Geheimnis der Form bei Richard Wagner* (*The Secret of Form in Richard Wagner*) between 1924 and 1933. The first introduced the concept of *Barform*, an *AAB* structure that Lorenz found central to Wagner's music at all levels, imparting dramatic momentum.

[2] A concept Wagner explained in a famous letter to Mathilde Wesendonck of 12 October 1859. Stating his dislike of the 'abrupt and sudden,' he argued that musical transitions should appear 'to come as a matter of course' through proper preparation. See *Selected Letters of Richard Wagner*, trans. and ed. by Stewart Spencer and Barry Millington (London: Dent, 1987), 475.

The departure of Manfredo brings us to what is perhaps the most lacerating page of the entire work – the episode in which Fiora mounts the battlements to wave her scarf at her departing lord. Inevitably one thinks of Isolde on viewing this scene, though the purpose of the scarf-waving is diametrically the opposite. But there is no mistaking the different states of mind communicated by the music. The heart-break of Montemezzi's scene is positively physical. The thudding *ostinati*, the shriek of the overblown clarinet, the ruthless march of the poignant melody – these things are worthy of the Verdi who created *Otello*. The brief entry of Avito is interrupted by a most moving episode, the coming of the handmaiden to deliver the casket containing the veil. Music and situation evoke some masterpiece of Florentine painting. Once more the heart-shaking music begins, this time intensified.

The scene between Avito and Fiora is the most elaborate of the work. Three great melodies stand out –

This last is an elaboration of the love melody heard in the first act. The duet ends with an intoxicating swirl of sensuously swelling music. Or rather, it suddenly breaks off, as the portentous theme of Archibaldo resounds. The music of the ensuing episode utilizes the means already familiar from the preceding scenes. It rises to a bitter climax and culminates in the scene of the strangling. Inevitably the music here calls to mind the murder of Desdemona.

The end of the scene, with the vengeful Archibaldo, carrying on his shoulders the body of Fiora, is a kind of march movement of heavy basses with a viola solo wailing above. This movement is carried over into the new prelude to the last act which Mr. Montemezzi wrote to replace the dozen bars of the old original introduction.[1] When the more elaborately developed prelude ends we hear what is at first an unaccompanied chorus of mourning, broken by a few solo episodes with poignant orchestral phrases. One hears in the choral writing the unmistakable influence of *Boris Godunoff*, just as in the music which accompanies the entrance of the stricken Avito and his song of lamentation one remarks the imprint of Debussy.

If it seemed that Montemezzi achieved the climax of poignancy and passionate expression in the second act he has risen above himself in the final words of Avito and Manfredo. The episode of Manfredo kissing the poisoned lips of Fiora climbs to such operatic climax as seemed incredible after the grandiose achievement of the second act.

---

1 As noted above, the new introduction to the third act, an inspired revision, was first heard at the Met's performance of *L'Amore dei Tre Re* on 7 February 1941, conducted by Montemezzi.

Virgilio Lazzari as Archibaldo and
Dorothy Kirsten as Fiora, 1948

15. Ethel Peyser and Marion Bauer, extract from *How Opera Grew: From Ancient Greece to the Present Day* (New York: G. P. Putnam's, 1956).

Verismo is Abandoned

Without exaggeration, Italo Montemezzi, born in Vigasio, Italy (1875–1952), proclaimed himself in his *L'amore dei tre re* (*The Love of Three Kings*) one of the greatest modern Italian writers of opera. He abandoned the realistic (verismo) school, and made deep impressions in both Italy and in America with this opera. […]

Love of Three Kings

This opera is kept moving in spite of its not having catchy tunes, like those of Puccini or Verdi. Montemezzi used new musical ideas in old romantic ways. He took an exciting and intense story, almost veristic in spots, and applied to it a continuous stream of melody, instead of breaking it up into separate songs. *Ecco!* Here is the first Italian who actually did what the Camerata in the seventeenth century tried to do, fit text to music.[1] It took nearly three hundred years to arrive at this pinnacle of Italian dramma per musica. Mussorgsky did it in his song-speech for

---

1 Earlier in their book, Peyser and Bauer state that: 'refugee scholars [from the East] stimulated and excited a real thirst for the Greek and Latin arts. In the beautiful palace of Count Giovanni Bardi (1534–1612) in Florence, they formed a club called the *Camerata*, or "People of the Chamber [or Room]"' (26). They do not explain how the Camerata failed in their quest to 'combine music and poetry [in a theatrical context] so that together they express the story' (27), but they later state of Gluck's *Orfeo ed Euridice* that it 'more nearly approaches the Greek pattern longed for by the Camerata than any seventeenth-century opera' (88). They also relate *Orfeo ed Euridice* to Debussy's *Pelléas ed Mélisande* (ibid).

Russia; Wagner did it to a certain extent for Germany; Debussy accomplished it for France to the fullest extent. Its tragedy is so much more elevated than the verismo operas that, with *Aïda* and *Otello*, *The Love of Three Kings* deserves to live forever. It is 'wear-ever' music and affects opera because it gives courage to writers to use the elevated style once more.

16. Harold C. Schonberg, *New York Times*, 26 February 1962.*

'The Love of Three Kings' Presented on TV by N.B.C. Opera

ONE OF the lesser-known operas of the Italian school was televised yesterday afternoon in a new production by the N.B.C. Opera Company. It was Italo Montemezzi's 'L'Amore dei Tre Re' – or, in the English translation by Joseph Machlis, 'The Love of Three Kings.'[1]

It has been about a dozen years since 'L'Amore' was at the Metropolitan. Before the war, the composer himself conducted several performances there; and, in the role of Fiora, Grace Moore had one of her best roles.[2] Ezio Pinza, too, was unforgettable as Archibaldo.

There must have been several reasons why the N.B.C. Opera Company turned its attention to this relatively obscure work. For one thing, it is not too long, and virtually the entire opera can be encompassed within an hour and a half (only one, traditional cut in the second act was used on this occasion). The libretto, as far as Italian opera librettos go, is tightly constructed and is full of sex.

---

* © 1962 The New York Times. All rights reserved. Used by permission and protected by the Copyright Laws of the United States. The printing, copying, redistribution, or retransmission of this Content without express written permission is prohibited.

1 Joseph Machlis (1906–98) was a professor at Queens College and the best-selling author of *The Enjoyment of Music* (1955). He translated and adapted many librettos for the NBC Opera Company.

2 Moore sang the role of Fiora on four occasions in the 1940–41 season, but did not return to the part.

There even are psychological overtones, so beloved in contemporary dramas involving sex. At the end of the opera, Manfredo gazes upon the bodies of his wife and the man who has deceived him. 'Why can I feel no hatred?' he asks. This might not be a line that will ring down the ages, especially in view of the standard love triangle that has come before, and also the heavy melodrama, but for Italian opera it is positively epochal.

The music has been described as Wagnerian, a statement that this writer finds hard to take. There may be some Wagnerian touches, but Richard Strauss also plays a part, and the choruses at the beginning of the last act are heavily influenced by 'Boris Godunov.' Nevertheless, there is some gorgeous melody in 'L'Amore,' and the second act is a minor masterpiece. It builds up to a terrific climax, and is packed full with an intense kind of rapture.

Literalism was the keynote of this production. There were the castle, stone battlements, the tower and a handsome cast. On the whole, the realities of the opera house governed the television conception. Thus, even though there were close-ups and fade-outs, long shots and one abrupt change of locale impossible in an opera house, the philosophy was completely traditional. As 'L'Amore' is a traditional opera, perhaps that was the only way to approach it.

What with a thoroughly experienced cast and a workable (though not very imaginative) translation, the opera made its point. From its beginning, it has been the aim of the N.B.C. Opera Company to sing in English, and to sing with enough clarity to make every word understood. These standards continue to prevail. The singers looked their parts, acted well, and sang with exemplary enunciation.

Thus, whatever musical values may have been lost in translation, the action and verbal meanings were clearly conveyed. For a television audience, these factors are of utmost importance. 'The Love of Three Kings' received a tidy, well-sung, well-prepared

Fiora (Phyllis Curtin) and Archibaldo (Giorgio Tozzi) in the NBC's *Love of Three Kings*

performance that, considering the intensity of the music, was bound to make an impact on its listeners. Considering the dearth of live music in television, this kind of program is most welcome – not only for what it represents, but, most important, for what it actually is. No apologies need be made; for 'The Love of Three Kings' turned out to be good entertainment as well as good music.

Of the cast, Giorgio Tozzi, in physical bulk and size of voice, was especially impressive. But Phyllis Curtin, Richard Torigi, Frank Porretta and Nicholas di Virgilio all successfully gave the lie to the belief that opera singers are buckets of wind surrounded by acres of flesh.[1] The light of intelligence was actually in their eyes.

Alfred Wallenstein was the fine conductor.[2] At the very moments that 'The Love of Three Kings' was being televised, he was in Carnegie Hall leading the New York Philharmonic. (The broadcast, of course, was aired from a video color tape.[3]) Life not only moves fast these days; it moves impossibly and illogically.

---

[1] The singers who took, respectively, the roles of Archibaldo, Fiora, Manfredo, Avito and Flaminio.

[2] This was the first occasion on which Wallenstein (1898–1983), a protégé of Toscanini, had conducted for the NBC Opera Company.

[3] This was still a new technology at the time. Most of the earlier NBC opera productions had been live broadcasts. The AMPEX video recorder was unveiled at the end of 1956, but it was not until the end of the decade that the NBC Opera Company started using it.

17. Winthrop Sargeant, *New Yorker*, 3 March 1962.*

Of Kings and Giants[1]

I HAVE BEEN listening to televised opera for quite a number of years, mainly to the performances provided by that adventurous organization the N.B.C. Opera Company, and have admired the ingenuity and artistry with which much of it has been done, as well as the integrity and stubborn idealism of this particular company's producer, Samuel Chotzinoff.[2] I am aware that the medium of television is capable of bringing opera to a much larger audience than that which regularly attends performances in opera houses, and I have been delighted by Mr. Chotzinoff's insistence on doing his operas in the English language – especially since he has nearly always chosen translations of the most skillful and effective sort. Yet I have been inclined to regard this form of operatic production as a substitute for the real thing. The television screen is unquestionably somewhat small for the purposes of opera, and the mechanics of sound production on television permit no end of adjustments in volume, which render lesser voices impressive and hence take away one of opera's incidental excitements. I must say, however, that last Sunday afternoon's broadcast of Italo Montemezzi's opera 'The Love of Three Kings' led me to revise some of my ideas on the subject. I have heard a number of performances of this work in various opera houses – where it has never been particularly popular – and have always found it rather dull and static, even when it was enlivened by striking stage personalities, such as Grace Moore and Ezio Pinza,

---

* © 1962 The New Yorker. All rights reserved.

1 'Giants' refers to the second section of Sargeant's column, devoted to the third volume of Stravinsky's conversations with Robert Craft, *Expositions and Developments* (1962).

2 For Chotzinoff, see introduction, p. 40.

whom I remember seeing in it at the Metropolitan.[1] In these performances, the opera has invariably seemed remote and formal – a sort of Italo-Germanic 'Pelléas et Mélisande,' with very little action and very little power to involve an audience's emotions. Sunday's broadcast, however, made me aware of subtleties in the work that had eluded me in the opera house, and caused me to realize for the first time what a wonderful opera 'The Love of Three Kings' is. And this revelation was due, in part, to the very limitations of televised opera that I have complained about. The small screen brought one into the midst of the action, and closeups enabled one to study the minutest changes in facial expression, with the result that what before had seemed remote and static became vital and touching. 'The Love of Three Kings' is, apparently, a very intimate opera – perhaps too intimate to be fully realized on the grand-opera stage. Television seems to be its ideal medium.

As set forth the other afternoon in full color, the opera proved so gripping that it must have left many of its auditors limp, if not actually in tears. Its theme is, of course, one of those eternal love-and-death affairs, owing something to 'Tristan und Isolde,' something to 'Pelléas,' and something to 'Romeo and Juliet.' Musically, it is a marvel, written in the final flush of the post-Wagnerian tradition, with a score far richer in hypnotic power that that of 'Pelléas,' and full of the noblest sort of expressiveness. I hope that, since it has been recorded on tape, the N.B.C. Opera will find occasion to repeat it.[2]

Much of the production's artistic success was undoubtedly due to its conductor, Alfred Wallenstein, one of the very few American maestros of top rank, and one whose extraordinary gifts are belatedly being recognized. Much of it was also due

---

[1] Moore and Pinza sang together in three performances of *L'Amore dei Tre Re* at the Met in February 1941.

[2] As noted in the introduction, it was repeated on 27 January 1963.

Giorgio Tozzi as Archibaldo

to the ingenious sets, by Ed Wittstein, and to Kirk Browning's superb stage direction, which stood up excellently under the microscopic scrutiny of the camera. The cast consisted of about as fine a group of American singing actors as could be assembled for such a purpose. Phyllis Curtin made an exceedingly handsome Fiora, and her good looks and naturalness of demeanor were perfectly suited to the understatement that television requires — better suited by far than the large-scale heroics of an old-fashioned prima donna would have been. Giorgio Tozzi, always a striking actor in tragic parts, was very impressive as the blind King Archibaldo. Richard Torigi had the dashing appearance and most of the capacity for sorrow and magnanimity that the role of the husband, Manfredo, requires, and Frank Porretta was effectively passionate as the lover, Prince Avito. Moreover, they all sang beautifully, or at least the microphones made them appear to do so (which is all that one could ask); as a matter of fact, whoever had charge of the balancing of sonorities among orchestra, chorus, and soloists turned in a flawless job. I have noticed that the activities of the N.B.C. Opera have been somewhat curtailed this season, and I think that this is a great pity and a further sign of cultural obtuseness on the part of those who have been given control of one of our great natural resources — the airwaves.[1] The replacement of these broadcasts by an additional dose of moronic claptrap would, I think, be a national tragedy.

---

1 *The Love of Three Kings* was the only new NBC Opera production in 1962. As noted in the introduction, soaring production costs had landed the company in financial difficulties, and it was disbanded in 1964.

Part Two:

The Other Operas

La Nave
(Premiered at La Scala, Milan, 3 November 1918)

Giovanni Gallurese
(Premiered at the Teatro Vittorio Emanuele, Turin, 28 January 1905)

La Notte di Zoraima
(Premiered at La Scala, Milan, 31 January 1931)

L'Incantesimo
(Premiered at Radio City, New York, 9 October 1943)

Montemezzi at the rehearsals for *Giovanni Gallurese*

The composer, seated, discusses a point with Tullio Serafin (the conductor) and Giuseppe Danise

La Nave

Chicago, The Auditorium Theatre, 18 November 1919

2 performances

Cast:

Basiliola	Rosa Raisa
Marco Gratico	Alessandro Dolci
Sergio Gratico	Giacomo Rimini
Orso Faledro	Vittorio Arimondi
Traba, the monk	Virgilio Lazzari

Director: Cleofonte Campanini
Stage and Costume Design: Norman Bel Geddes
Conductor: Italo Montemezzi

The Auditorium Theatre, Chicago, 1929
The Home of the Chicago Opera Company, 1910–1929

1. Karleton Hackett, *Chicago Evening Post*,
19 November 1919.

Sig. Montemezzi Scores Triumph in His New Opera

It was worth while bringing Montemezzi from away across the water for the opening of our opera season, and Campanini was justified of his works.[1] 'La Nave' is a tremendous score, far too important a work to attempt to grasp at a first hearing, yet one which leaves an indelible impression of power and sincerity. It is a somber drama and somberly told thru the music. The music is a great symphonic poem conceived on broad lines and sustained with force to the magnificent climax of the final act.

Montemezzi is a new voice come out of Italy, tho we already knew something of his force, one with far other aims than the school of the veristi of a generation ago and not even satisfied with the age old ideal of Italian music to charm by melodic grace and stir by dramatic power. He is a poet with a deeper conception of the meaning of music and with a command of his art which permits him to paint with sweeping strokes of power and beauty upon the widest canvas.

The individuals of the drama do not stand forth from the mass as the essential elements of the tale, but rather as the human bubbles floating on the surface of the mighty stream of life. In no modern work for the operatic stage has the chorus played so important a part. Last evening you felt in them the surge of the people, the energy of a race which was to grow into power by its own inherent strength, overcoming whatever of human evil and frailty might impede its path. The opera chorus has been one of the unmanageable

---

1 Hackett's allusion is to Matthew 11:19: 'wisdom is justified of her works.'

elements since the happy old days when it stood contentedly in two unconcerned lines as a mere convention, until composers in despair came frequently to do without it altogether. But Montemezzi had the imagination to find a use for the chorus again, and the swelling volume of choral tone rolled out thru the Auditorium with an elemental power which formed the background of his work.

He gave to the chorus tasks of extreme difficulty, but while difficult the music had meaning and could be sung by human voices after they had been drilled at it long enough. The manner in which the chorus sang last evening was a demonstration of their worth and of the training they have received.

The score was filled with beauty, for Montemezzi has the Italian birthright of spontaneous melody, tho expressed with the utmost freedom of modern thought. Not the graceful tune of pleasant prettiness, but rich, full melodies, singing thru the widest range of contrapuntal weaving and enharmonic change; not merely to delight the ear with passing charm, but to voice the deeper emotions.

One must have time to grow into comprehension of this score. With all its complexities there is power and design therein. The structural quality is there, firm and enduring and so able to wait for full understanding. At a first hearing it sounded as if there were portions of the prolog which might, with benefit, be condensed; and in the first episode, where Montemezzi for the moment got far from the people and the unfolding of the main theme, the music lost something of its vigor. But the last two episodes, or acts, as perhaps they would better be called, were magnificent. Things to hear and to absorb that the full power and beauty of the music might be revealed.

Rosa Raisa sang very beautifully in the prolog in which the music was especially grateful for her voice. Montemezzi has no mercy on his singers, having his own purposes in his mind, and demanding the utmost of which the human voice is capable. Yet he has the instinct for the voice, and while his music makes heavy demands they can be met if the singer have both the natural voice and the acquired skill. Mme. Raisa showed that she had them both. The first episode did not come out so well. The music was not so grateful, and the drama did not tell itself convincingly. If you knew the story you could understand what it was about, but for the general audience which had to catch it mostly by the eye it must have been nearly impossible. The sense of evil was not pervasive. Mme. Raisa must do something about the killing of the poor prisoners with those arrows which she shot from that slimpsy bow. When Eleonora Duse years ago shot those arrows in 'Francesca da Rimini' it seemed to me that she attained the apex of futility in female marksmanship,[1] but Mme. Raisa beat her record last evening. Mme. Raisa is too smart a woman not to find some way out of the difficulty no matter how stringent the police regulations may be about the use of dangerous weapons.

Her costumes were in excellent taste and she made a striking picture to the eye.

Mr. Dolci sang very well and played his part with dignity. Mr. Rimini was excellent. Mr. Arimondi, Mr. Lazzari and Mr. Rogerson deserve special words.[2]

---

1 Eleonora Duse created the title role in D'Annunzio's *Francesca da Rimini* – a play specially written for her – when it was premiered in Rome on 9 December 1901. She later brought it to America, where her company played it in Boston, New York and Chicago between October and December 1902.

2 William Rogerson sang the part of Orio Dedo, the Harbour Master.

Montemezzi rehearsing *La Nave*, 1919
(*L* to *R*) Dolci, Raisa and Rimini

It was rumored yesterday afternoon that quite a little gale had been blowing over the question of the stage settings, which served to heighten the general interest, as well as to show that the opera was functioning normally. When there is no excitement about an opera-house you may be sure that the organization is pretty nearly dead, consequently it was good news to hear that things were lively back of the stage.

As far as I am concerned, the stage settings were most gratifying to the eye, imaginatively conceived and making beautiful pictures. The setting for the prolog was symbolic of the ship and aided the audience in getting into the poetic mood. The ship of the final scene was quite a triumph of stagecraft, a tremendous affair which filled the entire stage, yet when the time came it moved down to the sea with impressive steadiness. Doubtless the settings were quite different from what Montemezzi expected, and perhaps another manner of doing the thing would have been just as effective and more to his mind. But as far as I am concerned Mr. Norman-Bel Geddes was entirely successful in his undertaking save for the technicality that he hardly left enough free space for the people on the stage. At times they had to be crowded together in a manner which must have taken considerable figuring on by the stage manager, but they were finally grouped into striking stage pictures.

Montemezzi received several ovations, especially after the first act, in which the singers had their full share. The performance was under his direction, and he showed genuine force as a conductor.

Of course 'everybody' was present, and there was a general air that the opera had begun this year under the most favorable conditions. There was not a vacant seat in the house and no tickets had been purchasable for days.

'La Nave' will be repeated next Monday evening, and if you wish to hear something of unusual power, something which will give you food for thought, you would better go.

William L. Hubbard
The most respected of the Chicago critics

2. William L. Hubbard, *Chicago Daily Tribune*, 19 November 1919.[1]

Composer Of 'La Nave' A 'Hit' As Opera Opens

Encores for Him and Raisa Testify to Audience's Approval

BRILLIANT, INTERESTING, successful. Thus might be described the opening night of the Chicago grand opera at the Auditorium last evening. An audience brilliant as no audience has been since wartime came was in attendance. An opera presented for the first time in America lent especial interest to the musical side of the evening. Successful were both performance and its reception by the audience so far as all the factors of the presentation itself and the applause bestowed on it were concerned. The audience came late, at least the major portion of it, but it all was there when the first intermission was at hand. At 8.12 a tall, slender, dark complexioned man appeared at the right of the orchestra pit, advanced quietly to the conductor's desk, and picked up the baton. He was Italo Montemezzi, the composer of 'The Ship' ('La Nave'), which was to receive its American premiere, and of 'The Love of Three Kings,' which has deservedly won high place in public esteem.

---

1 Hubbard considered *L'Amore dei Tre Re* to be 'the most sincere, most powerful, and most beautiful opera any modern Italian has given the world.' See his review, 'Mary Garden, in Italian Opera, Sings Brilliantly,' *Chicago Daily Tribune*, 10 January 1920, 13. He wrote a second review of *La Nave* for the *Chicago Sunday Tribune*, 23 November 1919. This can be found in the companion volume, *Essays On The Montemezzi-D'Annunzio 'Nave,'* 2nd edition, ed. David Chandler (Norwich: Durrant, 2014), 183–87.

He was recognized immediately and applause, spontaneous, hearty, and long continued, told him he was a welcome and honored guest. And throughout the evening after every curtain he not only shared with the singers the approval, but was given many recalls alone. It is said to have been the first time that the young Italian composer has conducted an operatic performance in public. There was never an evidence of this in his work last evening. He directs quietly and unostentatiously, but with a clarity of beat, a decision and with a fine supervision of both singers and instrumentalists that tell of the conductor born instead of made.

The orchestra flood that at times overwhelmed was due to no whipping up of the instrumentalists. Only by writing more lightly could this have been avoided. The fault must be charged, therefore, to the composer and not the conductor.

The audience received the new work and its presenting company with liberal evidences of approval. The recalls for Rosa Raisa, Mr. Dolci, and Mr. Rimini and their associates were numerous after every act, and while many in the public doubtless had little or no idea what the performance on the stage was really about dramatically, the pictures and the costuming were sufficiently gorgeous and novel to hold interest and arouse enthusiasm. For Mr. Norman-Bel Geddes, who mounted the opera, has supplied a scenic enframement that is strongly colorful, essentially modern, and generally appealing in its beauty and design.

Whether it is a setting best suited to the operatic needs of 'The Ship' is a question which may be left to later discussion.[1]

---

[1] Hubbard discussed it at greater length in his second review, where he strongly faulted its 'misapplied beauty.' *Essays On The Montemezzi-D'Annunzio 'Nave,'* 186–87.

It suffices tonight that all the scenes are impressive and compelling in their coloring and effect, and that the one in the Temple[1] and the final one showing the launching of the great vessel are truly exceptional.

As for the opera itself it consists of a prologue and three acts or episodes as they are styled. Only one of these is genuinely effective from grand opera viewpoint. This act, the one in the temple, has action and the clear elemental passions and their revealment that are essential for successful grand opera drama, especially where that drama is presented in language foreign to the hearer. The three other acts are talk instead of action and they therefore fail in effect.

Only by close studying of libretto and patient preparation could the public know what was being done on the stage, and it is but the tiny minority of our opera goers that troubles thus to prepare. The audience last night accepted all with the show of interest that becomes a well mannered grand opera audience, but only when some killing arrived in the third act did genuine attention and life make themselves felt. A drama which is written in the D'Annunzio manner with infinite attention to detail and filled with symbolism is not material for effective grand opera and if 'The Ship' fails to endure, it will be because the libretto is not suited for operatic use. The Montemezzi score is interesting, colorful, and contains much of beauty. It has abundant melody of the short phrased shifting kind that the majority of the modern scores contain and which is so skillfully used in the same composer's 'Love of Three Kings.'

---

1 The Second Episode, set in the Basilica.

These melodies are handled with admirable feeling for fine instrumental color and for the orchestral effect that enhances and intensifies dramatic action and emotion on the stage. It is music which must be heard more than once to estimate accurately its worth, but it may be set down at once as being interesting, effective, and often sensuously appealing.

The cast was a large one, but the weight of the performance rested chiefly on Rosa Raisa, Mr. Dolci, and Mr. Rimini. Miss Raisa as Basiliola, the avenging daughter, who turns seductress in order to achieve her purpose, had a rôle vocally intensely difficult and dramatically exacting. The music lies persistently high and only the splendid voice and exceptional skill of a Raisa could compass it as brilliantly as did she last night. In action the rôle lies outside the gifted soprano's best powers. The enchantress is not her line, and while she acted with intelligence and devotion, she did not convince.

Mr. Dolci sang the trying music of Marco with excellent tonal fullness and authority and acted the part acceptably. Mr. Rimini did not have so much to do as did his two associates, but he acted and sang in praise meriting fashion. Mr. Arimondi was excellent as the blind Orso, William Rogerson satisfactory as the Master, Mr. Lazzaro [sic] a thoroughly satisfactory Monk, and Arthur Boardman capital as Guaro.

3. Herman Devries, *Chicago American*, 19 November 1919.

Montemezzi and Rosa Raisa Win Honors in 'La Nave'; Opera Criticized

WHEN, IN OCTOBER, 1915, I reviewed in this column 'L'Amore dei Tre Re' upon its initial performance with the Boston Grand Opera Company at the Auditorium Theater, I said among other things:

'"L'Amore dei Tre Re," presented in Chicago for the first time last night, introduces to the local musical world a young Wagner.

'Ironical as it may appear, the crown of the great Teuton genius seems destined to repose on the brow of a Latin, Montemezzi.

'Will the name place Italy again upon the tablets of musical history as the torch bearer of a new and powerful creator?'[1]

After hearing 'La Nave' last night in its American premiere for the opening of the 1919–1920 Chicago season, I must in all honesty place my preference and my profound admiration with 'L'Amore dei Tre Re.'

Montemezzi's pretentious and stupendous 'Ship' does not transfer the musical affections one whit from the other opera's opulent beauty, inspiration and romantic appeal – for 'La Nave' has none of these.

Commands Consideration

And yet 'La Nave' commands consideration in its amazing formation. That a human brain could have conceived and

---

1 As noted above, *L'Amore dei Tre Re* was given its Chicago premiere on 6 October 1915, so Devries' review presumably appeared in the *Chicago American* the following day. Two or three issues of the paper were printed each day and unfortunately the one chosen for preservation and microfilming does not include the review.

accomplished so immense an orchestration, so complex a construction, so monumental a feat of technique, is unbelievable.

But we should not have heard 'La Nave' with singers and scenery. It would set more fittingly within the strings and the brasses of our orchestra. For 'La Nave' in my humble opinion is not an opera. It is a symphony.

'L'Amore dei Tre Re' rouses the longing for a rehearing. The more one listens to it, the more one wishes to hear it again.

Will 'La Nave' quicken that same desire? I doubt it, as I doubt that it will see as many performances as its lovely and more pliant predecessor.

However, let this be said – tradition presents many a tale wherein an initial hoot turned to applause. Many a first performance of what now stands immortal in music was greeted with unkindest criticism.

Perhaps in the case of 'La Nave' first criticism may not necessarily mean prophecy.

Montemezzi A Genius

Certain it is that Italo Montemezzi is a great musical genius.

He conducted his opera like the distinguished man of music he is.

He brought to his baton distinction, passion, energy and the orchestra responded gloriously.

First honors among the artists must go to that superb young soprano, Rosa Raisa. Not one bit burdened with the fact that Montemezzi has written his music for a soprano machine rather than for a soprano human, Miss Raisa sang the trying role of Basiliola with grace, charm, and glorious tone. Her matchless voice was again a ringing wonder of volume and luscious quality.

Her Basiliola was a magnificent piece of artistry – and her costumes revelations in rich color and design.

Rosa Raisa as Basiliola

Alessandro Dolci, who seemed slightly fatigued in the Prologue, rose excellently to the vocal requirements of the role of Marco in the last acts.

As for Giacomo Rimini, he is always the earnest, reliable, satisfying artist.

Although the role assigned to Virgilio Lazzari lies a trifle high for a basso, his fine, robust voice carried the dire music of 'Il Monaco Traba' splendidly.

Vittorio Arimondi, always a dependable artist, sang the few phrases of the blind Orso Faledro with authority.

Minor Parts Well Taken

The minor parts were all in excellent hands. Special mention is due Desire Defrere for his ringing tones in the Prologue.[1]

The audience packed the house from pit to dome and recalled the artists and the composer many times after each act. After the second act they brought with them Pietro Nepoti, the excellent chorus master, who is to be warmly lauded for the work of his men and women.

They were not a chorus – they were stars.

'La Nave' is richly mounted. The third act, Atrium of the Basilica, was a gorgeous spectacle and the finale, with its monster ship, was a very definite accomplishment in scenic wonder.

In closing, let me not forget to wish to our generalissimo, Cleofonte Campanini, a fruitful season.

---

1 Desire Defrere (1888–1964), a Belgian baritone who would have a long and distinguished career in America, had sung the role of the Boatswain's Voice (La Voce Del Còmito) heard at the very beginning of *La Nave*.

4. **Unsigned review attributed to Jeannette Cox,**
Musical Courier, 20 November 1919.

Chicago Hears American Premiere of 'La Nave'

CHICAGO, NOVEMBER 19, 1919. – Years succeed years and generally they seem alike. This state of things was true before 1914. The opening of an operatic season was yearly similar in brilliancy before 1914, but during the years of war a sort of gloom over the public mind was reflected in the more sombre vestments worn by the fashionable ladies of this city. After the rain, sunshine – after gloom, happiness; and the opening of the 1919–1920 season at the Auditorium was glorious. The society editor of the Musical Courier informed the writer that the gowns, furs and jewels displayed at the Auditorium on Tuesday evening, November 18, were the most magnificent ever seen in the home of opera in Chicago. More pleasant to record was that among the many auditors were recognized most of Chicago's leading musicians, who showed by their presence that money was plentiful among the tonal fraternity, as not only had they bought seats, but their garments and jewels compared most favorably with those worn by society leaders. For the opening night, General Manager Maestro Campanini decided to present a novelty composed by one of Italy's best known musicians – Italo Montemezzi, who at the conductor's desk presided over the destinies of 'La Nave' ('The Ship'), which had its world première at La Scala, Milan, last November.

The Plot

'La Nave' is a lyric drama in three episodes and a prologue. It is based on a drama in blank verse by Gabrielle [sic]

D'Annunzio, Italy's greatest poet of the present day. In preparing the libretto for Montemezzi's music, Tito Ricordi was forced to sacrifice three thousand lines, but it seems that by so doing he still thought he was able to maintain the action and the proper developments of the tragedy. 'The Ship' symbolizes the early struggles and the early successes of the Venetian state. In its properly dramatic circumference it deals with the passion of the two brothers Gratici for a woman, Basiliola, who remembers that her four brothers have had their eyes plucked out because of their surreptitious dealings with the Greeks. She swears bitter vengeance against the two brothers who are enemies of her house and succeeds in playing havoc by means of her own beauty and charm. Sacrilege, sin, and fratricide follow in the wake of her passion; but in the end righteousness wins over lust, and the woman pays the penalty of sin, while Venice continues once again on her way towards greatness, opulence and happiness. Those who believe that no musical drama could hold in itself any political significance would have only to hear 'La Nave' to think differently, as D'Annunzio, the propagandist, most assuredly had visions of Fiume when he wrote 'La Nave.'[1] Yet so well covered is the plot that only by minute inspection can it be realized that such dramas are conceived upon political inspiration.

The brothers, Marco and Sergio Gratico, are Venice in the allegory, and Basiliola is the woman who represents all the ills that may kill Venice in its birth. Listen to the last lines of the chorus:

---

[1] This is true only in the most general sense. D'Annunzio had long believed in the rights of Italy to the former Venetian possessions, but had shown no specific interest in Fiume before August 1919. John Woodhouse points out that 'he had not harped upon the name of Fiume as he had in the case of other "lost" cities' (*Gabriele D'Annunzio: Defiant Archangel* [Oxford: Clarendon P, 1998], 317).

Designs for the Prologue and Third Episode
Norman Bel Geddes

> Our country is on the ship!
> O Lord our God, redeem the Adriatic!
> Restore the Adriatic to Thy people!
> Give the Adriatic to the Venetians!
> Hallelujah! Christ shall reign!
> Christ and San Marco!
> Christ and Santo Ermagora![1]

With that final chorus the ship, boarded by Marco Gratico and his chosen comrades[,] glides into the water amid the exultation of the whole populace while the curtain falls and leaves the public amazed, not quite understanding the ambiguous plot; but those who had read the libretto carefully understood, and found behind 'La Nave' not only D'Annunzio the poet, but D'Annunzio the Italian patriot.

[An extended summary of the plot.]

This lengthy story of the plot was necessary as, even with it, those who do not understand Italian will have great difficulty in following the story. D'Annunzio is the Shakespeare of the day. He coins words, and indeed, it has been reported that there is today in Italy a D'Annunzio dictionary,[2] so no wonder the Auditorium audience was somewhat bewildered as to what was taking place on the stage.

The Music

Italo Montemezzi, best known in America by his 'L'Amore dei tre Re,' has written several other operas and symphonic works, and if, as prophesied here, 'La Nave' should have a short life on

---

[1] The quotation is from R. H. Elkin's translation of the libretto, slightly adapted.

[2] The scholar Giuseppe Lando Passerini (1862–1932) had indeed published *Il Vocabolario della Poesia Dannunziana* (1912) and *Il Vocabolario della Prosa Dannunziana* (1913).

the operatic stage, the fault will not be with the composer but with the librettist, as Montemezzi has written a masterpiece in this new opera. Probably a great admirer of Richard Wagner and Richard Strauss, Montemezzi, the great Italian composer, speaks Teutonically musically. He has written themes for every chorus. For instance, there is a carpenter theme, a sail maker's, and particularly one given to the millers – all combined in tremendous action. Then there is a seductive theme given to Basiliola, which on close examination resembles greatly that given to Salome in Richard Strauss's opera of that name, and there are many pages given to the tenor that demonstrates Montemezzi a fervent admirer of the man that made Bayreuth famous. A master musician, Montemezzi's orchestration is stupendous. Closely woven is his music. At times a stray melodious phrase is given to the singers or to the woodwind or strings, but more generally following the modern ideas in writing, Montemezzi is scrupulously symphonic in his treatment of the score. To him the singers are only part of his orchestra. He virtually sacrifices them, using them to add color to his tonal scheme. His musical palette is tinged with rainbow colors, mostly brilliant but at times sombre, and then his music is uninspired and even tedious. There isn't a single passage in the opera that will in the common term of the word become popular. There isn't a phrase that will be whistled. There isn't an excerpt from the opera that will ever be sung on the concert platform. There is nothing in it to popularize the opera, but there is a great deal that will make the musicians happy, as in it they will find many puzzles and problems well worth discovering. By his 'La Nave,' which is far inferior in the mind of this humble writer to his 'L'Amore dei tre Re,' Montemezzi has won added fame as an ultra-modern composer.

The Cast

'The days of the giants have gone by,' so they say, but giants are demanded by Montemezzi to sing his new work. It takes a Raisa for the role of Basiliola. She won, with the composer-conductor, first honors of the evening. The role is stupendous in its demand on the vocal chords. Written extremely high for the voice, Miss Raisa encompassed all the difficulties with the greatest ease. Her stentorian voice dominated over the orchestra even in climaxes which succeed repeatedly one another, testing the full vocal faculties of the singer, but Miss Raisa never flinched. She sang gloriously all through the opera, pouring out her golden tones with as great volubility at the close of the evening as she did at the beginning – a remarkable feat indeed when one is acquainted with the score. Dressed gorgeously, she made an alluring and seductive Basiliola, and histrionically she did admirable things. If the role of Basiliola demands a powerful voice, the same is true of the role of Marco, given to the tenor Dolci, one of the most popular tenors who have graced the Auditorium stage, an excellent musician who found the part of Marco Gratico a little too heavy for him, as it requires a Tamagno[1] to sustain the burden placed on the tenor by Montemezzi. That Dolci did as well as he did by the role is indeed a great credit to him, and it may be stated that no tenor of the day heard by this writer could have done better than he did, yet truly his voice sounded too light, as it is a lyric organ of great beauty, while a robusto tenor voice would make the role stand out in better light.

Sergio Gratico was capitally represented in the hands of Giacomo Rimini. He made the part live in the minds of the public, and vocally Mr. Rimini had seldom been heard to such advantage. His voice since last year has taken on much volume and he made the role stand out big in the episodes in which he figured.

Especially words of praise are due the work of Virgilio Lazzari as the Monk, although the part is not a big one. It was so effectively done as to make a great impression on the hearers, and the same may well be said of Orso Faledro, given to Vittorio

---

1 Francesco Tamagno (1850–1905), the Italian tenor who created the part of Verdi's Otello. His heroic voice was extremely powerful in its upper registers.

Cleofonte Campanini, 1913
Director of *La Nave* who brought
Montemezzi to America

Arimondi, who as ever made his presence felt. The other roles are so small as to necessitate no comment, yet they were entrusted to many popular singers of the company, including Constantin Nicolay, Vittorio Trevisan, Desire Defrere and Emma Noe.[1]

Italo Montemezzi, contrary to the general rule of composers being poor conductors, is quite efficient with the stick, and he made a stunning picture in the orchestral pit, conducting with great authority, elasticity and decision. After each episode, as well as after the prologue, he and the principal artists were recalled many times before the curtain.

Words of praise are due the chorus and orchestra, who were excellent, and they too should receive more attention from the reviewer, but space forbids giving them their due outside of stating once more that they were up to the high standard demanded from this opera company.

The only black spot in the opera was the scenery arranged by Norman-Bel Geddes. Even with a stretch of imagination it was impossible to understand what Mr. Geddes devised as the arsenal, for instance.[2] That scene, already difficult to understand for those who do not comprehend Italian, was made even more so by the picture presented by Mr. Geddes. Other scenes likewise were blurred in the minds of the people, due to scenic effects which hardly were in accord with the book. The launching of the ship was the best effect of the evening, but retrieved only in part the bad impression produced by previous scenes. The stage management, however, was not at fault and under prevailing conditions did itself proud.

---

[1] These singers sang the parts, respectively, of Lucio Polo the pilot, Simon D'Armario, the Boatswain's Voice, and 'The Voice.'

[2] This is a puzzling comment for D'Annunzio nowhere refers to an arsenal. It is most likely to refer to a misunderstanding of the scene with the pit in the First Episode.

Giovanni Gallurese

New York, Metropolitan Opera House, 19 February 1925

4 performances

Philadelphia, Academy of Music, 24 March 1925

1 performance

Cast:
Giovanni Gallurese... Giacomo Lauri-Volpi
Maria .... Maria Mueller (Müller)
Rivegas .... Giuseppe Danise
Nuvis, an old miller .. Giovanni Martino[1]

Director: Samuel Thewman
Stage and Costume Design: Giovanni Grandi
Conductor: Tullio Serafin

---

[1] In the Philadelphia performance Louis D'Angelo sang the part of Nuvis.

FIRE NOTICE.—LOOK AROUND *NOW* AND CHOOSE THE NEAREST EXIT TO YOUR SEAT. IN CASE OF FIRE, WALK (*NOT RUN*) TO *THAT EXIT*. DO *NOT* TRY TO BEAT YOUR NEIGHBOR TO THE STREET.   *Thomas J. Drennan, Fire Commissioner.*

METROPOLITAN OPERA HOUSE
GRAND OPERA SEASON 1924~1925
GIULIO GATTI-CASAZZA, GENERAL MANAGER

THURSDAY EVENING, FEBRUARY 19TH, AT 8.15 O'CLOCK

FIRST PERFORMANCE IN AMERICA

GIOVANNI GALLURESE
OPERA IN THREE ACTS
BY FRANCESCO D'ANGELANTONIO
(IN ITALIAN)
MUSIC BY ITALO MONTEMEZZI

GIOVANNI GALLURESE	GIACOMO LAURI-VOLPI
MARIA, DAUGHTER OF	MARIA MUELLER
NUVIS, AN OLD MILLER	GIOVANNI MARTINO
RIVEGAS, A CATALAN	GIUSEPPE DANISE
BASTIANO, COMRADE OF GIOVANNI	ANGELO BADA
A SPANISH OFFICER	MILLO PICCO
JOSE } HIRED FOLLOWERS OF RIVEGAS	{ ADAMO DIDUR
TROPEÁ }	{ VINCENZO RESCHIGLIAN
DON PASQUALE, INNKEEPER	POMPILIO MALATESTA
A SHEPHERD'S VOICE	MERLE ALCOCK

FOLLOWERS OF GIOVANNI, SPANISH SOLDIERS, MILITIA, PEASANTS AND POPULACE

Act II.—1. DANZA MONTANARA by FLORENCE RUDOLPH and CORPS DE BALLET.
 2. DANZA SARDA by ROSINA GALLI, Premiere Danseuse, and GIUSEPPE BONFIGLIO.
Dances Devised and Arranged by ROSINA GALLI

CONDUCTOR	TULLIO SERAFIN
STAGE DIRECTOR	SAMUEL THEWMAN
CHORUS MASTER	GIULIO SETTI
TECHNICAL DIRECTOR	EDWARD SIEDLE
STAGE MANAGER	ARMANDO AGNINI

NEW SCENIC PRODUCTION BY GIOVANNI GRANDI

Positively No Encores Allowed

PROGRAMME CONTINUED ON NEXT PAGE
CORRECT LIBRETTOS FOR SALE IN THE LOBBY
Hardman Piano Used Exclusively

1. William J. Henderson, *Sun*, 20 February 1925.

'Giovanni Gallurese' Premiere

Maestro Montemezzi's First Opera Is Produced at the Metropolitan

'GIOVANNI GALLURESE,' opera in three acts, book by Francesco d'Angelantonio, music by Italo Montemezzi, was performed at the Metropolitan Opera House last evening for the first time in this country.

The production was attended by a numerous audience and there was very much applause. But applause in the Metropolitan Opera House means less than it does in any other theater in the city since such large measure of it originates in partisanship. However, the new work deserved all it received, for it is an opera which, in spite of a banal libretto, contains much good and some beautiful music.

'Giovanni Gallurese' is Maestro Montemezzi's first opera.[1] It was produced in Turin in 1905. The story of the work has been told in this place.[2] The librettist fashioned it from the suggestions of a few venerable legends about a noble and untrammeled spirit which once haunted the crags of Sardinia, defying the laws of the Spanish usurper and occasionally from some secret eyrie potting a passing tyrant or two and using the proceeds to aid the deserving paupers of his country.

In the opera this Mediterranean Robin Hood has fallen in love with *Maria*, whom one *Rivegas* (inevitably a barytone) abducts. *Giovanni* rescues her only to learn that she thinks she has

---

1 This claim was made by many of the American critics, though in fact Montemezzi had earlier written the unperformed, one-act *Bianca* (1901).

2 Henderson's anticipatory feature on the opera, '"Giovanni Galurese" [sic] Thursday,' had been published in the *Sun*, 14 February, 4.

been carried off by the unspeakable *Gallurese*, whose very name fills her with horror. So the gallant rescuer gives a false name and the certain love duet follows.

Old Fashioned Libretto

Of course in the second act the barytone tells the tenor's real name and the maiden flees from his embraces. In the last act she buries her horror under an avalanche of mountain love and the barytone kills the tenor. It is all old fashioned opera libretto, of course, but it contains the well seasoned distribution of passions and motives which generations of composers have sung in musical or unmusical strains. One even thinks for the moment of *Ernani* who was also a high souled bandit, had a potent horn swinging at his side, and miserably perished in the last act.[1]

It was not in such surroundings that the muse of Montemezzi was to sing her deathless hymn. The libretto of this youthful opera is a workmanlike achievement, but out of such materials great lyric scores are seldom developed. Yet if this were the first of Montemezzi's works to be heard here, there would be a general proclamation of pleasure at the advent of a new talent.

The misfortune of 'Giovanni Gallurese' will be the insistent comparison of its art with that of 'l'Amore dei Tre Re.' Such a comparison will yield no valuable information and will work injustice to the early score. The opera just produced was first performed twenty years ago, or eight years before the tragedy of the three kings. The gropings of a young maestro after an individual medium of expression are perceptible. He faces the setting sun and the rising, and from neither does he get the glory of noon.

---

1 *Ernani*, Verdi's 1844 opera, based on a play by Victor Hugo. Several of the American critics of *Giovanni Gallurese* evoked a comparison with *Ernani*, which had been revived at the Met in 1921.

**Giovanni Gallurese (Lauri-Volpi),
Maria (Müller) and Nuvis (Martino) in Act 3**
The moment after Gallurese and Maria decide to marry

One hears occasionally the voice of the Verdi of swashbuckler days. Here and there is an echo of Ponchielli. And the shadow of Rossini, which crossed the path of almost every Italian composer after his day, sometimes stalks with ghostly tread among the peaks of Punta Bianca Spina.[1] But none the less the opera is made by a musician already in command of the technics of dramatic music, and the individual style of the later Montemezzi is frequently prominent.

Airs Have Firmness of Texture

In the weaving of the web there is no wavering, no uncertainty, no misfire. The dialogue is set forth in a vigorous and flexible recitative, the airs have firmness of texture, and clearness of melodic outline, the choruses are alive and proclaim themselves essential parts of the drama. The ensembles are written with boldness and a confident employment of the type of polyphony long established in Italy as the most adaptable to the stage.

Of course the opulence of opportunity in the second act is illusory. A party of convivial spirits at the *bettola*[2] on the right of the stage, the actors in the drama in the center, the choir in the church on the left, the villagers fringing the scene, and soldiers filing about are all parts of an ancient and well lubricated operatic machine. But Montemezzi handled it as if he had been sitting in the chauffeur's seat for a decade instead of for the first time in his career.

The promise of the future creator of 'Come tremi, diletto'[3] is heard first in the brazen proclamation which begins the score, the *Giovanni Gallurese* motif. This is one of the few definite

---

1 The highest summit in Sardinia.

2 Tavern.

3 'How you tremble, beloved.' Fiora's first words to Avito after their rapturous kiss in Act 2 of *L'Amore dei Tre Re*.

and purposeful attempts in the opera at representative themes. It is a passage which eloquently voices the patriotism and the pathos of the principal personage in the drama. It recurs with expressiveness when the outlaw gives *Maria* a false name, and with dramatic poignancy at the moment when *Gallurese*, in the midst of his most desperate trials, reveals fully the fineness of his nature. The melodic, harmonic and instrumental style of this theme are in a manner which became more familiar in the maestro's later creations. There is also a clearly demarked theme for the villain and others of less importance.

Duet Extremely Melodious

The duet which concludes the first act and which is a piece of supremely beautiful melody, is very much advanced toward the style of 1913. And throughout the opera the observant hearer will note phrases and especially cadences which came to be distinguishing marks of the true Montemezzi utterance. That this juvenile score would display the same penetration into the method of expression, the same nice choice of means, the same economy of material and the same extraordinary elevation of style was not to be expected.

But as already said, 'Giovanni Gallurese' must be judged by itself and not by comparison with 'l'Amore dei Tre Re.' Few modern Italian operas would stand that. This production of a young writer is indisputably the creation of a man of the theater, a musician whose whole mental bent is toward the construction of dramatic scores. He is plainly the child of Italy's three centuries of devotion to the lyric drama. And his music sings voluptuously. His pedestal is in the orchestra, his statue on the stage. There is no page in this score which stumbles in its movement. On the contrary an opulent vigor and a palpitating vitality often effectually disguise the conventionality of the material.

The impression made by the work as a whole is of a creation admirable in general construction, but as yet unformed in style, brilliant in spots, seldom weak or tremulous, and luxuriously vocal. There is no moment when the music rises to the heights of ecstasy reached by the maestro in 'l'Amore,' or sinks to depths of agonizing woe, but it is in general saturated with dramatic feeling and with the singular Italian instinct for theatrical style.

Instrumentation Is Admirable

The instrumentation is admirable, if not finished, in its methods. That of the same composer's later work exhibits a more fastidious choice of means. This leans toward the honored conventions of the modern opera house. Nevertheless it is always appropriate and often heightens the significance of the scene. The pictorial investiture of the work is inevitably stereotyped. Outlaws or brigands, mountains and pious peasantry offer little opportunity to escape from the peaks and valleys of 'La Sonnambula,' 'Dinorah' and 'William Tell,'[1] and the scene painter might have designed his three sets fifty years ago. However those which he has given us serve their purpose and might have been made somewhat more effective by the use of less antiquated methods of lighting than those employed at the Metropolitan.

About the performance not much need be said at present. Tullio Serafin conducted the work when it had its first performance in 1905 and he had the baton last night. He and Montemezzi were fellow students and have worked together in many things since the composer has been here at all the rehearsals. Yet this observer could not help feeling that the opera would have been

---

1 Operas by Bellini (1831), Meyerbeer (1859), and Rossini (1829), respectively. *Dinorah*, also evoked by Deems Taylor (see below, p. 258), had been revived at the Met on 22 January 1925.

Giuseppe Bonfiglio and Rosina Galli, the principal dancers in Act 2
Dressed in traditional Sardinian costume

helped by a little more vivacity in tempo here and there. The breath of life was never put into 'l'Amore' till Toscanini speeded up its movement, and since he dropped the baton it has never had quite the same thrill.[1]

Mr. Lauri-Volpi as the central figure was not satisfying either pictorially or vocally. His impersonation was wooden and his singing was often out of tune and badly phrased. Miss Maria Mueller sang the music of *Maria*, the heroine, commendably, but doubtless she was hampered by her first venture with Italian. She was not an ideal soprano for the part. Mr. Danise had a most unfavorable role in *Rivegas* and could make little of it. Mr. Martino discharged well his duties as *Nuvis*, the girl's father, and Mr. Bada was excellent as *Bastiano*, companion of *Giovanni*. There was some enjoyable dancing, with Miss Galli as the principal. Mr. Montemezzi was called before the curtain many times.

---

[1] Toscanini resigned his position as artistic director of the Met in 1915. Montemezzi himself, it may be noted, was opposed to Toscanini's 'speeding up' of *L'Amore dei Tre Re*.

2. Deems Taylor, *World*, 20 February 1925.

At The Metropolitan

IF 'GIOVANNI GALLURESE' had been heard here twenty years ago, when it was written, one might have said that it was a highly promising work by a hitherto unknown young Italian composer. Having heard it last night, instead, one can no longer call Montemezzi unknown, but one can still call his opera highly promising.

For it is astonishing to see how strongly 'Giovanni Gallurese' foreshadows 'L'Amore dei Tre Re.' Both scores exhibit the same simplicity of melodic and harmonic plan – a simplicity that does not keep the music from being strongly individual – the same talent for mirroring the dramatic action in the orchestra, and the same purity of taste and good sense of proportion.

'Gallurese' is merely not quite so individual, and does not attain the same sweep and poignancy of feeling as 'L'Amore dei Tre Re.' Considered purely as music, it is better than much of Puccini, and infinitely above the usual run of contemporary opera music by lesser lights.

But as an operatic entity 'Giovanni Gallurese' does not measure up so well. For two reasons, both connected with the book. It has a commonplace libretto, and the music does not fit the libretto in the only sense that would make it effective.

Another Outlaw

The story savors strongly of 'Ernani.'[1] Giovanni Gallurese, described masterfully in the libretto as 'a high-souled outlaw,' operating in Sardinia during the Spanish oppression of the seventeenth century, is in love with a shepherd's daughter, Maria,[2]

---

1 See above, p. 250, n. 1.
2 Maria is in fact a miller's daughter.

whom he rescues from an attempted abduction by the local Spanish tyrant, Rivegas. Maria, who reciprocates Giovanni's passion, does not know who he is, and thinks that Rivegas is Gallurese, whose very name she fears and hates. Whereupon the high-souled outlaw, attacked by the form of operatic imbecility that makes second acts possible, pretends that he is a simple shepherd lad.

Later, Giovanni and his followers rout the Spaniards and capture Rivegas, who blurts out Giovanni's name in front of Maria, who promptly recoils in horror. But the maiden eventually gets used to the fact that her lover is the Robin Hood of his day, especially after she sees how good he is to the poor. Just as the pair are preparing to fly to some safer land the scoundrelly Rivegas, whom Giovanni has imprudently released, shoots his liberator. Gallurese, desperately wounded, proceeds to sing himself to death, and Maria swoons upon his corpse in approved operatic style.

Not only is this story rather old hat, but it is written in the conventional recitative aria form of the middle Verdi period. Montemezzi's score, however, attempts to accompany it in the continuous style of post-Wagnerian music drama, with the result that the music is constantly at war with the libretto, so far as form is concerned.

The opening scenes last night, for instance, exhibited three characters entering, coming to the centre of the stage and explaining themselves to the audience in three separate arias, much in the fashion of 'Dinorah' or any other relic.[1] The music, however, obstinately refused to bow to this convention, so that the audience (or at least its more Latin constituents) kept breaking in with applause that the composer would not wait for.

'Giovanni Gallurese' is, therefore, neither good old-fashioned grand opera nor altogether effective music drama. Last night's

---

1 See above, p. 254, n. 1.

audience received it with loud signs of approval, but its effect upon future, less obviously friendly gatherings, is somewhat debatable.

A Competent Cast

The cast was fairly good but by no means brilliant. Mr. Lauri-Volpi did not seem to be entirely familiar with his role for he bungled his first entrance and made several minor slips during the evening. He was also inclined to shout a good deal and sang off pitch a considerable portion of the time. Mr. Danise was a vocally good, albeit rather subdued Rivegas. Miss Mueller sang with skill and sincerity but without much forcefulness. Her voice seemed a bit light for the role of Maria.

Nobody did much acting, except Miss Mueller, who was a convincing peasant girl, and Mr. Bada, who, as usual, turned a 'bit' into an achievement.[1] Most of the other principals confided their thoughts and passions exclusively to Mr. Serafin. The latter, by the way, gave a splendidly vitalized reading of the score.

The chorus sang exceptionally well and the ballets, while simple, were well conceived and effectively executed. The scenery was old-fashioned and uninteresting.

Mr. Montemezzi was in the audience and was called before the curtain after all three acts. After the second act he received an enormous laurel wreath, beribboned with the Italian colors. Mr. Serafin and Giulio Setti, the chorus master, shared the curtain calls with the cast.

---

1 Angelo Bada, a tenor, sang the part of Bastiano, Giovanni Gallurese's comrade.

Olin Downes, 1925
A central figure in Montemezzi's American reception

3. Olin Downes, *New York Times*, 20 February 1925.*

Montemezzi's Early Opera

THE PERFORMANCE of Italo Montemezzi's 'Giovanni Gallurese' last night by the Metropolitan Opera Company was the first presentation of this work in America. The occasion was given further distinction by the presence of the composer, called before the curtain after each act with overwhelming demonstration of enthusiasm, including wild cheers and bravos; sharing these tributes with the principal singers, with Tullio Serafin, the conductor; Mr. Setti, the admirable chorus master; Mr. Thewman, stage manager, and others of the Metropolitan staff who had contributed to the production.

This opera is Montemezzi's first work for the stage. It saw the light in Turin in 1905, when Mr. Serafin, as last night, led the performance. Only eight years separated it from 'L'Amore dei tre re,' the work on which the composer's reputation up to the present time has rested. A very important fact in the success of 'L'Amore dei tre re' was its superb libretto, a characteristic the opera does not share with 'Giovanni Gallurese.' 'Giovanni Gallurese' is an admirable example of [the] profound difference which a good or bad libretto exerts upon the product of the composer, and it is also of historic interest, as showing the astonishing evolution of Montemezzi from this early work to the achievement of the noble opera that was soon to follow.

The libretto of 'Gallurese' is the work of Francesco d'Angelantonio, a young Sicilian poet, a youth of means and ideals, but immature and probably without expert knowledge of

---

* © 1925 The New York Times. All rights reserved. Used by permission and protected by the Copyright Laws of the United States. The printing, copying, redistribution, or retransmission of this Content without express written permission is prohibited.

the stage when he planned his work. For the plot and situation are very naïve, and are not always adapted for musical treatment; the book expresses little that is real or varied in dramatic interest; it alternates between sentimentality and bald melodramatic romanticism. Giovanni Gallurese is one of the patriotic outlaws of Sardinia, nobly born, and in revolt against the tyranny of the Spanish invasion of the seventeenth century. He loves Maria, daughter of Nuvis, the miller. Gallurese is pursued by the treacherous Spaniard, Rivegas, who, of course, also desires Maria. In the first act Gallurese, whose name is the terror of the countryside, delivers Maria from the attempt of Rivegas to betray her. He proclaims his love and is rewarded by the passionate embraces of that lady.

This part of the opera has little action, consisting mainly of solos and a love duet. The second act is better for stage purposes. It shows a church and an inn, characteristic of many Italian operas, especially since 'Cavalleria Rusticana.' There are drinking choruses and religious choruses, much by-play, a vivid ensemble. There is the dancing of folk dances of the country. [Summary of the rest of the plot.]

As we have said, the interest and distinction of this opera lie principally in its relation to 'L'Amore dei tre re.' The first act is dramatically sleepy; musically it is not very original. It has, however, a certain atmosphere, a freedom from mere bombast, and a long melodic line which, if sugary and sometimes indicative of Puccinian influence, hints at the refinement and the plastic quality of the score of 'L'Amore dei tre re.' The score quickly exposes two principal motives – that of Gallurese and Rivegas, heard singly and in combination in later scenes. In this act the harmony and instrumentation are singularly for a period when Puccini was at the top of his fame in Italy.

In the same proportion as the second act is effective for stage purposes is it poor in its sheerly musical quality. The one exception is the music for the dances, which is of a folk flavor, very

Rehearsing the final scene in Act 3
Bastiano (Angelo Bada) and Maria (Müller) support the dying Giovanni Gallurese (Lauri-Volpi) as instructed by Samuel Thewman, the director

typical and freshly written. Thereafter the music is that of a young man quickly learning stage business and showing that if he had continued in the same direction in later operas he could probably have met the realists of Italy on their own ground and successfully competed with them. But this is not the true Montemezzi. His best measures occur in the introduction of act three, and in several episodes of this act which recall, musically and dramatically, the opening scenes. Nature, apostrophized by Gallurese in his first solo, has set the stage for this episode of blood and passion. Nature, at the last, is again serene and triumphant. The hills and the streams are as before. Humans have had their troubled day. There is the thought of the quiet and the beauty of the countryside, the all-enveloping shadows, the deepening sky, the passing of unhappy and pretty things. And it is in this mood that Mr. Montemezzi is most truly the precursor of the later composer who set to music what the public will not willingly relinquish, the noble and beautiful drama of Benelli.

The performance was principally conspicuous for the vivid and emotional portrayal of Maria by Miss Mueller, the splendid singing of the chorus, the admirable stage management and the playing of the orchestra under Mr. Serafin, who conducted with devotion and mastery. Miss Mueller, hitherto known in the Metropolitan as interpreter of Wagnerian rôles, had suddenly become the Sardinian woman, a picture to remember in her peasant garb, and one who gave her part a thrill which triumphed even over all obstacles. She was a dramatic reality, for all the incongruities of the situation in which she found herself; Lauri-Volpi, who was uncertain at beginning, sang at the top of his voice music which often deserved no better treatment; but there were places which a more thoughtful artist could have given poetry.

Mr. Danise's Rivegas was in keeping with the character and its lines. Mr. Bada, as Bastiano, provided one of the few effective moments by his taunting of Rivegas, in which he was assisted by a chorus which treated the stage Spaniard with contagious laughter and irrepressible gusto. It may be said that throughout the evening, as soldiers, drinkers or banditti, the chorus enjoyed themselves. The ensemble was excellent, the scenery of a conventional type, which, again, was fully justified by the opera. What else could be done with such an opera of outlawed noblemen, a la [sic] Ernani-horn and all; of swooning, popping guns and outraged innocence and bloody murder.

The wonder is not that the work is immature in its quality, but that it reaches the stage, and that, thanks to the composer's ability to write a melodic line and to score in a blatantly obvious manner for voices in solo or ensemble, it goes, in a fashion, across the footlights. These things seem to be the birthright of Italian composers. The enthusiasm of the audience, or a large section of it, mounted last night, until at the end of the duet of the dying Gallurese and Maria it drowned voices and orchestra with applause and bravos. For all that, this is an early and relatively unformed opera, frank in style, but usually undistinguished and weak in invention. Its interest is not inherent, but is due to the beautiful masterpiece which it preceded.

Mr. Montemezzi was presented with a wreath as a token of esteem and appreciation.

Giuseppe Danise as Rivegas

4. Lawrence Gilman, *New York Herald Tribune*,
20 February 1925.

A New Opera at the Metropolitan: Montemezzi's 'Giovanni Gallurese,' for the First Time Here

'GIOVANNI GALLURESE,' a 'historical melodrama' in three acts, is twenty years old. It was Montemezzi's first opera. He is said to have derived it from a youthful opus in one act, recasting it in its present form in 1904.[1] His librettist was Francesco d'Angelantonio, a literary compatriot who devised the book especially for Montemezzi. The opera was produced at the Teatro Vittorio Emmanuele, Turin, January 28, 1905, with Augusto Balboni as the bandit hero and Bice Corsini as Maria. Tullio Serafin, Montemezzi's classmate at the Milan Conservatory, conducted the performance, as he did last night.

Montemezzi's second opera, 'Hellera,' was produced at Turin in 1910.[2] 'L'Amore dei tre Re' – the work which made him celebrated and beloved in America – followed in 1913. His fourth opera, 'La Nave,' based on the play of D'Annunzio, was produced at La Scala in 1918 (Chicago heard it in the following year). He is now at work on a fifth, 'Paul and Virginia.'

Thus it will be seen that in choosing 'Giovanni Gallurese' for production the Metropolitan was going as far back in the history of this gifted composer as it could well reach. Doubtless there were good reasons for passing over Montemezzi's latest work, 'La Nave' (which it would have been interesting to hear), and

---

1 See above, p. 26.
2 *Héllera* was actually premiered at the Teatro Regio, Turin, on 17 March 1909.

for not awaiting the completion of 'Paul and Virginia.'[1] One cannot help wondering if Mr. Montemezzi himself was wildly enthusiastic over the resurrection of this early work. To be quite frank, we hope he was not.

We have too great a respect for the sensitive and imaginative musician who gave us the score of 'L'Amore dei tre Re' to be willing to believe that he still thinks highly of this relatively youthful indiscretion of his (he was almost thirty when it was produced). We know that composers – who, after all, are parents – are sometimes loath to repudiate even their feeblest offspring; and it is not difficult to understand their affection. But to have a sneaking fondness for a youthful work is not quite the same thing as assenting to its performance before a public which has acclaimed you as the author of a maturer and far worthier score. Yet there stood Mr. Montemezzi last night bowing happily from the stage of the Metropolitan, where a year ago he had been acclaimed as the composer of a masterpiece, his moving and beautiful 'L'Amore dei tre Re,' while many (one hopes) of his most discriminating friends among the applauding audience grieved for him sincerely, dismayed by this saddening revelation of his musical past.

We can think of nothing important to be gained by being politely euphemistic in this matter, nor do we trust our skill in such an endeavor sufficiently to attempt it. Therefore we see nothing for it but to speak what is from our standpoint the bleak and unhandsome truth – namely, that 'Giovanni Gallurese' is a tedious and commonplace opera, one of the most tedious and most commonplace, indeed, that the Metropolitan has mounted within our fairly long experience of its activities.

The story of the opera has been recounted more than once in

---

[1] There were in fact better reasons than Gilman could have imagined, for *Paolo e Virginia* was never completed.

this journal; so we need not rehearse it here.

D'Angelantonio's tale is quite as crude and unrewarding on the stage as one might judge it to be from a synopsis of the libretto. The quality of the text may be inferred from this passage in the song that Maria sings in the garden of the miller's cottage in the first act, which cannot be wholly perverted in the official English translation:

> Fair violets, I do not ask your fragrance sweet,
> Nor do I crave, O sun, thy flaming heat,
> Nor do I need, dear birds, your power of song
> To tell him he is fair and I have loved him long.[1]

It is all about like that – in the style of the lace-valentine literature of our dear, dead youth,[2] or of the Nick Carter romances of the same era.[3] That a text of this quality could have attracted the attention of the sensitive tone-poet who, only eight years later, was to choose Sem Benelli's superb drama for his 'L'Amore dei tre Re,' is simply incomprehensible.

---

[1] This is R. H. Elkin's translation; the original reads: 'Profumi a voi non chiedo – tenui vïole, / nè a te il possente ardor – fiammante sole; / non chiedo augelli a voi – melòde o canto / per dire a lui che è bello – e l'amo tanto!' The lines, crucially, are overheard by Gallurese, and represent D'Angelantonio's attempt to let Maria innocently express her feelings. Gilman is very misleading in suggesting that the libretto 'is all about like that.'

[2] Mass-produced Valentine's cards, often made with real or paper lace, and generally containing sentimental verses, became very popular in the late nineteenth-century. They were introduced into America by Esther Howland (1828–1904) around 1850.

[3] Nick Carter was a fictional detective created by John Coryell in 1886 who subsequently featured in hundreds of popular 'dime novels' and stories written by several different hands. He was primarily a detective, but his romantic and sexual adventures were frequently incorporated into the stories.

But composers of warm and high imagination have been known to transcend ridiculous libretti, turning out operas that we accept and delight in for their musical transfiguration of preposterous texts – Mozart in his 'Magic Flute' is only one of many who accomplished this impressive feat. Montemezzi cannot be numbered among the triumphant company. He has set d'Angelantonio's libretto to a score in which, for page after page, there is an unbroken stream of musical commonplaces.

The harmonic and melodic texture is as undistinguished as it is in Giordano and Zandonai at their feeblest. This music has most of the faults of the post-Verdian operas of the early years of the century, and none of their virtues. For expressive and finely molded and distinguished melody, it gives us those banal and sentimental cantilenas whose formulas Puccini and Mascagni and Zandonai and the rest have exploited ad nauseam; yet it gives us nothing of the characterizing vividness, the sharp dramatic definition, the warmth and fervor of lyric speech, which in Puccini (for example) at his best make his scores so potent and lovable and perdurable.

A fair sample of Montemezzi's style in 'Giovanni Gallurese' is that C major melody of incredible triteness and commonness which he puts in the mouth of his hero at Giovanni's words in the first act: 'Ne l'occhio tuo nerissimo, profondo, intravedo la vita,' etc.[1] The general level of the invention is about at that height. Sometimes the music goes a little above it; and once, as in the introduction and opening scene of the third act, between

---

[1] 'In the depths of your very dark eyes I sense life': Giovanni's words immediately after Maria has revealed her love for him. The melody Gilman objected to so strongly is reproduced opposite.

'Ne l'occhio tuo nerissimo ...'
Gilman found this a 'melody of incredible triteness and commonness'

Maria and her father, it becomes for a few pages delicate and fine-grained. But for the most part it is empty and sterile, when it is not worse. Nowhere does Montemezzi achieve the salient and moving and richly expressive speech that we had expected from the composer who, only a few years later, was to give us his 'L'Amore dei tre Re.'

Montemezzi has been quoted as saying that the music of 'Giovanni Gallurese' is 'melodious, but distinguished' – an amusing qualification, but scarcely a correct one. If he had said 'melodious but undistinguished,' he would have described it exactly. For there are various kinds of melodiousness. There is the melodiousness of 'Die Meistersinger,' and the melodiousness of 'Thaïs';[1] and so, also, there is the melodiousness of 'L'Amore dei tre Re,' and the melodiousness of 'Giovanni Gallurese.' Any one could have written the melody of Giovanni's 'Ne l'occhio tuo nerissimo' (though not every one would have been willing to sign it); but not many beside Italo Montemezzi could have written the melody of Fiora's 'Dammi le labbra e tanta ti daro di questo pace.'[2]

The Metropolitan's production of the work is animated and picturesque. The incidental dances in the second act, the singing of the chorus, the handling of the crowds, the costumes (the masculine sport suit was apparently invented in Sardinia about 1662) – these were some of the features that enlivened an unrewarding evening. Others were the singing and acting of that admirable artist, Angelo Bada, in the small part of Bastiano; the

---

[1] Massenet's *Thaïs* (1894) received its first performance at the Met in 1917, and immediately entered the regular repertoire there; Gilman deplored its popularity.

[2] 'Give me your lips, and I will give you of this peace': Fiora's words to Avito in Act 1 of *L'Amore dei Tre Re*. This was a favourite passage of Gilman's. See above, pp. 193–94.

ingratiating beauty and charm of Miss Mueller as Maria (though why, oh why will she never stop smiling in her love scenes?); and the unaffected and manly Giovanni of Mr. Lauri-Volpi – though Mr. Lauri-Volpi's acting was oversimplified, and he was too prone to imagine himself a human cornet: he seldom sang anything but fortes and fortissimos throughout the evening. Mr. Danise was as mild a mannered tyrant as ever crushed a people. Mr. Martino was acceptable as the old Miller. The scenery was conventional but fresh.

The true star of the performance was Tullio Serafin, whose conducting was electrifying in its power, its rhythmic and dynamic flexibility, its pervasive mastery and verve and authority. Surely he will be permitted to conduct for us a neglected work by a remarkable Italian composer: 'L'Amore dei tre Re,' by the late Italo Montemezzi.

The composer was present last night as the guest of the management. He appeared repeatedly before the curtain at the close of each act in response to the demonstrative applause of the audience, looking more than ever like a bashful McAdoo;[1] and after the close of the second act he was trailed by a lackey with a wreath (natural, not silver) beribboned with the Italian colors. Every one else was summoned before the curtain, too, and joy was unconfined. Mr. Montemezzi undoubtedly went to bed with the belief that this public does not know the difference between a fine opera and a mediocre one. But perhaps he was wrong.

---

[1] William Gibbs McAdoo (1863–1941); McAdoo, a prominent lawyer, was the United States Secretary of the Treasury between 1913 and 1918 and unsuccessfully attempted to win the Democratic nomination for President in 1920 and 1924.

Autograph quotation from *Giovanni Gallurese*, March 1925

('Oh con che calma eterna,' the hero's first words)

5. Ernest Newman, *New York Evening Post*, 20 February 1925.[1]

New Montemezzi Opera at the Metropolitan

MONTEMEZZI'S 'GIOVANNI GALLURESE,' which was produced at the Metropolitan last night for the first time in America, dates from 1905 – eight years before 'L'Amore dei Tre Re' – and is apparently his first opera. A good deal of water has passed under the bridge in these twenty years, and it is difficult for any musician to take 'Giovanni Gallurese' seriously at this time of day. What the motives were that induced an opera house like the Metropolitan to produce so poor a work I cannot even guess at. The general excuse given for reviving a bad opera is that it affords opportunities for this or that great singer. That plea will hardly hold good for last night's performance, for I have rarely heard worse singing in any opera house of repute.

The work is hardly a subject for criticism. There is not a thing in it, from the first word of the text to the last note of the music, that has not been staled and vulgarized by constant repetition. The story is of a romantic Byronic Sardinian outlaw, with a passion for declaiming about liberty, making *beaux gestes* when he has an enemy in his power, and rescuing beautiful maidens from the hands of ruffianly Spaniards. All this, which is faded enough in itself, is translated into the most faded idiom of Italian opera, verbal and scenic. The stage, in the first and third acts, is carefully planned for those romantic assaults and escapes and rescues that happen only in opera. In the second act we see one of those

---

1 Newman, who was British, was probably the only reviewer of the Met's *Giovanni Gallurese* who had not already seen *L'Amore dei Tre Re*. When he finally saw the latter opera in London in 1930, he judged that: 'There is hardly a single page of his [Montemezzi's] score that, as music, is fit to line Puccini's or the early Verdi's waste-paper basket; but almost all of it "comes off" on the stage.' See 'The Week's Music,' *Sunday Times*, 6 July 1930, 7.

churches that Italian architects so thoughtfully leave lying about the villages in order that the hero and the heroine and the villain may go about their work to the accompaniment of a hymn from the congregation. There are, of course, choruses of villagers, an innkeeper, an old heavy father, and a local ballet (which last night was the most enjoyable thing of the evening).

About the music it is almost impossible to write critically. All the scores of this school look exactly alike: open half a dozen of them at random, and you will think they are all by the same man, so unvarying is the distribution of minims and crotchets and quavers and semi-quavers, so regularly do the accents fall in the same place, so true to the family type are the melodies, so faithful are all the composers to the same three or four rhythms and the same half-dozen harmonies. The music of 'Giovanni Gallurese' is not bad music: it is simply negative music. It provokes no reactions either of attraction or of repulsion; it simply goes on and on and says nothing. It is a poor specimen of a poor genre. Now and then Montemezzi unconsciously challenges comparisons, and the result is disastrous.

No one can watch, for instance, the scene of the baiting of the captured Rivegas without being reminded of the scene of the baiting of the captured boyard in 'Boris Godounov': but to let one's thoughts fly from Montemezzi to Moussorgsky is to realize the gulf it has pleased Providence to place between one mind and another. The music of the opera in general is very singable, in the Italian sense of the word. The misfortune is that none of it is worth singing. There is not a melody in it that is not the commonest commonplace of the school to which it belongs; we know, from the moment a phrase starts, just where it will go and what it will do, and when the high notes will come and the orchestra will swell to a crude fortissimo.

Mr. Serafin, who conducted, had an anxious couple of minutes now and then with both principals and chorus, but he always steered them and us safely over the thin places in the ice. The performance, in truth, was only tentative in many places, but one is tolerant of this kind of thing on a first night. Madame Maria Mueller was a fairly sympathetic heroine and gave us some moderately good singing. Mr. Lauri-Volpi's voice I can still hear in imagination as I write this, eight hours after the performance ended. I cannot compliment him on being one of the best tenors I have ever heard, but I can lay my hand on my heart and say he is one of the very loudest; and for people who like this sort of thing, this is the sort of thing they will like. About the remainder of the singing the most charitable thing to do is to say nothing.

It only remains to add that the work and the performance were received with frantic enthusiasm.

Italo Montemezzi, famous composer, endorses the HARDMAN

In *L'Amore dei Tri Re*, Signor Italo Montemezzi composed one of the most notable operas Italy has produced in years.

And when *Giovanni Gallurese* opened at the Metropolitan last night, Signor Montemezzi again shared with the singers the applause of an enthusiastic audience....His latest score gives promise of being another enduring contribution to our operatic repertoire.

Like Gigli, Scotti, Rethberg and many of the great Metropolitan artists who interpret his works, Signor Montemezzi uses the Hardman, exclusively.

With quick, almost human responsiveness, the Hardman meets every mood of the most versatile performer. Its exquisite purity and clarity of tone guide these artists of the opera in perfecting each resonant, deep-toned note. And its unique durability, its structural staunchness keeps its tonal beauty unimpaired all through the years....The Hardman has for fourteen years held the coveted honor of being the Official Piano of the Metropolitan Opera House.

Not only is the Hardman moderate in price, but a small initial payment will place it in your home immediately.

HARDMAN, PECK & CO.
433 Fifth Avenue, New York City   47-51 Flatbush Avenue, Brooklyn

HARDMAN
EIGHTY-THREE YEARS OF FINE PIANO MAKING
PIANOS

Advert, New York *Sun*, 20 February 1925

6. Oscar Thompson, *Musical America*, 28 February 1925.

Early Montemezzi Opera Given First American Hearing

Italian Composer Is Center of Repeated Demonstrations at the Metropolitan When 'Giovanni Gallurese' Is Mounted – Score Contains Attractive Melody, Wedded to Outmoded Plot – Maria Müller, Lauri-Volpi and Danise in Chief Parts

ITALO MONTEMEZZI, tall, spare, and with hair silvering at the meridian of life, looked back twenty years to 'Giovanni Gallurese,' his first opera, when it was accorded its American première at the Metropolitan Opera House Thursday evening, Feb. 19. Summoned repeatedly before the curtain by a demonstrative audience, and presented with an enormous ornamental wreath, the distinguished Italian bowed and beamed his happiness after each of the three acts. It was a kingly reception which New York thus extended to the composer of its beloved 'L'Amore dei Tre Re,' but after the tumult and the shouting died, the impression left was that the demonstration was for Montemezzi more than for Thursday's opera, and that he was lionized because he wrote 'L'Amore,' rather than by reason of his authorship of 'Gallurese.'

Reversion to the earlier works of men who have won operatic fame after several preliminary ventures, long has tempted impresarios, and in this they are continually seconded by opera patrons, who fill their small-talk with speculations as to the nature of this or that early product of some celebrity, and with wonderings as to why opportunities of hearing these works are not forthcoming. Those with relatively brief operatic memories can recall experiments at the Metropolitan with Puccini's 'Le Villi,' Bizet's 'Pearl Fishers' and Rossini's 'L'Italiana in

Algieri [sic],'[1] as well as the more rewarding resuscitations of early Verdian scores. That success seldom has crowned these efforts to give vitality to works of the formative period of operatic masters, apparently is never a conclusive argument against further delving into the past. Always there remains the possibility that some amazing jewel will be found, one that was not properly appreciated when it first came to light either because it was in advance of its time, or because men did not recognize a diamond in the rough. We may yet hear Verdi's 'Nabucco' and Wagner's 'Die Feen' or 'Das Liebesverbot,'[2] having so recently experienced 'Ernani' and 'Rienzi.'[3]

Interest in the Metropolitan's acquisition of 'Giovanni Gallurese,' however, was not of the historical character to be found in most of the works referred to. Rather, it was a personal interest in Montemezzi, growing out of the abiding affection in which this public holds his 'L'Amore.' 'Gallurese' is much too recent to be of importance to the pedant or relic hunter, dating back only to 1905, when it achieved its première at Turin under the bâton of the same conductor who presided over the performance Thursday, Tullio Serafin. It is only eight years older than 'L'Amore' and must stand or fall as a modern work.

---

1 These operas had been staged at the Met in 1908, 1916, and 1919. *Le Villi*, though put on much earlier than the others, offered the most obvious comparison with *Giovanni Gallurese*.

2 Wagner's first two completed operas, composed 1833–34 and 1835–36; *Die Feen* was not performed in Wagner's lifetime, while *Das Liebesverbot* was only heard once; neither has been produced at the Met. It is strange to find Thompson associating them with Verdi's *Nabucco* (1842), the Italian composer's first great triumph, which the Met finally staged in 1960.

3 The Wagnerian Opera Company mounted a production of *Rienzi* at the Manhattan Opera House on 26 December 1923 – the first time the opera had been heard in New York since 1890; *Ernani*, as noted above, had been revived at the Met in 1921.

[Cast details.]

The performance given the novelty was a competent one, the details of which naturally take a place subordinate to a discussion of the character of the opera itself. The libretto by Francesco d'Angelantonio (the plot of which is briefly summarized in another column) is not badly made, so far as craftsmanship is concerned. But for operatic purposes, the choice of the subject is not a happy one. There is both too little and too much action, due to the circumstance that either nothing at all is happening, leaving the characters to sing the equivalent of old-fashioned solos and duets; or there is gunplay and an excess of scurrying about of a kind that does not lend itself naturally to musical expression.

'Giovanni Gallurese' resembles in details of its story both 'Ernani' and 'William Tell.' They sufficed for the dramatic requirements of the early part of the last century, but no composer of this era would think of setting the book of either. Montemezzi has taken their equivalent in 'Gallurese,' with the result that he has prejudiced his cause at the start. His subject is outmoded, his characters are cardboard figures with little human appeal, the arrangement of the text is such as to call for reactionary rather than advanced musical methods – for operatic set pieces instead of the semi-symphonic web of the post-Wagnerian music drama – and the very nature of most of these events (abductions, rescues, battles of musketry and eventual assassination) more or less hostile to musical investiture. Some one has said that there never has been a successful shot fired in opera. 'Gallurese' is about as badly off in this respect as 'La Navarraise.'[1] Like that work, it suggests a moving picture at times more than it does a lyric drama – but the films do such things far more convincingly. In physical heroics, opera singers usually are fortunate not to evoke laughter where least intended.

---

1 Massenet's opera (1894), written in response to *Cavalleria Rusticana*.

Montemezzi's music is not that of a half-fledged youth. He was thirty when 'Gallurese' was first sung. His musical gifts were those of a man mature both in ideas and craftsmanship, and it was his subject more than his lack of experience that kept 'Gallurese' from reaching the splendors of 'L'Amore.' The first act, devoted almost entirely to the soliloquies of the tenor and the soprano, and to the love music between them, is filled with warm, pulsating melody, much of it worthy of the hand that penned the melodies of 'L'Amore.' It is melody that will grow in the affections with rehearings. And it is orchestrated, for the most part, with a taste and mastery that Puccini and others of the latter-day Italian opera-makers have not equalled. But the music came to Thursday's audience as neither quite one thing nor the other – the railbirds[1] tried to applaud the vocal parts as they would old-school solos and duets, only to be hissed at by others intent on the symphonic continuity of the scoring.

In the second act, the composer set for himself a task foreign to his particular gifts. For two Sardinian dances he adapted or imitated native airs of vitality and charm, but for the violent action which followed the divertissement he found no suitable musical corollary. Even at the time when muskets are crackling behind the scenes, as the Spaniards and the followers of Gallurese are battling, there is no excitement in the scoring. The orchestra wends its way, rather sadly serene, or else halts altogether. Save for the dances, this is musically a very barren act. Nor has the composer been very happy in his apparent imitation of the accordeon, visibly (but silently) played by a member of the chorus in the 'Danza Montanara.' After 'Petruschka,' however, it is possible that even the real thing in accordeons would seem only a feeble and unconvincing imitation of itself.

The third act, in spite of the futility of the taunting of *Rivegas* – inevitably recalling Moussorgsky's stingingly vital treatment of the

---

[1] Standees.

somewhat similar scene of the maltreatment of the Boyar in 'Boris' (and in spite also of the ill-chosen gun play which brings on the final tragedy) has lyric moments approaching in beauty those of the first act, some of the music being in fact a partial repetition of the earlier themes. The love duet just preceding the assassination, with its climactic unison high B, is very good operatic writing of the 'Cavalleria'-'Pagliacci'-'Jewels of the Madonna'[1] order, but is much less aristocratic in its melodic inspiration than the music of *Giovanni* and *Maria* in the first twenty minutes of the opera.

There is a rather effective musical picture in the last act of the refugees wearily fleeing Spanish tyranny, and the very close of the opera, when *Maria* hovers over the dying *Giovanni*, brings a beautifully simple melody to the orchestra, expressive not so much of the human tragedy, as of the sorrowing solitude of the Sardinian hills. From the brazen solemnity of the very brief prelude to the first act, something of this brooding loneliness, a little sinister and ill-omened, invests the score. There is not much of characterization though there are recurrent themes in the music allotted to *Giovanni* and his adversary, *Rivegas*. Atmospherically, the music succeeds in suggesting its locale.

Miss Müller's *Maria* possessed the requisite vocal charm to yield to Thursday's audience the full beauty of this air, her earlier entrance song and plentiful duet passages with *Giovanni*. She enhanced the impression previously given that she combines with a very lovely voice a considerable measure of skill in its use. Her acting, however, again had details wanting in finesse, and she overemployed the expansive smile that has given a somewhat kittenish aspect to several characterizations doubtless intended to be naïve or simple.

---

1 *I Gioielli della Madonna* (1911), Ermanno Wolf-Ferrari's exercise in *verismo*, which once enjoyed great popularity in the Anglophone world.

Mr. Lauri-Volpi was vocally a very lusty outlaw, prodigal of ringing high tones and vigorous in action as well as song. Quantity of tone was not always matched by quality, however, and he had occasional difficulties with the pitch, especially during the sombre solo which opens the opera – perhaps the sturdiest music of the entire score. He must be credited with dying eloquently, and, with Miss Müller of making this scene distinctly more moving than similar tragedies in opera usually are. Mr. Danise did what there was to be done with the thankless part of *Rivegas*, and Mr. Bada and Mr. Martino were excellent in the small rôles of *Bastiano* and *Nuvis*. Merle Alcock's lovely voice was heard, faintly but tunefully, in the few bars of an off-stage Shepherd's song.

The settings were of the routine order that have come to be expected of Milanese and Viennese importations. The second act dances, led by Rosina Galli, Giuseppe Bonfiglio and Florence Rudolph were lively and colorful, but also of a routine savor. Routine, again, characterized the handling of the chorus and the disposition of the stage crowds. It was the presence of Signor Montemezzi that served to make this American première the event it proved to be.

La Notte di Zoraima

New York, Metropolitan Opera House, 2 December 1931

4 performances

Philadelphia, Academy of Music, 12 January 1932

1 performance

Cast:

Zoraima . . . . Rosa Ponselle
Muscar . . . . Frederick Jagel
Pedrito . . . . Mario Basiola
Manuela . . . . Santa Biondo[1]

Director: Alexandre Sanine
Stage Design: Joseph Novak
Costume Design: Lillian Gaertner Palmedo
Conductor: Tullio Serafin

---

[1] In the second and third performances she was substituted by Aida Doninelli.

METROPOLITAN OPERA HOUSE
GRAND OPERA SEASON 1931-1932
GIULIO GATTI-CASAZZA — GENERAL MANAGER

WEDNESDAY EVENING, DECEMBER 2, 1931, AT 8.30 O'CLOCK

DOUBLE BILL

FIRST TIME IN AMERICA

LA NOTTE DI ZORAIMA
OPERA IN ONE ACT
(IN ITALIAN)
BOOK BY MARIO GHISALBERTI

MUSIC BY ITALO MONTEMEZZI

ZORAIMA	ROSA PONSELLE
MANUELA	SANTA BIONDO
MUSCAR, A YOUNG INCA	FREDERICK JAGEL
PEDRITO, A SPANISH CHIEFTAIN	MARIO BASIOLA
LYOVAL, AN INCA INSURGENT	LOUIS D'ANGELO
FIRST INCA INSURGENT	ARNOLD GABOR
SECOND INCA INSURGENT	JAMES WOLFE
AN INCA PRISONER	GIORDANO PALTRINIERI
A VOICE	ALFIO TEDESCO

INCA INSURGENTS, SPANIARDS, A SPANISH CARAVAN

CONDUCTOR................TULLIO SERAFIN

CHORUS MASTER................GIULIO SETTI
STAGE DIRECTOR................ALEXANDER SANINE
STAGE MANAGER................ARMANDO AGNINI

TIME: About 1550
SCENE: The ruins of an Inca City, in Peru, after the first Spanish conquest
NEW SCENIC PRODUCTION BY JOSEPH NOVAK
COSTUMES DESIGNED BY LILLIAN GAERTNER PALMEDO

FOLLOWED BY

PAGLIACCI

POSITIVELY NO ENCORES ALLOWED
PROGRAM CONTINUED ON NEXT PAGE

CORRECT LIBRETTOS FOR SALE IN THE LOBBY
KNABE PIANO USED EXCLUSIVELY

1. William J. Henderson, *Sun*, 3 December 1931.

'La Notte di Zoraima' Is Sung

One-Act Opera by Ghisalberti and Montemezzi Brings New Laurels to Rosa Ponselle

THE SECOND novelty of the period of depression was produced at the Metropolitan Opera House last evening.[1] The work, 'La Notte di Zoraima,' is a one-act opera, book by Mario Ghisalberti, music by Italo Montemezzi, known to this public as the composer of 'L'Amore dei Tre Re.' The new opera, being short, served as a prelude to 'Pagliacci.' [Comment on *Pagliacci*.] If there was any news in last night's revelations it was somewhere in Montemezzi's recurrence. When he was brought back to us the last time, it was with 'Giovannni Galuresi [sic],' an opera of dismal character and brief existence.

It is customary to tell the story of a new opera. This story is not new. Montemezzi has bragged that he composed music to it because it packed into one capacious act every melodramatic antiquity of Italian opera.[2] The personages have changed

---

1 The first 'novelty' was *Schwanda, the Bagpiper* (*Švanda dudák*) by the Czech composer Jaromír Weinberger, performed at the Met on 7 November 1931.

2 Henderson apparently refers to a recent report by Olin Downes in the *New York Times*, which quotes an earlier report in that paper by Raymond Hall. It includes the following statement:

> 'I determined to set this story,' said Montemezzi, 'because it contains dramatic elements used in operas of every period. These elements are fundamental, clear, obvious and accessible to all. It is a drama universally understood. I believe its novelty derives from the manner of its treatment, particularly as shown by the dramatic and musical vision of the composer.'

See 'Montemezzi's "Notte di Zoraima,"' *New York Times*, 29 November 1931, section X, p. 8.

their names and put on other clothes, like the villain in Dixey's 'Adonis,'[1] but they are the same old puppets. Ecco: revolting Incas (1534 A.D.), defeated, scattered, bounding in and out of a ruined palace and an old temple, and towing along a very active heroine in love with a beaten and hunted hero.

Obverse side: Conquistadores (see Prescott's 'Conquest of Peru,' accurate enough for opera[2]), whose captain is smitten with the heroine, a woman of the enemy. See what's coming? When her hero and herself are cornered she says, 'Let my man go and I am yours.' The Spaniard falls for it. When he claims his reward she swindles him out of it by the pre-Adamite stage device of suicide. That is grand opera, or what the Italians call opera seria: people die. Opera buffa – they get married.

But the music? Well, let us describe this opera from above, a sort of birdman's view. It is made according to the method of today. There is much recitative of the modern Italian kind which stems from Verdi and has been affected by Ponchielli, Boito and lately by Puccini. There are no set airs, but several monologues and dialogues streaming out in phrases sometimes possessing spontaneity, but for the most part mechanically turned on the good old lathe. There is one good monologue for Manuela, the wife of the Spaniard, come to ask Zoraima to release her husband. This is written with feeling and with melodic dignity.

---

1 *Adonis*, a burlesque musical built around the many talents of Henry E. Dixey (1859–1943), opened at the Bijou Theatre on 4 September 1884 and went on to become the longest running show on Broadway to that date. It was periodically revived for the rest of the nineteenth century. The eponymous hero, played by Dixey, appeared in a long series of disguises. Henderson had been much involved with the world of popular musical theatre as a young man, and hence no doubt this reference, which must have been obscure to many of his readers in 1931.

2 William Hickling Prescott's *History of the Conquest of Peru* (1847) was a vividly imagined account of its subject, based on Spanish sources (Prescott had not been to Peru), and for decades had the status of a standard work.

Most of Zoraima's music is so violent, so strident and so wanting in repose that in the hands of almost any other singer than Miss Ponselle it would be hopeless. Fortunately there is considerable lyricism in the duet with Pedrito.

The duet for Zoraima and Muscar, the lover, is well shaped, but it is without inner fire. It is suitable, it is of the theater, and it is vocal, but that is all. The duet for Zoraima and the Spaniard Pedrito, is cut mostly from the same cloth. The choruses have good quality. They are an essential part of the dramatic web, not mere numbers for massed voices, and they are helped by good action and grouping.

There are some well scored orchestral passages to accompany that action which is without singing. Certain of these instrumental episodes have color as well as melodic interest. That accompanying Manuela's exit is admirable. The orchestration is generally good, though it is at no time distinguished or of that proudly patrician type which appears so often in the score of 'L'Amore dei Tre Re.' To name that opera again is to recall the heavy debt which 'La Notte di Zoraima' owes to it. One hears many phrases from the better work, and almost looks to see Archibaldo or Manfredo stride upon the stage. But the fine fiber of the earlier score is absent. The texture of this one is often rich, but also often coarse. The reminiscences are covered with a thin veil of midnight oil and are dank with the sweat of honest toil.

The most valuable possession of this opera is its vivacity of movement. It must be confessed that both duets are too long and that in them the work drags heavy feet; but the general impression is one of bustle and stir. The music runs well beside the action, the recitatives have animation and the ensembles assume a declamatory manner. But the thematic and harmonic materials of the score are too often commonplace to the hilt and one seeks in vain for a page of genuine musical invention.

The central scene in *La Notte di Zoraima*: an angry crowd calls for the death of Zoraima (Ponselle)

**Detail of Zoraima (Ponselle) and
Pedrito (Basiola) on the palace steps**

Traveling into the little known country of the Incas, and the period of the revolt not long after the death of Atahualpa,[1] the librettist rejoiced in the discovery of some period costumes to put on his characters. It was worth a journey to the Metropolitan to see Mr. Jagel in a Peruvian top hat and there can be no denying that it gave him an unusually heroic aspect. Miss Ponselle, in her mighty effort to look and act like a South American Indian of bygone times, turned herself out a half Selika and half Aida. She was a beautiful and uplifting spectacle. Mr. Basiola was a barytone; he could not help that; but he surely looked like Vasco di Gama from Meyerbeer's collection of marine curiosities. And the chorus with its feathers, its wooden guns and its savage leaps had apparently just escaped from 'L'Africaine.'[2] Later it appeared as a gang of cutthroats from the Spanish Main.

Joseph Novak, the scene painter, made a delightful excursion to the foothills of the Andes. The palace and the temple were discreetly done and made an excellent appearance against the snow clad cordillera in the distance. There were competent donkeys to carry the Spanish munitions up the mountains; but there were no llamas.

It was a night of splendor for Miss Ponselle. Never has her gorgeous voice swept its noble scale with greater certainty or more theatrical effect. If the opera does not retain a place in the repertory, it will be a pity, for it will be worth while to go occasionally to hear Miss Ponselle breathe the breath of life into Montemezzi's manufactured song. The music affords her scope for that sweeping phraseology and grandiloquence of style in

---

[1] Atahualpa (1497–1533), who was executed by Pizarro, was the last *Sapa Inca,* or emperor of the Inca Empire.

[2] *L'Africaine* (1865), Meyerbeer's grand opera, has a plot involving a romance between Vasco da Gama and Sélika, an African queen. *L'Africaine* was still in the Met's repertoire in the 1930s, and Ponselle had sung the role of Sélika many times.

which she is so impressive. The grand proportions of her voice are untrammeled, while it beautifully tempered itself to tenderer passages. There is no use blinking the fact that new roles for Miss Ponselle are greatly needed. This opera was probably produced in order to supply her with one, and for that reason we should hope that it will please the public.

We could wish that she had found better materials on which to expend her mock passions than Messrs. Jagel and Basiola, but we are reluctantly forced to the conclusion that the former's best asset was that towering headgear and the latter's the garments and whiskers of the celebrated navigator. One of the best vocal numbers in the score is the appeal of Manuela to Zoraima, but as sung by Santa Bionda it strangely suggested the perfect fitness of her name. The secondary roles were in well trained hands. Mr. Serafin conducted the performance with meticulous care and deep sympathy, and got everything out of the music that was in it.

Zoraima (Ponselle) and Muscar (Jagel)

2. Olin Downes, *New York Times*, 3 December 1931.*

Montemezzi Opera Is A Melodrama

'La Notte di Zoraima,' One Act Work, Has Its American Premiere at Metropolitan

Rosa Ponselle As Heroine

Little Opportunity for Singing Owing to Continuous Noisy Movement – A Poor Libretto

ITALO MONTEMEZZI's one act opera, 'La Notte di Zoraima,' the libretto by Mario Ghisalberti, was performed last night for the first time in America in the Metropolitan Opera House. The opera is poor as a libretto and a composition. The high tragedy of 'La Nave' and above all 'The Love of Three Kings' gives place to melodrama of the most out-dated sort and one that does not help the composer.

In fact it is hard to understand why or how the composer of 'L'Amore dei tre re' could accept such a libretto. The place and period of the piece are Peru after the first Spanish conquest. Zoraima, Inca Princess, driven with her lover Muscar from her throne, has been hiding in the hills, feigning madness, plotting vengeance. Muscar is waiting to waylay a Spanish convoy. Pedrito, the Spanish leader, cherishes a dark and Scarpian passion for Zoraima. He ambushes Muscar and wounds him. Muscar is hidden by Zoraima. Pedrito follows the fugitive, gun in hand. A disreputable crowd of compatriots follow on his heels, having

---

* © 1931 The New York Times. All rights reserved. Used by permission and protected by the Copyright Laws of the United States. The printing, copying, redistribution, or retransmission of this Content without express written permission is prohibited.

captured an insurgent, and ascertained from him Muscar's hiding place. Zoraima, to save Muscar, promises herself to Pedrito if he is set free. Pedrito dismisses the Spaniards, pledging his life that Muscar shall not escape. But the Incan Princess overcomes his hesitations by her beauty, and promises him sanctuary in the hills. Muscar is released. Leonora Gioconda Zoraima[1] waits for signal fires to show that he is safe and separated from his foes by blazing forests. Then she stabs herself and dies to slow music as Pedrito is bound by his enraged countrymen and presumably destined to execution. In all this trash – it is the fitting word for an absurd dramatic concoction – there is not a single real character or logical development, and if the atrocious English parallel of the Italian text in the libretto is an indication, it is the poorest kind of verse.

What could be done with this? Did Montemezzi, despondent because of the only partial success of other works, believe that his success lay in the road of shilling melodrama? Or was he, a poet by nature[,] a symphonist in opera, who nevertheless did not lose the beautiful lyricism which is his birthright, feel that brutal action and lurid denouement would fertilize his creative gift and result in a work of novelty and freshness of style?

He has preserved in this score the symphonic manipulation of motives, and written in a melodious and wholly undistinguished manner. The music is in greater part a distant echo of 'The Love of Three Kings.' In other pages it is passingly Wagnerian and passingly Verdi of the fat melodic manner of Verdi's early and more lurid period. The libretto would hardly admit of Montemezzi saying anything very distinguished in his score. The best music is that of the last quarter of the work, because here, at least, is drama of a sort, and the clash of personalities and emotions. But

---

1 References to *Il Trovatore* and *La Gioconda*, in both of which operas the heroine promises herself to the villain then disappoints him by committing suicide.

in no place has the composer struck a new note or equalled the earlier opera. The scene of exaltation and sacrifice could hardly have been convincing in its dramatic and literary quality to the artist and gentleman that Montemezzi is, and of course the music shows it. The libretto is a disappointment, the music is a disappointment, and it is hard to exonerate the composer, for he has exchanged his birthright for a mess of pottage.

This opera provides one important woman's rôle. It was taken by Miss Ponselle, who did not sing very well in the opening scenes, but in the last part of the opera gave pleasure by the rich quality and sonority of her voice and contrast of color. As an actress with a thankless part she was ineffective. One cannot blame Miss Ponselle that she was so long a-dying and emitting melodic loops of lament that neither deceived nor deeply impressed the audience. But it may be asked just what period her costume belonged to, and if it was truly the custom for Inca maidens to look for enemies in the bushes by raising the palm over the eyebrows and bending forward like effigies of Indian maidens which formerly adorned street corners and cigar stores. And it must be said that this is a poor and badly lighted production.

There is little opportunity for singing in this opera, which is one that apparently aims to distract by continual and noisy movement from beginning to end. Mr. Jagel did well with a few lyrical measures. Mr. Basiola blustered and for the most part shouted as the wholly unconvincing Pedrito. The parts of Manuela and Lyoval[1] are almost of equal unimportance; that of Manuela, mother of Pedrito's child, is dramatically superfluous and having not the slightest importance in the story. The one really effective moment was the onrush of the chorus with the insurgent prisoner, and the singing of the chorus remains one of the reliable and excellent features of a Metropolitan presentation.

---

1 Lyoval is, apart from Zoraima and Muscar, the only named Inca; his role is that of a reporter of news and carrier of messages.

The scenic production, the work of Joseph Novak, was ineffective, a shiftless mixture of styles. The costumes were not very much better. Mr. Serafin conducted with admirable mastery.

There was cordial applause at the end of the opera, which does not mean a great deal, because there is always applause after these performances. Last night was no exceptional rule. It would be a pleasure to record another triumph for the composer of 'L'Amore dei tre re,' which some of us regard as the finest quality of Italian music drama to have appeared since the days of Verdi. But last night the audience turned to that mainstay of Italian realism, 'Pagliacci.'

The cast which presented this opera was not distinguished, but it presented the opera with security, therefore effect, for this is a work of dramatic saliency and masterly structure. The stage director of 'Notte di Zoraima' was Alexandre Sanine, and for 'Pagliacci' Hanns Niedecken-Gebhard.

3. Lawrence Gilman, *New York Herald Tribune*,
3 December 1931.

Montemezzi's New Opera, 'La Notte di Zoraima,' Given at the Metropolitan

MONTEMEZZI'S EARLY opera, 'L'Amore dei tre Re,' still seems, in the light of our seventeen years' familiarity with it, a beautiful and moving work – beautiful, often, in its own right, despite its Tristanisms; for though Montemezzi's imagination was obviously kindled by the flame of Wagner's blazing score, he had things of his own to say to us that were well worth saying; and his passionate variation upon the old Greek theme of the tangled feet of Destiny will hold us absorbed whenever the Metropolitan again sees fit to let us hear it.

But in his newest opus, Montemezzi has disclosed no fresh enkindlement, from without or from within; he has merely warmed over yesterday's considerably diminished sustenance. Even borrowed inspirations may sound extremely well in the glow of the pristine ardor that impelled their original conversion; but their repetitions are diminishingly effective, and may cause one to think of Mark Twain's saying about what happens to tumblers who have lost their legs: 'these parties cease to draw.'[1]

Fiora's 'Dammi le labbra e tanta ti daro di questa pace,'[2] with its troubled ecstasy and sweetness, was affecting as one heard it in

---

[1] This comes from Twain's account of his conversation about opera with a German woman in *A Tramp Abroad*: 'with us [Americans], when a singer had lost his voice and a jumper had lost his legs, these parties ceased to draw.' *The Complete Travel Books of Mark Twain*, ed. Charles Neider, 2 vols (Garden City: Doubleday: 1966–67), 2:53.

[2] See pp. 193–94 for Gilman's earlier praise of this passage.

'L'Amore dei tre Re' – even though one was aware of its source in that welling spring of loveliness that flows exhaustlessly among the living shadows of King Mark's Cornish garden. But Muscar's love song in 'La Notte di Zoraima' – 'O mia Zoraima, tu sei bella'[1] – is quite another matter; and it is a typical instance.

Montemezzi was evidently haunted by the memory of that feature which gave especial poignancy to the melodic phrase as it occurred in 'Tristan' and in 'L'Amore dei Tre Re': the rise of the voice from the fourth to the sixth of the scale. But what was magical in 'Tristan'; what was apt and touching in 'L'Amore dei Tre Re' because of the reminiscent glow behind the notes, as well as because of the freshness of the setting, is merely flat and tame in 'La Notte di Zoraima.' The glow has gone; the setting is worn and tarnished.

And those dactylic rhythms with which we became so familiar in 'L'Amore dei tre Re': they are utilized in the new score, but with how much less point and vitality and seizingness!

Montemezzi has been quoted as saying that in this new work (which is separated from 'L'Amore dei Tre Re' by seventeen years or so, and from 'La Nave' by about a dozen) he 'had no desire to change his style'[2] – which rather misses the point. A really vital artist does not deliberately set about 'changing his style'; rather, he grows in power and flexibility, adapting his manner of speech to whatever new subjects he undertakes. One of the miracles of Wagner's art, for

---

[1] A line from the big duet between Zoraima and Muscar. In the published libretto, interestingly, it is simply 'Zoraima, tu sei bella' ('Zoraima, you are beautiful'), suggesting that the composer added the 'O mia' found in the vocal score.

[2] Olin Downes, in the *New York Times* for 29 November 1931, quoted Montemezzi as saying: '"La Notte di Zoraima" does not represent a change of style, as compared with my previous operas. I am using the same esthetic canons as before …' See above, p. 287, n.2.

Manuela (Biondo) and Zoraima (Ponselle)

example, is its self-containment and integrity in each of its different manifestations: so that, when he quotes in 'Die Meistersinger' a motive from 'Tristan,' you could not possibly mistake it for anything but a deliberate importation from another work.

What one hoped for and expected from Montemezzi, after his long silence, was evidence of a deepened and more adaptive talent, a power of expression individualized, enriched, matured. Signs of these things are not easily discernable in 'La Notte di Zoriama.' The old clichés recur with disheartening regularity: those formulas that are here not merely canned Wagnerian heat, but warmed-over Montemezzi – which is quite a different thing. Montemezzi seems to have lost whatever gifts of melodic and harmonic eloquence he once possessed; and his rhythms have grown flabby. He fits out his dying heroine with a kind of pocket 'Liebestod': but what feeble stuff it is with its insipidity and flatness, its sentimental platitudes that have been the small change of the salon composer for half a century!

Montemezzi is a sincere and highminded artist; but, alas, sincerity and highmindedness do not butter the parsnips of creative art.

Even the book of 'La Notte di Zoraima' affects us with the stale odor of spilt librettoese. The central idea of the plot – that of a desperate woman saving her endangered tenor lover by promising to yield herself to the lecherous barytone who has the lover in his power, and then cheating her creditor by suicide – is at least as old as Ponchielli's 'La Gioconda'; and the fact that Montemezzi's librettist, Mario Ghisalberti, lays the scene of his one-act melodrama among the oppressed and embattled Incas of sixteenth century Peru, thus making it necessary for Miss Ponselle to get herself up in an unbecoming Indian costume and complexion, does not help commend the work to this observer.

The Metropolitan has given the opera a production that is distinguished only by the singing of Miss Ponselle, who, as the proud and desperate Incan maiden who preserves Mr. Jagel and double-crosses Mr. Basiola, is on the stage most of the time, thus giving us many welcome opportunities to hear her triumphantly solvent voice. Mr. Jagel as her lover, Mr. Basiola as the desirous Spanish commander, and Mr. Serafin in the orchestra pit, render unto Montemezzi the things that are his. The others need not be specified; nor would public happiness be increased by dwelling upon Mr. Novak's deeply depressing scenic conception of the ruins of an Incan palace destroyed by the Spanish *conquistadores*.

And 'La Notte di Zoraima' is one of the works that the Metropolitan stepped over 'Elektra' to pick up![1]

---

[1] *Elektra* was finally given its Met premiere exactly a year later, on 3 December 1932, when it was enthusiastically acclaimed. Its previous absence from the Met stage had long rankled with those who felt the Met's repertoire should be more modern and experimental, and a performance by the Philadelphia Grand Opera Company on 30 October 1931 seemed to highlight the Met's backwardness.

Rehearsing the central scene: Alexandre Sanine (pointing) directs the cast of *La Notte di Zoraima*

4. Oscar Thompson, *New York Evening Post*, 3 December 1931.

With Ponselle as Inca Princess, Montemezzi's New 'Notte di Zoraima' Has American Premiere at Metropolitan

ECHOES OF one of the most admirable Italian operas written since the death of Giuseppe Verdi resounded in the Metropolitan last night. The opera thus echoed was Italo Montemezzi's 'L'Amore dei Tre Re.' The echoes were the same composer's 'La Notte di Zoraima.' The former has been in and out of the Metropolitan repertory for eighteen years. Now, as last season, it is out. The latter had its first American performance on this occasion, in succession to the world premiere which took place in Milan as recently as January 31 of this year.

'La Notte di Zoraima' is a one-act work, of less than an hour's duration. Tullio Serafin conducted the American premiere and appeared before the curtain in acknowledgment of the usual cordial applause, in company with the stage director, Alexandre Sanine, and the chorus master, Giulio Setti. The chief singers were Rosa Ponselle, Santa Biondo, Frederick Jagel and Mario Basiola. For these there was a procession of joint recalls, with the Zoraima of the evening also appearing alone. Vocally the titular role may be considered a fortunate one for Miss Ponselle; perhaps more so than Fiora in 'L'Amore,' the part with which she opened the Metropolitan season three years ago.

The composer, who once received a wreath at a performance of 'L'Amore' at the Metropolitan,[1] remained in Europe; but Mrs. Montemezzi, who is American by birth,[2] was present to hear

---

1 See above, pp. 183–84.

2 Katherine Montemezzi was born Kate Levy in Hartford, Connecticut, on 17 May 1885. The family changed its name to Leith during the First World War.

the cordial applause bestowed on her husband's fifth operatic work. Besides 'L'Amore,' one other had preceded 'La Notte di Zoraima' at the Metropolitan, without, however, leaving any very enduring memories. That other, 'Giovanni Gallurese,' slumbers beyond any probability of a reawakening. It was Montemezzi's first opera and it came too late. 'L'Amore dei Tre Re,' which had preceded it to these shores, forced upon it comparisons the earlier work could not withstand. 'La Notte di Zoraima,' a better opera than 'Giovanni Gallurese,' now must face these same comparisons. They shelved 'La Nave,' the Montemezzi opera produced in Chicago some ten or twelve years ago.

Whether the new work introduced to the Metropolitan will alter Montemezzi's apparent destiny to be rated a one-opera composer, may require more than today's critical verdicts to determine. Indications last night were that the Metropolitan subscribers enjoyed, within the bounds of moderation, the melodious and deftly written score. They might have enjoyed it more twenty years ago. 'La Notte di Zoraima' represents a type of opera or music-drama that has somewhat lost its vogue. The term, 'continuous melody,' no longer means what it once meant. The arioso style that evades the set number but aims similarly at a melodic goal belonged to the nineties and the early years of the new century. 'L'Amore dei Tre Re' summed up for Italy what Frenchmen and Germans, from Massenet to Schreker and Strauss, were once assumed to be striving for. It was and remains a superior work. It said more, in 1913, than 'La Notte di Zoraima,' coming freshly into an altered world, can hope to say in 1931.

The similarities are not far to seek. The new opera has the same type of long-breathed melody. It employs repeatedly those ostinato effects that gave personality as well as stir to some of the episodes of 'L'Amore.' The blind Archibaldo's staggered chords are recalled in moments of apprehension and foreboding. The orchestral timbres recall inevitably the love of Fiora and Avito, with that touch of remoteness, that suggestion of distance, that in some manner became a part of the musical landscape, so to speak, of the earlier score. Even the offstage voice of the tenor in the new opera brings back something of an unforgettable aura – the aura of Sem Benelli's medieval Italy rather than the Peruvian locale of 'Notte di Zoraima.'

This Peruvian locale, with its commingling of conquering Spaniard and insurgent native, gives the opera some visual resemblance to 'L'Africana [sic].'[1] In appearance, Zoraima is a blood sister to Selika. The action, however, approximates the second act of 'Tosca.' There is a similar excess of it. In one bulging act is compressed enough for four acts of Scribe and Meyerbeer.[2] The characters scarcely have opportunity to become acquainted with one another. Mario Ghisalberti's libretto hustles every one, including Montemezzi, on to the final tragedy, without pausing long enough to develop the stage characters beyond the puppet stage. They love, they rage, they die – at least Zoraima does, and she is the opera. But they build no affection, they remain virtually cardboard figures. It is otherwise with 'L'Amore.' There, Manfredo, Avito, Archibaldo and Fiora are all human personages. There is an almost equal division of sympathy between those four.

This lithographic Zoraima is an Inca princess, who loves Muscar, the dethroned Inca king. Pedrito, leader of the Spanish conquerors, desires Zoraima. When Muscar is wounded, Zoraima gains safe-conduct for him by agreeing, Tosca-like, to yield herself to the Spaniard. She toys with him until her people

---

1 See above, p. 292 and n. 1.
2 The librettist and composer of *L'Africaine*.

have set a great forest fire that is to make certain her lover's escape, whereupon, she stabs herself and falls dead at Pedrito's feet. She is his – but distressingly dead. Traversed at a more leisurely pace, this story might not have seemed so obviously a made-to-order, rubber stamp affair, and conceivably it could have taken on its measure of human appeal.

The wonder is that Montemezzi found opportunity to develop the number of lyric accents he did. There is some fairly extended and familiar-sounding love music for Muscar and Zoraima. Manuela, a Spanish woman deserted by Pedrito, tells of her wrongs in an arioso-scena of considerable length. Zoraima's premonition of death for her lover takes a similar form. There are even moments when something of symphonic expansion is attempted: brief intermezzi appear between the flights and pursuits of characters across the stage. For the reviewer, the most effective writing in the score is the first chorus of the natives, plotting an attack on a Spanish convoy; and an ostinato that ushers the Spaniards off the stage after Zoraima has taunted Pedrito into asserting his power of command.

The performance, if one of only moderate effectiveness, may be assumed to have given the work opportunity to assert its best qualities. Miss Ponselle sang better than she acted and acted better than she posed. We thought her tone in such passages as that beginning 'Fanciullo, ti tormenti,'[1] much more alluring than the blandishments by which Pedrito was won over. That worthy was not a particularly imposing example of the fiery conquistador, as bodied forth by Basiola; his singing was adequate, if nothing more. Jagel's agreeable tenor took on an additional fullness, and

---

[1] This passage occurs in Zoraima's final exchange with Pedrito: 'Fanciullo … / Ti tormenti di dubbio e d'amore' ('Child … / You are tormented by doubt and love').

Miss Biondo, who had an unfortunate appearance as Nedda last year before she was ready for it,[1] did some very pretty singing in the supplication of Manuela. The chorus and orchestra and some of the stage groupings merited praise. But the conflagration at the close would scarcely have passed muster as a really good bonfire. A panoramic setting, of the traditional order, and credited to Joseph Novak, sufficed to picture the mountain background of the tale.

---

[1] In fact, Santa Biondo made her Met premiere as Nedda in *Pagliacci* in 1929.

Tullio Serafin, 1931
Conductor of *Giovanni Gallurese*
and *La Notte di Zoraima*

5. Deems Taylor, *New York American*, 3 December 1931.[1]

New Montemezzi Opera Presented At Metropolitan

ITALO MONTEMEZZI's one-act opera, 'La Notte di Zoraima' (Zoraima's Night), the first stage work that the composer of 'L'Amore dei Tre Re' has given us in several years, had its first American hearing at the Metropolitan last night. Montemezzi's past works have all been full-length, three-act productions. 'Zoraima' is his first essay in a short form.[2]

Forsaking his famous librettist, Sem Benelli (New York still remembers 'The Jest,' as well as 'L'Amore,'[3]) he wrote the present piece in collaboration with a young Italian poet, Mario Ghisalberti.

[Summary of the plot.]

The score bears the familiar earmarks of the composer of 'L'Amore' – flowing, melodious music, direct, almost naive in its appeal, simply harmonized, grateful to the voice, distinguished by a sincerity and intellectual honesty that keeps its simplicity and tunefulness from any suspicion of cheapness. It is well and discreetly orchestrated. Mr. Serafin's subtle and beautifully lyric reading of the score, by the way, was one of the high marks of last night's performance.

---

1 This review only appeared in late editions of the paper, and was reprinted in the morning edition for 4 December.

2 Montemezzi's unperformed first opera, *Bianca* (1901), had also been in one act.

3 Edward Sheldon's adaptation of *La Cena delle Beffe* as *The Jest* was produced in New York in 1919 and proved very successful, with 256 performances. It was of course misleading to suggest at this juncture that Benelli had ever been, in the sense implied here, Montemezzi's 'librettist,' though he would eventually produce the libretto for *L'Incantesimo*.

If the opera lacks a measure of the musical and dramatic strength of some of Montemezzi's other works, the fault can be laid largely at the door of the librettist. The story, as the above synopsis indicates, is as old as the hills. Meyerbeer would have understood it perfectly, although he might have found it rather lacking in novelty. Nor is it given any new twist by its literary treatment. The characters not only do the familiar operatic things. They are the familiar operatic characters – two-dimensional puppets, with no flesh and blood beneath their costumes save what is provided by the singers.

Montemezzi's has never been a vitally dramatic talent. The readiest adjective that comes to mind in connection with his music is 'gentle.' He is happiest, one feels, in quiet scenes of dreamy, not too impassioned, lyricism (the tender opening love scene of 'L'Amore,' for instance).

In 'L'Amore dei Tre Re' the power of Benelli's poignant and searching drama carried him along whether or no, forced him to write gripping dramatic music almost in spite of himself. But Ghisalberti, though he may be a good poet, is neither a good story-teller nor a clever dramatist. Not only is his story hackneyed, but its manner of telling is thoroughly old-fashioned, action being spun out almost to the vanishing point in order to afford plenty of time for arias and duets.

These latter Montemezzi supplies, and many of them have quality and distinction (they are not 'spotted' as separate numbers, of course; 'Zoraima' is not as old-fashioned as that). What he does not supply are [the] power of characterization and driving power that the libretto lacks. As a result, the work lacks vitality, and the warmth of human probability.

The performance was excellent. Both Miss Ponselle and Frederick Jagel were ideally united, vocally, and made the cardboard lovers at least a pleasure to hear. Mario Basiola, too, did lyric and histrionic justice to the villainous Pedrito. Mr. D'Angelo's Lyoval was only a bit, but he made a vivid one.

The production gave us a chance to see what Alexander Sanine, the Metropolitan's Russian stage director, could do. He did enough to give us an appetite for more. The book baffled him – would baffle Stanislavsky;[1] but the grouping and the individual pantomime of the chorus were graphic and naturalistic.

The audience was large, and friendly.

---

1 Constantin Stanislavsky (1863–1938), the great Russian actor and theatre director. Two of his former students, Richard Boleslavsky and Maria Ouspenskaya, had founded the American Laboratory Theatre in New York in 1925, and his ideas had gained considerable currency in America. Sanine had worked with Stanislavsky in Russia.

Alexandre Sanine, 1931
The Director of *La Notte di Zoraima*

(Photograph inscribed to Filippo Crispano)

6. A. Walter Kramer, *Musical America*, 10 December 1931.

Montemezzi Opera Is Given Premiere At Metropolitan

'La Notte di Zoraima,' One-Act Work on Incan Theme, with Libretto by Ghisalberti, Has First American Hearing in Double Bill – Rosa Ponselle Hailed in Beautifully Sung Portrayal of Leading Role – Skillfully Written Score in Post-Wagnerian Style Abounds in Drama

To its Wednesday evening subscribers the Metropolitan Opera Company revealed its second novelty of this season on the evening of Dec. 2, when it mounted for the first time in this country Italo Montemezzi's one-act opera 'La Notte di Zoraima' ('Zoraima's Night'), given its premiere last season at La Scala in Milan.

Ever since this Italian composer's 'L'Amore dei Tre Re' was disclosed to us at the Metropolitan on Jan. 2, 1914, under the baton of Arturo Toscanini, we have had the highest regard for his creative gift, one which, despite its leanings on music of the past, won us by its individual and poetic quality.

This is Signor Montemezzi's first opera since 'L'Amore.'[1] He is no prolific bestower of musical notation on score paper; but he is a thoughtful composer. At a time when so many choose to seize our attention with countless compositions, ill-considered and too often uninspired, he is to be greatly prized.

'La Notte di Zoraima,' a setting of a well contrived libretto by Mario Ghisalberti, has much to recommend it. It is genuine music of the stage, music that fits the action, that has a true dramatic stripe, that can boast a spontaneous lyricism in a day

---

[1] Kramer was obviously forgetting *La Nave*.

when younger and less gifted men prefer rather to decry melodic naturalness than to write it, – assuming that they can!

Difficult Art Form

Nothing is more difficult for a composer than to give definite musical shape to his characters in a one-act opera. To an extent, this is Montemezzi's problem in this work, which lasts something short of an hour, but he has on the whole managed it skillfully. His music is strongly contrasted, the love scene with Muscar warm, the finale with Pedrito stirring in its hidden implications. As in 'L'Amore' he employs a single tenor voice on 'Ah!' backstage as an orchestral instrument, a bit which would be even more telling, did it not recall the previous one so strongly, though the music itself is different.

The treatment of the chorus, both the Inca insurgents and the Spanish followers of Pedrito, exhibits a master hand. The scene in which Pedrito orders the mob to leave the scene is one of the most vivid we know. The orchestra mutters along with the crowd as it withdraws, making the Spanish conquistador swear that he will be responsible to them with his life for Zoraima, whom they wish to kill.

Vividly Dramatic Score

Frankly, the treatment of voices and orchestra is Wagnerian, as is the idiom of much of Montemezzi's musical utterance. But it is no slavish imitation; it is a musico-dramatic speech, which this composer has conceived following in its general line the Wagnerian 'endless melody,' made his own and Italianized in the process. One can not fail to recognize it as Montemezzi; nor can one but rejoice in his ability to refrain from the things which have in popular opinion been characteristic of so much Italian opera, namely, banality and coarseness of musical expression.

There is an exceptional aristocracy in Montemezzi's musical speech, nowhere more discernible than in his treatment of those passages which are conversational, the equivalent of what was once a recitative. These have less of that medieval color than do corresponding portions of 'L'Amore,' for the excellent reason that this drama's atmosphere is totally different.

Resemblances to other composers crop up here and there, as they always do and probably always will, few of them conspicuous ones, save the phrase of Pedrito, 'L'anima mia balza verso di te,'[1] which is a sequence that stems from Strauss's 'Rosenkavalier' waltzes. For in this work Montemezzi recalls himself more than he does others. There is a big sweep in his climaxes, a romantic glamor, a terribly sincere feeling through it all, which ought to give it a place among the few one-act operas that remain in the repertoire.

Ponselle a Striking Protagonist

Rosa Ponselle makes of the Inca princess, Zoraima, a figure of appeal and sings her music gloriously. Her voice is ideally suited for it (or vice versa, if you prefer) and her golden tones over the pulsing orchestra were among the most ravishing of musical moments of the season. In her dramatic conception of the role, she again gave evidence of her claim to distinction in that department.

In the ungrateful role of the Inca prince, Muscar, Frederick Jagel acquitted himself with credit. Not so much can be said for Mario Basiola as the Spanish captain Pedrito, lacking in distinction vocally and dramatically. Santa Biondo was more than admirable in voice as Manuela. Louis d'Angele [sic] as Lyoval, and Alfio Tedesco and Giordano Paltrinieri, were both satisfying,

---

[1] 'My soul leaps toward you.' This passage occurs in the episode where Zoraima promises herself to Pedrito.

the former in the off-stage phrases, the latter as the Prisoner. Messrs. Gabor and Wolfe completed the cast.

The orchestra under Tullio Serafin played unusually well, in fact at times with superb eloquence. Giulio Setti's chorus sang its music with assurance, a result of his fine training.

Stage Direction Undistinguished

The stage under the direction of the new Russian, Alexander Sanine, was below the level of the other departments' achievements. There was too little coordination of movement and unnecessarily clumsy groupings. The scene painted by Joseph Novak suggests anything but the ruins of a palace. Nor does a back drop of this kind mean anything to us. That sort of thing was out of date twenty years ago.

We could forgive much, if there were an attempt to suggest the conflagration, which Zoraima has prepared with her followers early in the opera, and which after her words 'Un dono d'amore t'offrirò!'[1] bursts into flame, as the chorus rushes in, saying that the forest is on fire and destroying everything. Here all the Metropolitan does is to let loose a little stage steam (is it from Wagner's 'Magic Fire'?) tinted red. The whole stage should light up, back drop and all. Montemezzi gives explicit directions in his score. Why will composers' – including Wagner's – directions be disobeyed?

---

[1] 'A gift of love I offer you!' Montemezzi apparently rearranged the line that in the libretto appears as 'T' offrirò un dono / d'amore.'

L'Incantesimo

NBC Broadcast From Radio City, New York, 9 October 1943

Cast:

Giselda . . . . Vivian Della Chiesa
Rinaldo . . . . Mario Berini
Folco . . . . Alexander Sved
Salomone . . . . Virgilio Lazzari

Conductor: Italo Montemezzi

Studio 8-H, Radio City, 1940
L'Incantesimo was broadcast from here

1. Olin Downes, *New York Times*, 10 October 1943.*

Montemezzi Opera In Radio Premiere

'L'Incantesimo' Given by NBC, With Composer Conducting – Poem is by Benelli

Work Suited To Medium

Vivian Della Chiesa, Alexander Sved, Berini and Lazzari Heard With Symphony

THE WORLD premiére of Italo Montemezzi's latest opera, 'L'Incantesimo' was given by the National Broadcasting Company, the composer conducting the performance, yesterday afternoon in Studio 8-H in Radio City. This is by far the most representative opera by a contemporaneous composer which has been introduced on the air; it is a work especially adaptable to broadcasting. It was very enthusiastically received. It is beautiful music.

The singers were Vivian Della Chiesa, soprano (Giselda); Mario Berini, tenor (Rinaldo), Alexander Sved, baritone, of the Metropolitan Opera Association (Folco), and Virgilio Lazzari, basso, of the same institution (the Magician). The performance was one of general eloquence, especially on the parts of Miss Della Chiesa and Mr. Berini, and Mr. Montemezzi led with the authority of a central conception of the music. The admirable orchestra was that of the NBC Symphony.

The circumstances which brought this work to the NBC and America are significant. The poem of 'L'Incantesimo,' by Sem Benelli, the same poet who precipitated Montemezzi's greatest

---

* © 1943 The New York Times. All rights reserved. Used by permission and protected by the Copyright Laws of the United States. The printing, copying, redistribution, or retransmission of this Content without express written permission is prohibited.

opera up to date, the internationally accepted 'L'Amore dei Tre Re,' was completed in 1933, and Montemezzi, then in Italy, began work on the score. It is said, and easy to believe, that he, who had none too good previous relations with the Mussolini Government,[1] found the atmosphere there intolerable for creative work, so that the new scored lagged. In 1938,[2] Mr. Montemezzi came to America, where he has since lived. He completed 'L'Incantesimo,' including the orchestration, last summer at his home in California.

Little Dramatic Action

The opera is short, consuming some forty-five minutes in performance, and for the reasons of paucity of dramatic action, poetical mood and a glamorous lyrical style exceptionally adapted to radio performance. Indeed, it is less an opera for visualization than a symphonic poem, with low voices and at the end a very brief choral passage entering as component parts into the symphonic line and surge of the music.

---

[1] It is actually difficult to position Montemezzi in relation to the Fascist regime. Through the 1920s and '30s he wrote a series of scraping letters to Mussolini and members of the Fascist bureaucracy, mostly concerned with getting *La Nave* staged. These can be read in Fiamma Nicolodi, *Musica e musicisti nel ventennio fascista* (Fiesole: Discanto Editore, 1984), 412–27. On the other hand, Montemezzi collaborated with Benelli, who was out of favour with the regime, and *L'Incantesimo* itself seems to incorporate a level of anti-Fascist symbolism. Moreover, Montemezzi neither sought nor obtained a position from the Fascist authorities, and his decision to attend a Toscanini concert in Lucerne in 1938 can be understood as an indirect but unmistakable protest against Italy's rulers: see Harvey Sachs, *Music in Fascist Italy* (London: Weidenfeld and Nicolson, 1987), 230. It is clear that once in America Montemezzi stressed his anti-Fascist credentials; but Downes' suggestion that he had brought on himself the active disfavour of Mussolini's government – at least before his decision to leave Italy – appears to be exaggerated.

[2] In fact, in 1939.

Montemezzi (seated) rehearsing
L'Incantesimo with (*L* to *R*) Mario Berini,
Vivian Della Chiesa and Alexander Sved

For the stage the 'plot' would be weak, if not unintelligible in terms of sheer dramatic development. But this hardly matters when the essential drama is told by the music.

And that is what happens. There is the immediate musical establishment of atmosphere; there are prevailing moods – two principal moods, practically one, the tragical being just sufficiently touched to heighten the lyrical sweep and glow of what is essentially the same tonal speech which Montemezzi made glorious in 'L'Amore dei Tre Re' ('The Love of Three Kings') and for which, in Benelli's new poem, he finds a corresponding incentive.

The story? The husband, Folco, and the wife, Giselda, sit in the great room of a medieval castle in northern Italy, while a February tempest raged outside. They are waiting for the visit of Rinaldo, a former rival of Folco's for his wife's hand, and a magician with whom Rinaldo has been studying, since their marriage. From this man Folco seeks an interpretation of a strange thing.

Hunting, Folco has slain a grim wolf, and then, the ardor of the chase upon him, had turned and speared a gentle doe that was coming toward him, when, lo, as the animal fell, he thought it had his wife's face! Folco secretly fears the appeal of the younger Rinaldo to his wife, and Rinaldo knows the supreme transforming power of love, which can effect any miracle.

The magician's rede is that if Folco goes back into the forest, finds the slain doe, and, if it still has for him his wife's face, is strong enough to bring the victim back to the castle, his love is secure. If not —? While he is away Rinaldo of course makes love. Giselda, moved, and greatly agitated, tries to jest. If love had the power he claims, then she would fain he exorcised the bitter weather, and brought spring to her, and the ardor of Rinaldo is felt in the music.

Voice of Folco Heard

The voice of Folco, harsh, apprehensive, is heard outside. He has found nothing. And now the magic is aworking. Outside are heard the songs of birds. Nature awakens. The sun disperses the clouds, the fields blossom, the songs of birds are heard. And Giselda's soul bursts its bonds, and she apostrophizes love's power.

It is evident that in his score Mr. Montemezzi has said nothing that is new since the score of 'L'Amore dei tre re' – a similar theme. His lyricism has the same ardent pulse and sweep of line – a lyricism less coarse and vital, perhaps, than that of Puccini or other Italian realists, but wholly poetical in color and exaltation, without grease, and superbly vocal. In other words, we have in the finest pages of 'L'Incantesimo' the same priceless melodic substance, so scarce today in music; the same Italianate song in terms of translated symphonism, which made 'L'Amore'; the same freedom from dross and poetic sentiment. Just some more of it, which is splendid, and likely to be of wide popular appeal.

One thing is lacking in this radio production which should promptly be provided. That is a good English translation, for listeners who need to understand what the music is talking about, especially when they tune in too late to hear the introductory explanation of the story. For this will bear repetition.

At the end of the performance Mr. Montemezzi received a thunderous tribute from audience and orchestra, too, which his music had fairly earned.

Then, the second after, came the announcement of important, gratifying and murderous war news[1] – a transition, if ever there was one, symbolic of today, but also symbolic of the fact that something else but murder had been done by a poet and a composer and broadcast in humanity's cause to the world; and that some day the song, and not the murder would have the last word.

---

[1] There is a striking and poignant probability that this 'murderous war news' concerned the Allied advance into Italy, against stiff German opposition, which was dominating headlines at the time (see illustration overleaf). A second possibility is that it concerned the Russian advance toward Kiev.

Front page of the New York *Sun*, 9 October 1943

L'Incantesimo was broadcast as the Allies pushed towards Rome

2. Viva Liebling, *Musical Courier*, 20 October 1943.

Montemezzi Opera Premiered by NBC

It is a pleasure to announce that Italo Montemezzi's new opera, L'Incantesimo, premiered Oct. 9 by NBC, is one long stretch of melody from beginning to end. To be able to sit back and let the music flow around me, without having either to consult a chart as to its form or keep in mind its social significance, was reason enough to be grateful to its composer.

There were vague rumors that the plot, slightly on the complex side, has some deep underlying political meaning.[1] If so, there is certainly no sign of it in the music, which is gloriously and uninhibitedly lyrical. It rises throughout to unashamedly poetical and passionate climaxes and makes one wonder why so many of our contemporary composers are frightened out of their wits by any hint of melody.

The opera lasts forty-five minutes. Like L'Amore dei Tre Re, the melodic line is continuous, in the Wagner-Strauss tradition. There are no set arias, and the orchestration is more symphonic than operatic in form. The three high moments of the work are reached in Folco's narrative, the love duet between Rinaldo and Giselda, and Giselda's final apostrophe to the miracle of love. A brief choral interlude is introduced effectively just before the end.

Whether, because of its lack of dramatic action, the opera would be highly effective on the stage, remains to be seen. However, because of its symphonic quality, it could and should have many performances by symphony orchestras. An English libretto might be provided, as it is difficult to keep the story in mind throughout.

---

1 This 'deep' meaning is certainly there if Giselda is understood as, at some level, a personification of Italy, just as Fiora was in *L'Amore dei Tre Re*.

Alexander Sved, Vivian Della Chiesa, Mario Berini and Virgilio Lazzari threw their whole souls into the performance, no doubt stimulated by the superb playing of the NBC Symphony Orchestra. Folco's narrative, as sung by Alexander Sved[,] was a gem of taste and beautiful phrasing. One understands why Montemezzi was so insistent about obtaining Sved for the part.[1] It is hard to imagine anyone singing it better.

Vivian Della Chiesa, who has been sorely missed from radio, sang Giselda with warmth, tenderness and luscious beauty of tone, and Mario Berini seconded her brilliantly as Rinaldo. Lazzari made an impressive Salomone.

---

[1] Liebling had published an anticipatory feature on *L'Incantesimo* in the previous issue of the *Musical Courier* (5 October), largely concerned with detailing the story, and noted that 'Alexander Sved ... has been chosen by Montemezzi for the role of Folco.'

3. Oscar Thompson, *Musical America*, October 1943.

New Montemezzi Opera Has Radio Premiere

Composer Conducts First Hearing of His 'L'Incantesimo,' With Text By Sem Benelli – Vague Symbolism of Book a Barrier to Stage Performance – Score Both Melodic and Symphonic

IN HIS newest opera, 'L'Incantesimo,' which Italo Montemezzi has composed to a poetic text by Sem Benelli, author of the play that served the Italian composer as libretto for 'L'Amore dei Tre Re,' Montemezzi has repeated himself. But he has done this so beautifully and so expertly that his score is a treasurable one. Whether it will ever see the operatic stage is conjectural, especially since its radio premiere at the hands of the NBC on Oct. 9 seemed to argue the weakness of the literary subject matter as a theme for dramatic production.

With the composer himself conducting, and with Vivian della Chiesa, Mario Berini, Alexander Sved and Virgilio Lazzari as soloists, the NBC Symphony gave the most sonorous eloquence to the orchestral score, which is of the symphonic richness of 'L'Amore.' The singers coped competently with their tasks, but were often overshadowed by the surging, soaring climaxes of the instrumental ensemble, which shared with the vocalists the melodic exfoliations and often compelled the singers to give to their music all the power of voice they could summon forth in their effort to be heard.

Unlike 'L'Amore,' the words of 'L'Incantesimo' were written to be set to music, and they were intended for Mr. Montemezzi's particular use. The libretto contains as much of vague symbolism and a kind of philosophy as it does of drama,[1] and the upshot

---

[1] For the symbolism, see above, p. 327, n. 1. The 'philosophy' concerns the contrasting effects of the selfish, brutish, possessive love of Folco and the generous, patient, redemptive love of Rinaldo.

is a text more suitable for a cantata, it would seem, than for an opera in the stage sense, though in performance the work occupies more than 40 minutes.

Little or No Characterization

Folco, husband of Giselda, and Rinaldo, a former lover, are in some degree personifications – the one of brute force, the other of ideal love. Giselda herself is a colorless figure, for whose edification a minor miracle is worked, so that she sees spring aglow in the midst of winter. The magician Salomone is merely so much machinery, though he discourses eruditely – if scantily – on the meaning of love and the opera's particular parables. It all seems to end nowhere and the characters are never real. Their emotions are the orchestra's – the composer's and Sem Benelli's – scarcely their own, though they have important melodic passages to sing. There is little or no characterization.

This last is as true of the music as of the text. The composer simply had no opportunity to set one character differently from the others, as he had with blind old Archibaldo in 'L'Amore dei Tre Re.' As personages, Giselda, Folco and Rinaldo are indefinite figures, yet the music of all of these is warm and soars ecstatically.

Montemezzi is a melodist – an Italian melodist. He is true to his birthright in what he writes for the voice. But he is also a master of the orchestra, and, unlike so many of his countrymen – including the popular Puccini – he builds a symphonic structure; it has a web that is the main fabric of his score; the voices are spun into this web or suspended above it.

The Old Charge of Wagnerism

It is this that raises again the old and erroneous charge of Wagnerism. The score is Italian – in feeling, in color, in emotion, in sensuous lyricism. There is in it more that suggests a

ARENA di VERONA

ENTE AUTONOMO SPETTACOLI LIRICI

XXX STAGIONE: 19 LUGLIO - 17 AGOSTO 1952

LA GIOCONDA
DI A. PONCHIELLI

BORIS GODUNOV   LA TRAVIATA
DI M. MOUSSORGSKY   DI G. VERDI

CAVALLERIA RUSTICANA
DI P. MASCAGNI

L'INCANTESIMO
DI I. MONTEMEZZI
IN PRIMA MONDIALE

BALLETTI
DELL' I. B. DI LONDRA

CALENDARIO DEGLI SPETTACOLI

Sabato 19 Luglio - LA GIOCONDA	Domenica 10 Agosto - LA TRAVIATA
Domenica 20 Luglio - BORIS GODUNOV	Martedì 12 Agosto - L'INCANTESIMO
Mercoledì 23 Luglio - LA GIOCONDA	CAVALLERIA RUSTICANA
Sabato 26 Luglio - BORIS GODUNOV	GAIETE' PARISIENNE
Domenica 27 Luglio - LA TRAVIATA	Mercoledì 13 Agosto - IL LAGO DEI CIGNI
Martedì 29 Luglio - BORIS GODUNOV	*(International Ballet)*
Giovedì 31 Luglio - LA GIOCONDA	Giovedì 14 Agosto - LA TRAVIATA
Sabato 2 Agosto - LA TRAVIATA	Venerdì 15 Agosto - L'INCANTESIMO
Domenica 3 Agosto - LA GIOCONDA	CAVALLERIA RUSTICANA
Martedì 5 Agosto - LA TRAVIATA	GAIETE' PARISIENNE
Giovedì 7 Agosto - LA GIOCONDA	Sabato 16 Agosto - LA BELLA ADDORMENTATA
Sabato 9 Agosto - L'INCANTESIMO	*(International Ballet)*
CAVALLERIA RUSTICANA	Domenica 17 Agosto - IL LAGO DEI CIGNI
GAIETE' PARISIENNE	*(International Ballet)*

Verranno effettuati TRENI TURISTICI a cura delle Ferrovie dello Stato

INFORMAZIONI: Soprintendenza dell'Ente autonomo spettacoli lirici Arena di Verona: VICOLO SCUOLE COMUNALI n. 7 tel. 3520 - Telegrammi: ENTEARENA VERONA - Ufficio turistico: ARCOVOLO n. 5 tel. 3204 - Ente Prov. Turismo, Casa Giulietta, tel. 5065 e presso tutte le Org. turistiche e Agenzie di viaggio

Diffusione autorizzata dalla Questura di Verona in data 5 Marzo 1952 n. 19444

TIP U.COUTELLA-VERONA

L'Incantesimo was first staged in 1952, in Verona

glorified Mascagni than Wagner, though it is perfectly possible to find individual phrases that in their contours recall Wagner or Strauss. The structure certainly is not Wagnerian in the sense that it is built upon the repetition of leading motives.

But if its lyric blood is that of Mascagni, Leoncavallo and Puccini, it runs a more aristocratic course, both in its basic inspiration and in the employment of a technique superior to theirs in the refinements of the musical art. Like that of 'L'Amore,' the music of 'L'Incantesimo' has a patrician cast.

Whether there is a lasting place in radio for a score as complicated and as difficult to perform as 'L'Incantesimo' is by no means assured. One can only rejoice that in the world today – and living among us in America – is a composer who can write music of such worth and appeal. With this rejoicing, there goes the regret that he has not found a warmly human and theatrical text that might have enabled him to compose an opera that would at least stand besides his 'Tre Re.' He has not gone beyond the earlier work in 'L'Incantesimo,' or equalled it in dramatic poignancy. But he has shown that he is still an artist.

4. Marion Bauer, *Musical Leader*, November 1943.

Montemezzi's New Opera

ONE OF the most important broadcasts of the young season, was the premiere of the opera 'L'Incantesimo' (The Enchantment) by Italo Montemezzi, the noted composer of 'L'Amore dei Tre Re.' The librettist was Sem Benelli who had also written the older opera which has been performed at the Metropolitan and elsewhere frequently. The new opera was written in this country and the composer has often expressed his joy at finding himself far from the atmosphere of Fascist Italy to have a haven in a land where an artist could create unfettered by restrictions on personal freedom. For the first time an opera by a composer of his rank has been given its world premiere by radio. Previous to this NBC has presented two operas which it commissioned: Menotti's 'The Old Maid and the Thief' and George Lessner's 'The Nightingale and the Rose,' both of which were successful.[1]

'L'Incantesimo' represents Montemezzi's finest style of beautiful lyricism, rich harmonization and splendid orchestration. There is no attempt at ultramodern idiom which would not be a true expression of the composer's type of writing. But this work is sincere and natural music written by one whose greatest success was achieved early in the 20th century. The score is frequently impressionistic and sometimes reflects Wagnerian harmonies, but the entire effect is beautiful and noble. The cast included the Metropolitan baritone, Alexander Sved, in the role of Folco, Mario Berini, tenor, in the role of Renaldo [sic], and Vivian della Chiesa, well known American soprano, of radio, concert

1 *The Old Maid and the Thief* had been broadcast on 22 April 1939; *The Nightingale and the Rose* on 25 April 1942. The NBC's involvement with radio operas actually went back several years further to Charles Wakefield Cadman's *The Willow Tree*, apparently the first opera specially written for the radio medium, broadcast on 3 October 1932.

and opera, who sang the role of Folco's young wife Giselda; the role of the magician, Salomone, was sung by Lazzari, also of the Metropolitan. The action of the opera takes place in the castle of Folco at the foot of the Alps in Italy. The time is the Middle Ages. Montemezzi conducted the NBC Orchestra and the soloists in an excellent performance. It is to be hoped that the public will have the chance to see the opera staged in the near future.

Appendix 1: Plots

The Plots of Montemezzi's Operas

(presented in the United States)

L'Amore dei Tre Re

Background:
Forty years ago, at an unspecified period in the Dark Ages, Archibaldo was one of the leaders of a barbarian army invading Italy. Eventually he conquered the province of Altura, the people of which made peace by marrying their princess, Fiora, to Archibaldo's son, Manfredo. Fiora had previously been engaged to the Italian prince Avito. Despite the marriage, there is an on-going insurgency in Altura, and Manfredo is often away attempting to suppress the rebellion. Archibaldo himself no longer leaves his castle: he has become blind. Fiora has resumed her relationship with Avito, and Archibaldo is very suspicious of her. The action takes place in Archibaldo's castle.

Act One:
Shortly before dawn, Archibaldo, unable to sleep, comes into the great hall of the castle which leads onto a terrace overlooking the valley below. He is expecting Manfredo's return. Flaminio, his servant, leads him to sing of his great love of Italy, and his former desire for conquest, before persuading him to go back to bed. Avito and Fiora appear from her room, talking of their love. After a long kiss, Avito slips away. Archibaldo, suspicious, returns to the hall and catches Fiora before she is able to get back to her room. She denies that she has been talking to anyone, and says she has come out to look for Manfredo. Archibaldo does not believe her, and when news arrives of Manfredo's arrival, he tells her to go back to bed. Father and son greet each other warmly, and Manfredo reports that the insurgency is nearly defeated. Fiora, reappearing, greets Manfredo coolly; he expresses his grief that he cannot win her love.

Act Two:
In the afternoon, a few days later, Manfredo says farewell to Fiora on a terrace high on the castle walls. He begs her, for the sake of his love, to wave to him with a scarf as he leads his army back to the war. Touched by his affection, she agrees. He leaves, and soon afterwards a handmaiden brings a casket containing the white scarf to be waved. Fiora reluctantly climbs onto the castle wall to wave it, but Avito appears below, disguised as a guard, and she is torn between her duty to her husband and the passionate declarations of her lover. At last she comes down to Avito, and they share a long kiss. Archibaldo disturbs them; Avito slips away, but his departure is heard by the blind king, who accordingly begins to interrogate Fiora. Flaminio announces that Manfredo is returning. Fiora admits to Archibaldo that she has been with her lover, but says she will reveal more only to Manfredo. Archibaldo, fearing that Manfredo will pardon her, becomes angrier and angrier and finally strangles Fiora. Manfredo, who has returned worried by the fact that Fiora stopped waving the scarf, enters to discover her dead. He is sad rather than angry to learn of her treachery. Archibaldo promises further vengeance on the unknown lover, and they enter the castle, Archibaldo carrying Fiora's dead body.

Act Three:
In the evening of the same day, Fiora's body has been laid out in the crypt of the castle chapel. People of Altura have gathered to express their sorrow for her loss and to talk of vengeance. They leave when they see Avito approaching. He sings of his sorrow and his love, then kisses Fiora's lips, after which he feels a terrible faintness. Manfredo enters and announces that, at Archibaldo's command, a powerful poison had been spread on Fiora's lips. Manfredo himself is unable to feel any hatred for the dying Avito, and he too kisses Fiora, throwing himself on her body. Archibaldo enters, believing the lover has been caught, and finds his son about to expire.

La Nave

Background:
The action takes place on an island in the Venetian estuary around 552 A.D. The early Venetians are building their city, while fighting for independence from the Byzantine Empire. They have recently revolted against their Tribune, Orso Faledro, who stands accused of extorting

property from his fellow Venetians and secret dealings with the Greeks. Orso and four of his sons have been blinded.

Prologue:
The people are awaiting the arrival of the Gratico brothers from the war. They want to make Marco Gratico their next Tribune and Sergio Gratico their next Bishop. Basiliola, the beautiful daughter of Orso Faledro, arrives just before the Graticos and is appalled to discover the fate of her father and brothers. The Gratico brothers arrive bringing news of their success in war and recovery of holy relics; they are acclaimed as Tribune and Bishop. Basiliola offers to dance the 'dance of Victory' for Marco, but collapses, sobbing.

First Episode:
Basiliola approaches a pit in which those out of favour with the new Gratico regime are kept prisoner. The prisoners accuse her, knowing she is now the lover of Marco Gratico. Basiliola is eventually so outraged that she seizes a bow and starts shooting the prisoners, who beg for death. They are all killed. A monk, Traba, enters to denounce Basiliola and predict her downfall. When Marco Gratico appears, Traba upbraids him too, saying that he is 'in the hands of a woman' and betraying his great destiny. Basiliola demands vengeance on Traba, but Marco merely tells him to go away. Before he leaves, Traba reveals that Basiliola is also a lover of Sergio. Marco is suspicious of Basiliola, but is seduced and distracted by the pictures of foreign conquest she paints for him. They bury their differences in a long kiss.

Second Episode:
Sergio Gratico is holding a distinctly unchristian feast in his church. Basiliola dances seductively before his guests. There is an intrusion of people demanding that the church be purged of 'fornicators and idolaters,' and that Sergio lose his office. Marco Gratico arrives to interrupt a tense standoff; he orders his men to arrest Sergio, but the Bishop responds with threats, and the two brothers, incited by Basiliola and the people, agree to a single combat that will decide Sergio's guilt or innocence. The fight takes place in the church. Sergio, despite being aided by Basiliola, is defeated and killed. Alarms sound, and news arrives that Giovanni Faledro, Basiliola's oldest brother, is leading an attack on the city. Marco orders Basiliola to be bound, then leaves to organize the defence.

Third Episode:
Venice has been successfully defended. The big ship *Totus Mundus* is ready for launching. Marco Gratico explains to the people that he will expiate the sin of killing his brother by banishing himself on the ship. They respond enthusiastically, calling on him to 'Redeem the Adriatic!' Basiliola, still bound, interrupts to request a 'glorious death.' Marco orders that Basiliola be fixed onto the ship as a figurehead. This is done, and as the people sing a chorus of praise, the ship slides into the water.

Giovanni Gallurese

Background:
The action takes place in Sardinia in 1662, near the end of the period when the island was ruled by Spain. Giovanni Gallurese is a notable outlaw, having killed a Spanish nobleman who insulted him. He and Maria, a miller's daughter, have secretly fallen in love, though they have not spoken, and Maria has no idea who he is. Rivegas, a Spaniard, has become infatuated with Maria.

Act One:
Rivegas and two of his Spanish cronies attempt to abduct Maria from outside her father's house. Her cries are heard by Giovanni Gallurese, who rescues her, killing one of the Spaniards and causing the others to flee. He learns that Maria and her father believe the abductors to have been Giovanni Gallurese and his men: outlaws of whom they are deeply afraid. Embarrassed by this, Giovanni gives a false name when they ask him who he is, and pretends to be a shepherd. He initially refuses to enter their house, but when he hears Maria singing of her love for him he reveals his own love, and there is a scene of rapturous mutual understanding.

Act Two:
A few days later a lively crowd has gathered outside a temporary inn to celebrate the festival of Saint Antonio. There is much drinking and dancing and Rivegas is a prominent figure in the crowd. Giovanni and Maria are ecstatically reunited, but then Giovanni hears Rivegas denouncing Giovanni Gallurese and telling of how he, Rivegas, had rescued Maria from an attempted abduction by the outlaw. Giovanni, furious, wants to confront Rivegas, but he is restrained by his friend

Bastiano, who himself reveals the truth. Rivegas is publically humiliated, but then realizing that Giovanni is there, he hurries off to get soldiers to arrest him. One of the other Spaniards panics and reveals the presence of the famous outlaw to the crowd. The people disperse quickly and Giovanni comforts a frightened Maria. As Rivegas and Spanish soldiers approach, Giovanni calls his men and takes to the mountains, to Maria's astonishment. She watches from a distance as the outlaws defeat the Spaniards. As Giovanni and his men return with the captured Rivegas, she asks Giovanni who he really is. He still attempts to conceal the truth, but his identity is revealed by Rivegas. Maria flees in horror.

Act Three:
Immediately afterwards, Maria and her father return home, with Maria in a state of confused agony. Giovanni and his men enter with the captured Rivegas, who they taunt before Giovanni interrupts to describe the ideal of 'Liberty' that inspires his actions. The other outlaws want to kill Rivegas, but Giovanni insists that he be allowed to go free. Maria, who has watched all this, declares her continuing, unconditional love for Giovanni, and the lovers, now alone, plan to emigrate together. Rivegas, however, has obtained a gun and shoots Giovanni from behind before attempting to rape Maria. Maria, following Giovanni's instruction, manages to sound his horn three times: this recalls his followers, who kill Rivegas. Giovanni dies, his final words being of love and liberty.

La Notte di Zoraima

Background:
Peru has been conquered by the Spanish, but Muscar, the dethroned Inca king, is leading an active insurgency. Muscar's affianced lover, Zoraima, widely supposed to be mad but in fact quite rational and assisting the insurgency, is living in a ruined palace. Pedrito, the married captain of the Spanish, is hunting Muscar and also infatuated with Zoraima.

Single Act:
Inca insurgents visit Zoraima to confirm the plan for an ambitious raid on a Spanish munitions convoy; afterwards they will escape to the mountains, and set fire to the forest behind them. There is only

one problem: a rumour that Pedrito is waiting to ambush Muscar. The Incas leave to prepare for the attack, then Muscar himself visits Zoraima. She warns him about Pedrito, but he refuses to change the plan, and promises to marry Zoraima on the following day. They sing of their love. He leaves. Manuela, Pedrito's wife, then visits Zoraima to beg her for assurance that she, Zoraima, is not her husband's lover. Zoraima assures her she would never love Pedrito. Soon after Manuela leaves, a shot rings out; Zoraima is full of foreboding, and soon afterwards some Incas bring in the wounded Muscar, shot by Pedrito. They report that they are being pursued by the Spanish, and Zoraima hides them in the palace. Pedrito arrives, convinced that Muscar is there; he accuses Zoraima of treachery and threatens to rape her. They are interrupted by the arrival of a motley crowd of Spaniards demanding Zoraima's death: the crowd has obtained information from a prisoner that she is hiding Muscar. Pedrito gets them to leave by staking his own life for those of Muscar and Zoraima. After they have gone, Zoraima admits that the wounded king is in the palace, but she offers to become Pedrito's lover if he will let Muscar go free. Pedrito, torn in his feelings, finally agrees. Muscar is conveyed away. Zoraima plays for time with Pedrito, then, when the forest bursts into fire as a signal that Muscar is safely in the mountains, she stabs herself and dies. The Spaniards return, astonished by the fire, and seize Pedrito, accusing him of treachery.

L'Incantesimo

In the case of *L'Incantesimo* I reproduce here a summary which Montemezzi himself must have approved, and that he quite possibly prepared. This was published ahead of the broadcast performance and clarifies a few details not clear in the libretto:

> The action takes place in the Middle Ages, in the castle of Folco, at the foot of the Italian Alps. Folco and his young wife Giselda have just finished dinner in the great hall. Folco inquires of a servant if Count Rinaldo has arrived. Giselda asks if her husband doubts her love, that he has invited her former suitor after so long a silence. Folco replies that he merely wishes to ask Rinaldo about his magician, Salomone, and whether he can

interpret something strange that has befallen.

Rinaldo arrives with Salomone, to whom Folco tells his story. During a hunt he had followed a wolf and killed him. Then he saw a hind, and was about to kill her, when the face of the hind turned into the face of Giselda. Too late, he struck. What, he asks Salomone, does this portend?

Salomone interprets it by saying that Folco is full of pride and ignores the real meaning of love. As Folco protests, Salomone declares he can prove his love by digging up the hind he has killed and, if he finds Giselda's corpse instead, he must carry it through the storm to the castle. Folco leaves to do this.

Rinaldo tells Giselda he still loves her, but Giselda is not convinced. However, as Rinaldo continues to plead his love, Giselda declares that if he can make Spring appear during this Winter storm she will believe and be his.

The scene darkens, Giselda is afraid. Outside Folco's voice is heard, and Rinaldo has disappeared. Folco enters and asks Salomone where Giselda is. Salomone points to her, but Folco sees only the hind where his wife is standing.

Suddenly the call of Spring is heard, Folco and Salomone disappear and as the Spring dawns outside, Giselda sings a hymn in praise of love.[1]

---

[1] *Musical Courier*, 5 October 1943, 8.

Appendix 2: Biographies

Biographies of Montemezzi's American Critics

(featured in this collection)

ALDRICH, Richard. Born 1863 in Providence, Rhode Island. Graduated magna cum laude from Harvard in 1885, where, as well as taking regular humanities courses, he studied music with John Knowles Paine and wrote musical criticism for the *Harvard Crimson*. After graduating, Aldrich commenced a career in journalism with the *Providence Journal*, then moved to Washington around 1889 as private secretary to the junior senator from Rhode Island. While in Washington he wrote music criticism for the *Washington Star*; this attracted the attention of the *New-York Tribune*, which appointed him assistant music, art and literary critic in 1891. At the *Tribune* he was a colleague of Henry E. Krehbiel. When William J. Henderson left the *New York Times* to go to the *Sun* in 1902, he recommended Aldrich as his successor. Apart from a brief period in the First World War, when he joined military intelligence, Aldrich served as the chief music critic of the *Times* until 1923, when, disillusioned by the direction modern music was taking, he retired. With Krehbiel, Henderson and Henry T. Finck, Aldrich made up a powerful quartet of leading New York music critics, but he was gentler and less opinionated than the others. Mark N. Grant judges that 'Aldrich was mild, assiduous, scholarly, comprehensive – the archetypal boilerplate *New York Times* writer.'[1] Unlike the others, too, he was not devoted to book publication, though he did publish *A Guide to Parsifal* (1904), *A Guide to the Ring of the Nibelungen* (1905) and *Musical Discourse* (1928), the last a collection of his writings for the *Times*. The composers Aldrich most admired were Bach and Wagner; he had a particular dislike for Berlioz, and little time for Italian opera before *Rigoletto*. Here his customary mildness sometimes deserted him: a severe account of Bellini's *Il Puritani* in 1906 prompted an angry response from one Italian reader: 'Is not this

---

[1] *Maestros of the Pen: A History of Classical Music Criticism in America* (Boston: Northeastern UP, 1998), 98.

gentleman [Aldrich], among the numerous Teuton-trained critics who afflict New York, the most "arrrabiato" [rabid]?'[1] After his retirement from the *New York Times*, Aldrich spent a year in London, reviewing for the London *Times*. Thereafter he continued to write on music on an occasional basis, while building up and cataloguing his enormous music library (later donated to Harvard). He died in Rome in 1937, while on a visit to his younger brother.

BAUER, Marion (Eugénie). Born 1882 in Walla Walla, Washington, of French parentage. The family moved to Portland, Oregon, in 1890, and Bauer graduated from St. Helen's Hall (later Oregon Episcopal School) in 1899. She then went to New York to live and study music with her older sister, Emilie Frances Bauer (1865–1926). She continued her music studies in Paris in 1906–07, where one of her teachers was Nadia Boulanger (who taught her in exchange for English lessons). On her return to New York, Bauer still continued to study with a variety of teachers, supported by her sister and family. She started publishing songs and piano pieces regularly in the 1910s, and by the early 1920s had earned a reputation as a promising composer of radical and modernist tendencies. The illness and death of her sister Emilie in 1926 changed Bauer's life. She joined the music faculty of New York University the same year, and took over her sister's position as the New York correspondent to the Chicago *Musical Leader*. Bauer taught music history and composition at New York University until her retirement in 1951; she also taught at the Juilliard School between 1940 and 1944, and often taught summer courses at other institutions. In 1933 she published an influential defense of modernist music, *Twentieth Century Music: How it Developed, How to Listen to It*. She also co-authored three books with the popular writer Ethel Peyser (listed separately). By the 1930s Bauer was no longer associated with the avant-garde, but she was respected for her intelligent, elegant compositions, and much admired as a teacher. She died while on vacation at South Hadley, Massachusetts, in 1955.

BROEKHOVEN, John (Andrew) van. Born 1852 in Beek, Holland. It is not clear when he came to America, but he played viola in the Theodore Thomas Orchestra, dissolved in 1888. Broekhoven then taught at the Cincinnati College of Music between 1889 and 1899, while also conducting local symphony orchestras. He composed a good deal

---

[1] 'An Italian Friend's Protest,' *New York Times*, 9 December 1906, 5.

of music, including a one-act opera, *A Colonial Wedding*, performed in Cincinnati in 1905, and a full-length opera, *Camaralzaman*, apparently unperformed. He specialized in vocal training, on which he published several books, as well as writing for a number of musical periodicals. Broekhoven moved to New York in 1905 to work mainly as a singing teacher. He died at the home of his nephew in Columbus, Ohio, in 1930.

COX, Jeannette. Cox served as the Chicago correspondent to the *Musical Courier* from the 1910s to the 1940s. No other information about her is currently available.

DE KOVEN, Reginald. Born 1859 in Middletown, Connecticut. In 1872 his family moved to England, where in 1880 he graduated from the University of Oxford with a degree in modern history. De Koven then studied various aspects of music in Germany, Austria, and Italy, including composition with Richard Genée in Vienna. He returned to America in 1882, settling in Chicago, where he initially worked in a brokerage firm. In 1884 his marriage to Anna Farwell, the wealthy daughter of a senator from Illinois, gave him the financial security to pursue a career as a composer – a career which soon proved very lucrative in its own right. His first operetta, *The Begum* (1887), was successful; his third, *Robin Hood* (1891), was a sensation, and established De Koven as the leading American composer of operetta. Apparently on the basis of his success as a composer, he was invited to pursue a second career as a newspaper critic, something he did for many years, despite not needing the income. He reviewed for the *Chicago Evening Post* from 1889 to 1892, and then, on moving to New York, continued with the *New York World* until 1897, while also writing for *Harper's Weekly* 1895–97. In 1897 De Koven moved to Washington, D.C., where he founded and conducted the short-lived Washington Symphony Orchestra in 1902. Subsequently moving back to New York, he commenced his second stint as a critic, returning to the *New York World* in 1907. He stayed there until 1912, then took a second break from criticism, before becoming music critic for the *New York Herald* in 1918. As a critic, De Koven was mainly interested in opera and operetta, and he championed popular Italian and French operas against the more highbrow critics. In 1907 he predicted that '[o]peras like *Faust* and *Carmen* will be played and enjoyed when the dramas of the *Ring* are forgotten.'[1] In 1918 he stated that *Aida* was his favourite

---

1 Quoted in Grant, *Maestros of the Pen*, 173.

opera, for it was 'the richest in spontaneous melody.'[1] Views like this put him at odds with such Wagnerian critics as Henry E. Krehbiel and Henry T. Finck, who tended not to take him seriously, though when he joined the *Herald* Krehbiel welcomed the appointment of 'an expert of demonstrated merit' as a specialized music critic.[2] As a composer, De Koven never repeated the immense success of *Robin Hood*, but *Rob Roy* (1894), *The Highwayman* (1897) and *Maid Marian* (1902) all proved very popular. His later operettas were, by his own standards, mostly failures, and late in his career he turned to opera with *The Canterbury Pilgrims* (1917), produced at the Met, and *Rip van Winkle* (1920). He died on a visit to Chicago, to attend a performance of the latter opera, in 1920.

DEVRIES, Herman. Born 1858 in New York. His family moved to France while he was a child. Devries studied at the Lycee Condorcet, Paris, and also took singing lessons with Bizet. He made his professional singing debut in June 1879 as the Grand Inquisitor in Meyerbeer's *L'Africaine* at the Opéra, Paris. Devries generally sung bass roles, but later in his career sometimes took baritone roles, too. He enjoyed a reasonably successful singing career, culminating in his singing at the Met for two seasons between 1898 and 1900. Devries retired from singing in 1900 and moved to Chicago, where he established himself as a leading singer teacher and the music critic for the *Chicago American*. He died in Chicago in 1949.

DOWNES, Olin. Born 1886 in Evanston, Illinois, as Edwin Olin Quigley, but grew up in privileged circumstances in New Jersey. His father was imprisoned for forgery in 1895; his mother then obtained a divorce and changed the family name to Downes. The effects of this scandal made higher education impossible for Downes, but he studied music privately and developed considerable proficiency on the piano. In 1906 he was appointed music critic of the *Boston Post*, a downmarket newspaper which boasted one of the largest circulations in the country. Here Downes was initially very influenced by Philip Hale, dean of the Boston music critics, but he developed a more popular style of writing than that employed by most of his older peers. He

---

1 Augustin Lardy, 'New York's Music Critics Talk Shop Out of Hours,' *New York Herald Magazine*, 22 December 1918, 2.

2 Ibid.

continued at the *Post* until 1924, then moved to New York to succeed Richard Aldrich as the chief music critic for the *New York Times*. With the deaths and retirements of most of the older critics around this time, Downes soon found himself in a dominant position in New York, his main rivals being the aging William J. Henderson and the more highbrow Lawrence Gilman. Downes was not a particularly subtle critic, but he was very good at communicating enthusiasm. He saw his work in terms of building and educating the audience for classical music, though he also showed appreciation for ragtime and jazz. Downes became best known for his passionate championship of Sibelius's music and Toscanini's conducting. He was also enthusiastic about the music of Brahms and Strauss, and showed a more measured taste for that of Debussy, Prokofiev and Shostakovich. He had a particular dislike for Mahler and Stravinsky. In opera, Downes greatly admired Wagner, but he also appreciated a much wider range of opera, and indeed operetta, than the older critics. Here, as with instrumental music, he could position himself with the 'ordinary' music lover and against the highbrows. Of *Il Trovatore*, for example, he wrote: 'What melody! What emotional power! In spite of its tortuous narrative, in spite of the old-fashioned conventions ... the music has a pulse, a thrill, that neither time nor custom nor hand-organs can stale.'[1] In addition to his newspaper work, Downes published *The Lure of Music* (1918), *Symphonic Broadcasts* (1931) and the posthumous *Sibelius the Symphonist* (1956). He continued to write for the *New York Times* until his death in New York in 1955.

FINCK, Henry T. (Theophilus). Born 1854 in Bethel, Missouri, of German parentage. The family moved to Aurora, Oregon, in 1862. Finck graduated from Harvard in 1876, and promptly accepted a commission to report on the first Bayreuth performance of the complete Ring Cycle for the New York *World*. Returning to Harvard for graduate study, he won a fellowship which allowed him to study philosophy and psychology in Berlin, Heidelberg and Vienna between 1878 and 1881. His goal at this time was to be a professor of philosophy, but on his return to the United States Finck accepted a position as music critic for the New York *Evening Post*, a job which in the early years involved a good deal of general editorial work. He stayed with the *Post* until summer 1924, establishing a reputation as one of the leading and most influential music critics of the day. Alongside his journalism, he

---

1 *The Lure of Music* (New York: Harper, 1918), 44.

wrote many books, the most significant being *Wagner and His Works* (1893), on which he worked for seventeen years. Other books on music include *Chopin and Other Musical Essays* (1889), *Songs and Song-Writers* (1900), *Edward Grieg* (1906), *Grieg and His Music* (1909), *Massenet and His Operas* (1910) and *Richard Strauss: The Man and His Works* (1917). Alongside such works, Finck also published books on diet, gardening and the history of romantic love. Among other composers, he championed Bach, Gluck, Weber, Schumann, Schubert, Chopin, Liszt, Tchaikovsky, MacDowell, Grieg and Massenet. Towards the end of his life he described Chopin as 'the peer of any composer Germany ever produced, Bach and Beethoven and Wagner not excepted.'[1] He had a great antipathy to Brahms and a dislike of Richard Strauss. In opera Wagner was always his hero, but he considered *Carmen* 'the best opera' apart from Wagner's later works,[2] and he had a particular enthusiasm for Massenet's operas. Finck, who wrote many of his reviews in collaboration with his wife, prided himself on being the most amiable of the major East Coast critics, and he regarded Krehbiel, with whom he liked to disagree, as his chief rival. Finck retired in 1924, disillusioned by the direction modern music was taking. He died in Rumford Falls, Maine, in 1926.

GILMAN, Lawrence. Born 1878 in Queens, New York. His education was completed at the Collins Street Classical School in Hartford, Connecticut, where he studied art. In 1896 Gilman commenced a career in journalism, working as an illustrator for the *New York Herald*. In this period he studied music intensely, making himself an expert on modern music in particular. In 1901 he became the music critic for *Harper's Weekly*. The following decade was his most productive; while the older New York critics were still generally suspicious of post-Wagnerian developments in music, Gilman undertook to familiarize American readers with the new music of the day in a series of lucid and groundbreaking studies: *Phases of Modern Music* (1904), *The Music of Tomorrow* (1907) and *Edward MacDowell: A Study* (1908). He was interested in music that expressed extramusical ideas, and his enthusiasm for opera led him to become a champion of Wagner, Strauss and Debussy. He published *Debussy's 'Pelléas and Mélisande'* (1907), *Strauss's Salome* (1907), *Aspects of Modern Opera* (1909) and, much

---

1 'James Huneker, Virtuoso of the Paragraph, Friend of the Arts,' *Evening Post*, 19 February 1921, 10.

2 Lardy, 'New York's Music Critics.'

later, *Wagner's Operas* (1937). After 1910 Gilman, whose health was poor, was forced to slow down, but he continued to write reviews for the rest of his life. In 1913 he moved to the *North American Review*, where he served as music, drama and literary critic. In 1923, after Henry E. Krehbiel's death, Gilman succeeded him as music critic for the *New-York Tribune* (it became the *Herald Tribune* the following year); he held this position until his own death. Though driven by a desire to popularize the music he loved, Gilman struck others as singularly unworldly, and much more than his peers he tended to present great music as akin to religion, with himself as hierophant. To this end he developed a highly literary style of writing, full of imagery and metaphor; to some readers it was intoxicating, to others convoluted and pretentious. Nevertheless, Gilman's judgments were generally astute, and his critical standing was very high, especially from the mid-1920s after the deaths or retirements of most of the more senior critics. He died at his summer residence in Sugar Hill, New Hampshire, in 1939. To many it seemed the end of an epoch. Leonard Liebling described Gilman as 'the last of the great critics of a bygone era.'[1] Miles Kastendieck felt that '[a] period of American musical criticism is definitely closed. ... He [Gilman] was the last of [those] who created what has been called the golden age of musical criticism in this country.'[2]

HACKETT, Karleton (Spalding). Born 1867 in Brookline, Massachusetts. Graduated from Harvard in 1891 and later studied music in Florence, London and Munich. He obtained a position as a vocal teacher at the American Conservatory of Music, Chicago, later serving as the Conservatory's vice-president and (from 1931) president. Alongside his teaching and administrative work, Hackett was the music critic for the *Chicago Evening Post* from about 1907 to 1932, when the paper ceased publication. He won a reputation as one of the leading Chicago critics. A great enthusiast for opera, Hackett led the campaign that established an opera company in Chicago, and in 1934 he became the president of the Chicago Grand Opera Company. He also published a slim volume entitled *The Beginning of Grand Opera in Chicago (1850–1859)* (1913). He died in Chicago in 1935.

---

1 Quoted in Grant, *Maestros of the Pen*, 277.

2 'Philharmonic Will Dedicate Program This Afternoon to Memory of Gilman,' *Brooklyn Eagle*, 22 October 1939, 6.

HALE, Philip. Born 1854 in Norwich, Vermont. The family subsequently moved to Northampton, Massachusetts, where, by the age of fourteen, Hale was serving as the organist of the Unitarian Church. He entered Yale in 1871 and graduated in 1876. He then studied law in Albany, New York, and was admitted to the New York bar in 1880. During these years Hale was employed as an organist at St. Peter's Episcopal Church and wrote music criticisms for the *Albany Times* and *Albany Express*. In 1882 he abandoned law in favour of music, studying in Germany 1882–85 and in Paris 1885–87. Returning to America in 1887, he moved back to Albany, where he continued to serve as an organist and to write musical journalism. In 1889 he moved to Boston, accepting posts as an organist-choirmaster at the First Unitarian Church of Roxbury and as a music critic for the *Boston Home Journal*. In 1890 he moved to become music critic for the *Boston Journal*, and in 1893 he was appointed music and drama critic of the *Boston Herald*, a position he held until his retirement in 1933. In 1901 Hale started writing programme notes for the Boston Symphony Orchestra; these notes, which sometimes grew very long, were soon regarded as critical masterpieces and held in very high regard by other critics. Hale's newspaper criticism was witty, erudite, informal and always individual. He was not afraid to change his mind. In his early career he was essentially a classicist and denounced Liszt, Berlioz, Wagner and Strauss. In later years he enthused about all these composers, Wagner apart, for whom he only ever showed a guarded appreciation. Unlike his New York peers, Hale felt that German music was too dominant in America, and he campaigned for more French and Russian music to be heard. He championed Debussy above all other modern composers; he also admired Prokofiev, but had no time for Stravinsky or Schoenberg.[1] Although Hale was less well known to the public than the major New York critics, his standing among his peers was unmatched. Huneker called him 'stupendous.'[2] Oscar Thompson hailed him as 'the dean of deans' as a newspaper music critic.[3] And after Hale's

---

1 Information about Hale's life and critical views is taken from Jean Ann Boyd's Ph.D. dissertation, 'Philip Hale, American Music Critic, Boston, 1889–1933' (University of Texas at Austin, 1985). This is much the fullest study of Hale to date.

2 See above, p. 2.

3 'Music,' *New York Evening Post*, 18 November 1933, 24.

death, William J. Henderson, the last survivor of this brilliant generation, judged that: 'In music he [Hale] can be paired only with the dazzling Huneker. These two men were unlike in most things but alike in their remoteness from conventionalism and routine in musical criticism. ... Philip Hale had a truly great mind.'[1] Hale died in Boston in 1934.

HENDERSON, William J. (James). Born 1855 in Newark, New Jersey. Contributed to local newspapers as a teenager. Graduated from Princeton in 1876 and began working for the *New-York Tribune* as a general reporter. In the late 1870s he abandoned journalism to help his father manage the Standard Theatre in New York, an experience which gave him a lifelong interest in popular musical theatre. Henderson returned to journalism in the 1880s, rejoining the *Tribune* in 1882, then becoming a general reporter for the *New York Times* the following year. Despite being largely self-taught in music, he soon started writing reviews of musical events, and in 1887 replaced Henry Schwab as the *Times*'s chief music critic. Within a few years Henderson established himself as an exceptionally well-informed critic of great descriptive power. His interest was primarily in opera, and his detailed analyses of particular singers' performances became famous, as did his witty, devastating put-downs of anything he considered substandard. His reputation was consolidated with a series of books aimed at a wide public: *The Story of Music* (1889), *Preludes and Studies* (1891) – a book largely concerned with Wagner and dedicated to Henry E. Krehbiel – *What is Good Music?* (1898), *How Music Developed* (1898) and *The Orchestra and Orchestral Music* (1899). Henderson's other passion was the sea, and he wrote a good deal of nautical fiction – *Sea Yarns for Boys* (1893), *Afloat with the Flag* (1894), *The Last Cruise of the Mohawk* (1897) – as well as *Elements of Navigation* (1895), a book used as a training manual by the U.S. government. By 1900 Henderson had a reputation as a music critic second only to Krehbiel's, and in 1902 he moved to the New York *Sun*, in exchange for a much better salary. He continued to publish prolifically: *Richard Wagner, His Life and His Dramas* (1901), *Modern Musical Drift* (1904), *The Art of the Singer* (1906) and *Some Forerunners of Italian Opera* (1911). Henderson was devoted to the Germanic tradition of music, as consummated in Wagner, though he was less partisan than Krehbiel, and when asked about his favourite music in 1918 he suggested 'that there is so much

---

1 'Music and Musicians,' *Sun*, 3 December 1934, 10.

good music in the world that no man can say what is most worthy of praise, or even advance a preference, especially if one is a music critic.'[1] For much of his career Henderson tended to be ranked second to Krehbiel among the New York critics, but there were those who judged him the older man's equal or superior. Oscar Thompson later stated his belief 'that W. J. Henderson was the greatest music critic America has produced, [even] though Henderson, himself, waved that distinction on to Krehbiel.'[2] Henderson outlived all the other major critics of his generation, and 'like a gnarled oak in a forest of saplings'[3] continued to write for the *Sun* until shortly before his suicide in New York in 1937.

HUBBARD, William L. (Lines). Born 1867 in Farmersville, New York. Grew up in Kinmundy, Illinois, and (from 1880) in Chicago. Graduated from the Lake View High School and in 1885 obtained a job as a bookkeeper for the *Chicago Evening Journal*, for which newspaper he also started writing music criticism. Hubbard served as music critic for the *Chicago Tribune* between 1891 and 1893, before moving to Dresden for five years to study piano, singing and composition. He returned to Chicago in 1898 and established himself as a singing teacher, the following year also reassuming his position as music critic for the *Tribune* (he would later serve, for a time, as the literary and drama critic, too). Hubbard was the general editor of, and major contributor to, the 12-volume *American History and Encyclopedia of Music* (1908–10), at the time the most ambitious work of its kind, and one to which Henry E. Krehbiel and William J. Henderson both contributed. Hubbard had a particular interest in opera, of which he considered Wagner the greatest exponent, and he wrote most of the short chapters on the standard operas for the *History and Encyclopedia*. Between 1912 and 1915 he served as publicity manager for the Boston Opera and gained a considerable reputation for his illustrated talks on particular operas (including *L'Amore dei Tre Re*). Hubbard had the highest reputation of any of the Chicago critics of his time. In the 1920s he retired to the Grossmont Art Colony in California, where he died in 1951.

---

1 Lardy, 'New York's Music Critics.'

2 'An American School of Criticism,' *Musical Quarterly* 23 (1937), 428–39, p. 439.

3 Winthrop Sargeant's description, quoted in Grant, *Maestros of the Pen*, 93.

HUNEKER, James Gibbons. Born 1857 in Philadelphia. Attended the Broad Street Academy, Philadelphia, between 1865 and 1872, then began a five-year apprenticeship in law, during which he discovered his great love of music. In 1875 Huneker started piano lessons with Michael Cross, one of Philadelphia's leading piano teachers, and also started writing music reviews for the Philadelphia *Evening Bulletin*. After further studies in France, 1878–79, Huneker settled in Philadelphia as a piano teacher. In 1885 he began writing for *Etude* music magazine. In 1886 he moved to New York and soon established a double career as a piano teacher at the National Conservatory of Music and a critic for the *Musical Courier* (continuing to write for *Etude*, too). By the 1890s his confident, informed, witty and unstuffy writing had won him a wide following; much in demand, he showed himself capable of immense amounts of work. In addition to writing for the *Courier* and *Etude*, he served as a music and drama critic for the New York *Recorder* from 1891 to 1895, in the same capacity for the *Morning Advertiser* from 1895 to 1897, and as a music critic for *Town Topics* from 1897 to 1902. His reputation was consolidated at the turn of the century with the publication of two acclaimed books, *Mezzotints in Modern Music* (1899) and *Chopin: The Man and His Music* (1900); Huneker considered the latter his masterpiece. These established him as one of America's top five or six music critics, but the subsequent growth of his reputation had much to do with the fact that he revealed himself much more than a music critic. In 1900 he started working for the New York *Sun* as the principal music critic; in 1902 he switched to become the paper's drama critic; and in 1906 he switched again to become the art and literature critic. His credentials for such wide-ranging criticism were established in a series of impressive studies: *Iconoclasts: A Book of Dramatists* (1905) dealt with dramatic criticism; *Egoists* (1910) with literary criticism; *Promenades of an Impressionist* (1910) with art criticism. Huneker also wrote on a freelance basis for many periodicals and continued to write extensively on music too, as well as devoting much time to editing music, including the piano music of Chopin. In his final years he began to concentrate more narrowly on music again, serving successively as a music critic for the *Philadelphia Press* (1917–18), the *New York Times* (1918–19) and the New York *World* (1919–21). Always a bohemian in his basic attitudes, Huneker was renowned for his heavy drinking, brilliant conversation and supposed sexual adventures: he was far more of a celebrity than any other American music critic had managed to be. Huneker's favourite composer was Chopin, and he was a prominent champion of Brahms and Strauss, describing the latter in 1901 as the greatest living musician and greatest orchestrator in the history of music. His opinions on many other composers are difficult to establish, as he often made contradictory statements about them, seeming to accept that contradiction could be an inherent part of an open critical attitude, and also relishing a playful, puckish, critical persona; William J. Henderson referred to him as an 'arch jester.'[1] Behind the jokes Huneker was much more open to new music than the other leading American critics of his generation. His great importance lay in his ability to make music criticism into literature and to make it an integral part of a wider culture. Mark N. Grant concludes that 'Huneker was doubtless the most influential and most widely read by other writers and intellectuals of all the music critics in our [the United States'] history.'[2] Huneker died in Brooklyn, New York, in 1921.

KRAMER, A. (Arthur) Walter. Born 1890 in New York, the son of an Austrian-born music teacher, Maximilian Kramer, who taught him music. Graduated from the City College of New York in 1910. Kramer had published a *Gavotte* for violin as early as 1908, and his main goal was to establish himself as a composer. From 1910 to 1922, however, he also served as a critic and editor for *Musical America*. From late 1922 to 1925 he travelled in Germany, Switzerland, Italy and France, experiencing a great deal of music and composing extensively. On returning to New York, Kramer rejoined *Musical America* and served as its editor-in-chief from 1929 to 1936. From 1936 to his retirement in 1956 he was the managing director of the Galaxy Music Corporation. Kramer published over three hundred compositions, in many genres, but though, as a critic, he advocated for American opera, he never attempted one himself. He was asked about his views on music in 1926, and it was reported that 'In the field of orchestral music Kramer feels that the highest peaks have been attained by Beethoven, Wagner, Strauss and Debussy. Of contemporary composers he thinks Ravel, Malipiero, Sibelius, Schoenberg, Bax and perhaps Vaughan Williams and Gustav Holst most important.' When it came to songs, 'Brahms and Hugo Wolf are the masters.'[3] Kramer died in New York in 1969.

---

1 'Miss Garden and Miss Farrar, Artistic Rivals, Discussed,' *Sun and New York Herald*, 1 February 1920, 18.

2 *Maestros of the Pen*, 106.

3 John Tasker Howard, *Studies of Contemporary American Composers: A. Walter Kramer* (New York: J. Fischer, 1926), 18, 20.

KREHBIEL, Henry E. (Edward). Born 1854 in Ann Arbor, Michigan, of German parentage. He grew up there and (from 1864) in Cincinnati. An extraordinary autodidact, Krehbiel had no higher education and little formal instruction in music. Nevertheless, through intense private study he made himself a major authority on music and music history. Between 1872 and 1874 he studied law at a local law practice, but gave it up to work as a general reporter and sometime music critic for the *Cincinnati Gazette*. In 1880 he published his first book, *The Technics of Violin Playing*, translated from the German of Karl Courvoisier. Perhaps this led to the invitation he received the same year to edit New York's weekly *Musical Review*. After a month or so in New York he accepted a better offer to become assistant music critic to the *New-York Tribune*. In his first years with the *Tribune* Krehbiel also did general reporting and editorial work, but in 1884 he succeeded John R. G. Hassard as chief music critic and could devote himself wholly to writing on music. By the end of the century he had established himself as 'the most esteemed and influential music critic America had yet seen.'[1] Alongside his journalism, Krehbiel taught music, lectured at the Institute for Musical Art (later the Juilliard School), and wrote programme notes for the New York Philharmonic Society, the Music Art Society, and many concerts and recitals. In addition he found time for an extraordinary amount of research; as his friend Henry T. Finck put it admiringly, 'He was a simply enormous worker.'[2] His major publications include *Studies in Wagnerian Drama* (1891), *How to Listen to Music* (1897), *Music and Manners in the Classical Period* (1898), *Chapters of Opera* (1909), *The Pianoforte and Its Music* (1911) and *Afro-American Folksongs: A Study in Racial and National Music* (1914). The major project of his last years was a translation of Alexander Thayer's *Ludvig van Beethovens Leben* expanded with new material from Thayer's papers (1921). In the latter part of his career Krehbiel was widely known as 'The Dean,' and after his death Richard Aldrich described him simply, but uncontroversially, as 'the leading music critic of America.'[3] Huneker, William J. Henderson and Finck may have been at least equally insightful and brilliant, but none of them matched Krehbiel's single-minded devotion to music and its study.

---

1 Grant, *Maestros of the Pen*, 81.

2 'H. E. Krehbiel A Music Critic For 48 Years,' *New York Evening Post*, 21 March 1923, 7.

3 'Henry Edward Krehbiel,' *Music and Letters* 4 (1923), 266–68, p. 266.

He believed music criticism could be objective and scientific and had an absolute faith in his own judgments. After his death, Finck wrote of him: 'While we shared our adoration of Bach, Schubert, Wagner, and a few other composers, our ideals in general were widely apart. For non-German geniuses like Chopin, Liszt, Grieg, Tchaikovsky, Bizet, Gounod, Verdi, he had little esteem; Liszt, indeed, he hated as the devil hates holy water...'[1] There was some truth to this, but, *pace* Finck, Krehbiel was an important champion of Tchaikovsky and later Mussorgsky, as well as an ardent admirer of Dvořák. His excited response to *L'Amore dei Tre Re* shows how open he was to new, 'non-German' music in the last decade of his life, even as he denounced the more consciously modernist music of Strauss and Schoenberg. Krehbiel died in New York in 1923.

LIEBLING, Leonard. Born 1874 in New York, of German parentage. Graduated from the City College of New York in 1897. Liebling then went to Berlin to study music, taking composition classes with Heinrich Urban (1837–1901) as well as piano lessons with several leading teachers, for he hoped to be a concert pianist. In 1902 he returned to New York, earlier than he had intended, to escape the determined matrimonial intentions of a German heiress.[2] He found that he could not support himself as a pianist, and soon joined the staff of the *Musical Courier*. Liebling proceeded to become the editor-in-chief of the publication in 1911, a position he held until his death. Between 1923 and 1936 he also served as the music critic of the *New York American*, though Deems Taylor briefly took over in 1931-32. Like many of his American contemporaries, Liebling was conservative in his critical opinions, devoted to the German tradition, and suspicious of modernism. In 1932 he declared: 'For me, Bach, Beethoven, Brahms, Wagner, and all the acknowledged rest in the truly legitimate line of royal succession, remain my exalted and undying heroes. ... if music does not make the appeal of beauty, what is it but a succession of more or less skillfully contrived sounds?'[3] He was known for his strong, forthright opinions, as well as his witty style. He died in New York in 1945.

---

1 'H. E. Krehbiel Painted By a Candid Friend,' *New York Evening Post*, 31 March 1923, 6.

2 'Hunted by Heiress Mr. Liebling Fled,' *New York Herald*, 31 July 1902, 6.

3 'Confessions of a Music Critic,' *Proceedings of the Music Teachers National Association* 27 (1932), 133–36, pp. 134–35.

LIEBLING, Viva. Born in New York in 1910, the daughter of Leonard Liebling. She graduated from St. Agatha's Girls School in New York and completed her education in Europe. Having studied painting with the commercial artist Penrhyn Stanlaws (1877–1957) in New York, Liebling pursued a career as a portrait painter in Europe and America. In 1934 she married a wealthy Spanish banker and moved to Majorca, but returned to New York after the outbreak of the Spanish Civil War two years later. Her husband, a prominent supporter of the Franco insurgency, was killed in an accident in 1938. Liebling started a second career as a writer around 1940, and in 1943 joined the staff of her father's *Musical Courier*, where she wrote the column on radio music. She died in New York in 1944.

NEWMAN, Ernest. Born 1868 in Everton, Lancashire, United Kingdom, the son of a tailor. Graduated from University College, Liverpool, in 1886, having studied English literature, philosophy and art. Newman was largely self-taught as a musician and authority on music, and he worked as a clerk in the Bank of Liverpool from 1889 to 1903. He became known as a music critic with his first books, *Gluck and the Opera* (1895) and *A Study of Wagner* (1899). These were successful enough for him to make the decision to pursue a career as a full-time music critic. He started with the *Manchester Guardian* in 1905, then moved to the *Birmingham Post*, where he worked from 1906 to 1919. Newman was appointed music critic of the *Sunday Times* in 1920 and stayed there until his retirement in 1958, but between October 1924 and March 1925 he accepted a position as guest critic for the *New York Evening Post*, following the retirement of Henry T. Finck. His wife later recalled, with English understatement, that 'He [Newman] was not very impressed with the performances he saw at the Metropolitan Opera, and he caused a certain amount of annoyance by saying so.'[1] Alongside his journalistic activities, Newman published major studies of Elgar (1906), Hugo Wolf (1907) and Richard Strauss (1908). *Wagner as Man and Artist* followed in 1914, *The Unconscious Beethoven* in 1927, and the four volumes of Newman's magnum opus, *The Life of Richard Wagner*, between 1933 and 1947. Newman won a reputation as the leading British music critic of his time. His critical allegiance was primarily to the tradition of German music from Mozart to Strauss; on Italian music he was often scathing. He died at Tadworth, Surrey, in 1959.

---

1 Vera Newman, *Ernest Newman: A Memoir by His Wife* (London: Putnam, 1963), 47.

APPENDIX 2: BIOGRAPHIES   357

PARKER, H. T. (Henry Taylor). Born 1867 in Boston, Massachusetts. Educated at Harrow School, England. Entered Harvard in 1886 but left in 1889 without a degree. While there he helped edit the *Harvard Monthly* and joined the Mermaid Club, a group of enthusiasts for literature and, especially, drama. Parker worked as a secretary to Sherman Hoar (1860–98), the Massachusetts politician, before moving into journalism. At some time in the 1890s he served as the dramatic critic for the New York *Commercial Advertiser*, but he did not settle into regular work of this nature until 1905, when he was appointed the dramatic and music critic of the *Boston Evening Transcript*, a position he held for the rest of his life. He also reported on theatre in Boston for the *New York Times*. Parker became known for the length and very literary quality of his reviews; he believed his ornate style was chiefly influenced by Latin and by the English of the great historian Francis Parkman (1823–93).[1] He was admired and feared for the very impressionistic and partisan nature of his criticism, and in time wielded great influence. He achieved a reputation among the Boston music critics second only to that of Philip Hale, but had a higher standing still as a drama critic, and was unusual in approaching opera at least as much from a dramatic as from a musical point of view. In 1922 Parker published *Eighth Notes: Voices and Figures of Music and the Dance*, a collection of his writings for the *Evening Transcript*. He also began a book on opera after Wagner, but did not complete it. He died in Boston in 1934.

PEYSER, Ethel (Rose). Born 1887 in New York. Graduated from Columbia University with a BSc degree in 1908. She began writing for various magazines on a wide range of cultural and housekeeping topics, and at different times served on the editorial staffs of the *New-York Tribune*, the *New York Evening Mail*, *House and Garden Magazine* and *Everyland* (a children's magazine). Peyser's interests gradually settled more firmly on music, and in the 1920s she began working on a series of collaborative books with Marion Bauer, starting with *How Music Grew: From Prehistoric Times to the Present Day* (1925). There followed *Music Through the Ages* (1932) and *How Opera Grew: From Ancient Greece to the Present Day* (1956). These books were all aimed at the popular market and enjoyed considerable success. Peyser seems to have done most of the actual writing, Bauer helping with research and evaluation. Peyser died in New York in 1961.

---

1 David McCord, *H.T.P.: Portrait of a Critic* (New York: Coward-McGann, 1935),16.

PEYSER, Herbert F. (Francis). Born 1886 in New York. Lived in Germany and France between the ages of six and fourteen. Graduated from Columbia University in 1909. In his student years Peyser was already fascinated by music criticism, and wrote unpublished reviews of the many musical performances he saw, also copying out Henry T. Finck's reviews of the same performances. In 1909 he joined the staff of *Musical America*, for which he wrote until 1920. Peyser later wrote for the *Evening Post, New York Telegram, Musical Observer* and other publications, but, unmarried and apparently supported by family money, he did not need the security of a regular position as a music journalist. In 1930 he moved to Europe, living successively in Berlin, Vienna and Paris, and acting as a correspondent to several American publications, including the *New York Times*. In 1939 he returned to New York and again joined the staff of *Musical America*. In the 1940s he began writing programmes for the New York Philharmonic, some of which developed into full-scale introductory booklets to particular composers. In his final years Peyser also worked on a book, *Masters of the Orchestra from Bach to Prokofieff*, with Louis Leopold Biancolli; this was published in 1954. As he neither held a regular position at one of the major newspapers, nor published books (for most of his career), Peyser was less prominent than some of his peers, but they accepted him as an equal in knowledge of music. William J. Henderson praised him as 'one of New York's most scholarly writers on music,'[1] and Olga Samaroff claimed in 1927 that 'there is no better informed writer on music in this city [New York] or any other.'[2] He died in New York in 1953.

SARGEANT, Winthrop. Born 1903 in San Francisco. He studied the violin in San Francisco and Europe, and in 1922 joined the San Francisco Symphony Orchestra as its youngest member. Sargeant moved to New York in 1926 to play first with the New York Symphony Orchestra, and then, from 1928, with the New York Philharmonic (under Toscanini). After his move to New York he began writing music criticism, and in 1930 decided to give up his career as a performer in order to try and establish himself as a critic. He began writing for *Musical America* in 1931, then became the music critic for the *Brooklyn Daily Eagle* in 1934. He briefly moved to the *New York American* in

---

1 'Unfinished Schubert Composition Played for First Time in New York,' *Sun*, 5 December 1928 [n. pag.].

2 'Music,' *Evening Post*, 23 February 1927, 5.

1936, before taking up a post as music editor for *Time* magazine in 1937. While at *Time* Sargeant consolidated his reputation as a critic with *Jazz: Hot and Hybrid* (1938), a pioneering and influential technical study of the jazz idiom. In 1945 he became a senior writer for *Life*, then in 1949 moved again to become the music critic for the *New Yorker*, the publication with which he is most associated. In 1958 he published another well-received book, *Listen to Music*, a collection of his *New Yorker* articles. Sargeant found a role for himself as a very witty, highly readable critic with basically conservative, anti-modernist views about music. He championed contemporary composers who seemed loyal to tonal traditions of composition, and often ridiculed determined avant-gardists and the cults surrounding them. Stravinsky, who Sargeant had little time for, nicknamed him S. D. Deaf. Sargeant's reputation was highest in the 1950s, when for a time he was one of the most admired United States critics; thereafter he gradually lost influence as younger critics painted him as reactionary and advocated for composers he had disparaged. Sargeant retired from the *New Yorker* in 1972, though he continued to contribute music criticisms on an occasional basis. In his later years he devoted much of his time to an English translation of the *Bhagavad Gita*, published in 1979. He died in Salisbury, Connecticut, in 1986.

SCHONBERG, Harold C. (Charles). Born 1915 in Washington Heights, New York. Having shown great musical ability as a boy, he decided he wanted to be a music critic after attending a performance of *Die Meistersinger von Nürnberg* just before his twelfth birthday. In 1936, while an undergraduate at Brooklyn College, Schonberg began writing reviews for the *Musical Advance*. After graduating in 1937, he entered the graduate school of New York University to study music; he was taught there by Marion Bauer. Schonberg obtained his M.A. in 1938 with a thesis on the musical and literary significance of Elizabethan songbooks. In 1939 he became an associate editor and record critic for the *American Music Lover*. During the war years he served in the United States Army Airborne Signal Corps, and was based in London. Returning to New York in 1946, Schonberg became a music critic for the New York *Sun*, a paper for which he served as a regular news reporter, too. He also began contributing reviews to the *Musical Courier*, *Musical Digest* and the British publication *Gramophone*. He moved to the *New York Times* in 1950, becoming that paper's record editor in 1955, and senior music critic in 1960. In the following decade Schonberg established himself as New York's leading music critic with a series of critically acclaimed and very successful books: *The Great Pianists* (1963), *The Great Conductors* (1967), and *The Lives of the Great Composers* (1970). After the 1966 demise of the *New York Herald Tribune*, of which Paul Henry Lang (1901–91) had been senior music critic, Schonberg 'wielded sovereign power in New York'[1] and was feared and admired for his incisive, impartial reviews. His stature was confirmed in 1971 when he became the second winner of the Pulitzer Prize for Criticism. Schonberg's primary interest was in piano music and its performance, and his appetite for opera somewhat limited; nevertheless, he wrote hundreds of opera reviews in the course of his career, and had clear critical standards, judging *Tristan und Isolde* and *Otello* the greatest operas in the German and Italian traditions respectively. He retired from his position at the *New York Times* in 1980, but continued to write occasional criticism for the paper, and produced several more books in his retirement. Norman Lebrecht has described him as '[p]robably the most widely read music critic of the pre-web world.'[2] Schonberg died in New York in 2003.

SELDES, Gilbert. Born 1893 in Alliance, New Jersey. Sent to the prestigious Central High School, Philadelphia, in 1906, and entered Harvard in 1910. At Harvard, Seldes wrote many reviews and essays for the *Harvard Monthly*, and also served as one of the editors of the magazine. His interests at this time were in literature and philosophy, but after graduating in 1914 he obtained a job as the music critic for the Philadelphia *Evening Ledger*. His biographer, Michael Kannen, comments briefly: 'Seldes had no prior experience or training in music. His musical tastes would evolve from classical to a strong preference for jazz and popular tunes by the later 1920s. ... He admired Wagner's music a great deal in 1910 ... but not at all in later years.'[3] With his literary training, Seldes tended to approach opera from a dramatic rather than a musical point of view. In 1916 he moved to London to work as a war correspondent and never returned to conventional musical criticism. After the First World War he returned to America

---

1 Grant, *Maestros of the Pen*, 280.

2 'How to prolong a critical condition,' *The Age*, 7 December 2009. Online at: <http://www.theage.com.au/>.

3 *The Lively Arts: Gilbert Seldes and the Transformation of Cultural Criticism in the United States* (New York: Oxford UP, 1996), 413, n. 40.

and became the associate editor of *Collier's Weekly* and then, from 1920, the managing editor of the celebrated literary monthly, *The Dial*, for which he also wrote the theatre column and many book reviews. His work at *The Dial* brought Seldes into close contact with many leading literary and artistic figures. His interests, however, had steadily come to focus more on popular culture, and he began writing about cinema, revues, jazz, popular songs, novels and theatre with a depth of serious analysis not attempted before. This led to his most significant and influential book, *The 7 Lively Arts* (1924). Later in life Seldes continued to be an influential critic of popular culture while also writing novels and plays and doing much work for radio and television. He died in New York in 1970.

SESSIONS, Roger (Huntington). Born 1896 in Brooklyn, New York. He spent most of his childhood at his family's ancestral home in Hadley, Massachusetts. Academically precocious, he entered Harvard at the age of fourteen, graduating in 1915 at the age of eighteen. In 1913 he started writing for the student-authored *Harvard Musical Review*, founded the previous year. His biographer, Andrea Olmstead, suggests that Sessions' 'fundamental attitudes about music' revealed in these early writings 'did not significantly alter over the next seven decades.'[1] After leaving Harvard, Sessions studied composition with Horatio Parker at Yale and with Ernest Bloch in New York. Between 1917 and 1925 he taught at Smith College and at the Cleveland Institute, where he was Bloch's assistant. He first became known as a composer with his incidental music for *The Black Maskers* (1923), but it was not until the 1950s that Sessions gained acceptance as one of the major American composers of the century. Between 1926 and 1933 he lived mainly in Italy. On his return to the United States, he became a professor of music at Princeton in 1935, moving to Berkeley in 1944, then back to Princeton in 1953, where he continued to teach until his retirement in 1965. He is widely regarded as the most important American teacher of composition of his era. Sessions had long been fascinated by opera, especially after his experiences in Europe, but did not produce one himself until he wrote *The Trial of Lucullus* in 1947. He then went on to compose *Montezuma*, an opera he worked on for fifteen years; it was first performed in Berlin in 1964, and given its United States premiere in 1976. Like much of his music, Sessions' operas are written in a modernist idiom which only appeals to a very small audience,

---

1 *Roger Sessions: A Biography* (New York: Routledge, 2008), 68.

despite the dramatic profundity of the works themselves. In later life Sessions published a number of academic books, starting with *The Musical Experience of Composer, Performer, Listener* (1950). He died in Princeton in 1985.

STEVENS, Otheman (Abel). Born 1857 in New York. Stevens apparently had no tertiary education and by 1880 he was working as a farmer in San Gabriel, Los Angeles, while living with his elder sister and her husband. Between then and the end of the century he moved into journalism and newspaper editing, working mainly for the *Los Angeles Herald*, a paper he served 'for many years ... in various capacities,'[1] while also acting as the Los Angeles correspondent to the *San Francisco Examiner*. It was presumably his connection with the latter paper, owned by William Randolph Hearst, which led to his becoming a staff writer for Hearst's new *Los Angeles Examiner* in 1903, where he was the dramatic critic in addition to writing on politics and current events. Stevens became very well known in Los Angeles, partly because a good deal of his writing was concerned with encouraging the growth of civic pride there. He continued to write for the *Examiner* into the 1930s. He died in Los Angeles in 1936.

TAYLOR, Deems. Born 1885 in New York. Graduated from New York University in 1906 with a liberal arts degree. For many years Taylor supported himself mainly through journalism, while also writing light verse and light music. He began a more thorough study of composition in the 1910s, and established himself as a serious composer of great promise with *The Chambered Nautilus* (1914) and especially *Through the Looking Glass* (1919). Taylor had almost no experience of music criticism when he applied to succeed the just deceased James Gibbons Huneker as music critic for the *World* in 1921, but after a two week trial he obtained the position and in his four years at the *World* gained a formidable reputation as a witty and informed critic of a wide range of music. Don Seitz, the business manager of the paper, told Taylor's father that his son 'brought the *World* more readers than any other man they ever had.'[2] In 1925 Taylor gave up regular criticism so that he would have more time to compose. Much of the next six years was devoted to two operas, *The King's Henchman* (1927) and *Peter Ibbetson*

---

1 'Stevens' New Job,' *Los Angeles Herald*, 7 May 1900, 3.

2 Quoted in James A. Pegolotti, *Deems Taylor: A Biography* (Boston: Northeastern UP, 2003), 130.

(1931), both premiered at the Met; the former proved the most successful serious opera written by an American to that date. Taylor also served briefly as the editor of *Musical America*, 1927–29. He returned to full-time reviewing with the *New York American*, serving as the paper's principal music critic 1931–32, but in 1931 he also made his debut as a radio commentator, and his success at this soon caused him to abandon traditional reviewing. As the commentator for the Met and the New York Philharmonic in the 1930s, Taylor 'reached a larger, more diverse audience than any other music critic in our [United States] history before or since.'[1] In 1937 he also published a very successful book, *Of Men and Music*, a collection of his radio talks. Taylor was a truly household name after his appearance as the Master of Ceremonies in Disney's *Fantasia* (1940), and his celebrity allowed him to establish himself as a television personality in later life. As a critic, Taylor was notably less partisan than most of his colleagues: he judged individual works rather than composers. He died in New York in 1966.

THOMPSON, Oscar. Born 1887 in Crawfordsville, Indiana. His family moved to Seattle when he was two. Educated at a private Academy of Dramatic Arts, he initially intended to pursue a career as a singer, but at the age of sixteen he got his first job as a reporter with the Seattle *Times*. From then until 1917 Thompson worked for a series of newspapers, first as a reporter, then as an editor, in Seattle and (from 1909) in Tacoma. In 1917 he enlisted in the army and served in military intelligence until the end of the First World War. In 1919 Thompson's career as a music critic commenced when he was employed full-time by *Musical America*. He later served as an associate editor of the publication, and from 1936 to 1943 as the editor-in-chief, in succession to A. Walter Kramer. Thompson's authoritative and genial brand of criticism won him the plaudits of his New York peers, and in 1928 he accepted a second position as chief music critic for the *Evening Post*. In 1934 he resigned this and moved to the *New York Times*, where he was a colleague of Olin Downes. In 1937 he moved to the *Sun*, where he succeeded William. J. Henderson. Through the 1920s it appeared that Thompson might be content with a distinguished career in music journalism, but the full extent of his ambitions was revealed in the 1930s, when he started producing a whole series of introductory and encyclopedic works on music aimed at a wide audience: *Practical Music Criticism* (1934), *How to Understand Music* (1935), *A Tabulated Biographical*

---

1 Grant, *Maestros of the Pen*, 174.

Dictionary of Music (1936), *The American Singer* (1937), *Great Modern Composers* (1941), and, as editor, the *International Cyclopedia of Music and Musicians* (1939). He also published a more specialized study of a composer he found particularly interesting: *Debussy: Man and Artist* (1937). Thompson was eclectic in his enthusiasms and did not display the unswerving allegiance to the German tradition found in many of the older American critics. He was valued by his peers for his encyclopedic knowledge of musical history, his extraordinary memory of performances he had witnessed, even decades before, and the scrupulous fairness of his judgments; he was considered, in Miles Kastendieck's words, 'the embodiment of all that is fair-minded and wholly objective in musical criticism.'[1] He died in New York in 1945.

VAN VECHTEN, Carl. Born 1880 in Cedar Rapids, Iowa. Attended the University of Chicago 1899–1903 where he was able to pursue his interests in music, theatre and art, and where he wrote for the *University of Chicago Weekly*. After graduation, Van Vechten obtained his first job as a general reporter and columnist for the *Chicago American*. In 1906 he moved to New York and obtained a job as assistant music critic at the *New York Times* (under Richard Aldrich). In 1907 he took an extended leave of absence and travelled to Europe to extend his knowledge of music, opera and the visual arts. On his return to New York in 1909, Van Vechten resumed his position at the *Times*, and also began to write dance criticism for the paper. In 1913 he left the *Times* to become the drama critic for the *New York Press*, but the following year he gave up that position, too, and decided to become a freelancer, knowing he could draw on family money if necessary. For the remainder of the 1910s Van Vechten lived a very bohemian life, concentrating his efforts on a series of books about music (parts of which were usually published earlier in newspapers and periodicals): *Music after the Great War* (1915), *Music and Bad Manners* (1916), *Interpreters and Interpretation* (1917; extended edition 1920), *The Merry-Go-Round* (1918) and *In the Garret* (1919). These books made him almost no money, and in 1920 he decided to abandon criticism; after writing two popular books on cats, he embarked on a second career as a novelist in the 1920s. Although Van Vechten achieved great success as a novelist, a series of inheritances in the late 1920s made him completely independent financially, and in 1932 he abandoned writing altogether to commence a third career

---

[1] 'Oscar Thompson, Sun's Music Critic, Was Steadying Force in Criticism,' *Brooklyn Eagle*, 6 July 1945, 10.

as a portrait photographer, at which he again excelled. As early as the 1910s Van Vechten showed a great interest in African American culture, and in later years he befriended many African American artists and did much to promote their work. As Mark N. Grant states, Van Vechten 'was both one of the last of the great cultural critics who put classical music at the forefront of general artistic culture, and the first in the line of crossover critics who looked to Afro-Asiatic cultures for replenishment of the Western tradition.'[1] In 1916 he was already declaring that 'Wagner is becoming just a little bit old-fashioned.'[2] He died in New York in 1964.

---

1 *Maestros of the Pen*, 294–95.

2 'Shall we Realize Wagner's Ideals?,' *Musical Quarterly* 2 (1916), 387–401, p. 387.

Also Available

Essays On The Montemezzi-D'Annunzio *Nave*

Italo Montemezzi
Ugo Navarra
Adriano Lualdi
Ildebrando Pizzetti
Bruno Barilli
Guido M. Gatti
Domenico De Paoli
Raffaele Mellace

Edited by David Chandler
Translations by Monica Cuneo   Foreword by Duane D. Printz

This groundbreaking study is now available in a revised and expanded second edition containing reviews and essays by 28 critics on the opera Montemezzi considered his masterpiece.

www.ingramcontent.com/pod-product-compliance
Lightning Source LLC
Chambersburg PA
CBHW032058090426
42743CB00007B/162